European Sustainable Carriage of Goods

This work discusses the rapidly developing European transport policy on sustainable freight and the connected efforts initiated by the European Commission (EC) on greening transport by the means of contract law.

Greening transport has been a central goal for the EU for decades. The main problem has been, and still is, that far too much carriage of goods within the EU is performed unimodally, by road carriage alone. This has caused severe problems particularly in central Europe, where both trade and environment is suffering from an ineffective transport industry with growing problems of congestion and pollution. A modal shift in transport from mainly road-based to a form of transport in which more environmental friendly modes such as rail, inland waterways and seaborne transport are integrated into one transport chain, is hence an objective of the EU. If successful, this model could then be extended to the international transport community.

The key question raised in this book is whether the traditional role of contract law is changing to such an extent that the parties involved must take external interests into account. In the case of the EU's efforts to enhance sustainable carriage of goods within its realm, the author explores whether governmental interference is necessary, or if we can trust that the parties will integrate environmental issues into their contracts because there is a demand for such clauses. The different proposals for an EU regime on multimodal contracts of carriage are discussed in this context.

This book will be of great relevance to academics and practitioners with an interest in EU law, transport law, environmental law and maritime law in general.

Dr Ellen Eftestøl-Wilhelmsson is an associate professor in law at the Scandinavian Institute of Maritime Law, University of Oslo, Norway and a docent of civil law and research manager for the InterTran research group at the Faculty of Law, University of Helsinki, Finland.

IMLI Studies in International Maritime Law

Series Editor: Professor David Joseph Attard, Director of the IMO International Maritime Law Institute

The IMO International Maritime Law Institute (IMLI) was established under the auspices of the International Maritime Organization, a specialised agency of the United Nations.

The Institute is an international centre for the training of specialists in international maritime law. It contributes to the development and dissemination of knowledge and expertise in the international regime of merchant shipping and related areas of maritime law and the general law of the sea, with special reference to the international regulations and procedures for safety and efficiency of shipping and the prevention of marine pollution. For further information on the Institute please visit its website at: www.imli.org.

The series is dedicated to publishing original, scholarly contributions which analyse key issues in international maritime law. The works published in the series will be of interest to an audience of students and scholars in maritime law, maritime lawyers and barristers, and professionals in the shipping industry.

Available Titles:

Limitation of Liability in International Maritime Conventions
The Relationship between Global Limitation Conventions and Particular Liability Regimes
Norman A. Martínez Gutiérrez

Serving the Rule of International Maritime Law
Essays in Honour of Professor David Joseph Attard
Edited by A. Martínez Gutiérrez

Extension of Coastal State Jurisdiction in Enclosed or Semi-enclosed Seas
A Mediterranean and Adriatic Perspective
Mitja Grbec

European Sustainable Carriage of Goods
The Role of Contract Law
Ellen Eftestøl-Wilhelmsson

European Sustainable Carriage of Goods

The role of contract law

Ellen Eftestøl-Wilhelmsson

Routledge
Taylor & Francis Group
LONDON AND NEW YORK

First published 2016 by Routledge

2 Park Square, Milton Park, Abingdon, Oxfordshire OX14 4RN
711 Third Avenue, New York, NY 10017

Routledge is an imprint of the Taylor & Francis Group, an informa business

First issued in paperback 2018

British Library Cataloguing in Publication Data
A catalogue record for this book is available from the British Library

Library of Congress Cataloging-in-Publication Data
A catalog record for this title has been requested

ISBN: 978-1-138-79670-6 (hbk)
ISBN: 978-1-138-61442-0 (pbk)

Typeset in Galliard
by Apex CoVantage, LLC

“Those who cannot change their minds cannot change anything.”

George Bernard Shaw

Contents

Preface and acknowledgments

"I would like the lawyers to tell me what the law should be, and not what it is."
Beatrice Ask, Swedish Minister of Justice,
at a seminar in Helsinki 28 April 2014

This book discusses how the rules on international carriage of goods should be changed in order to enhance sustainable carriage of goods within the EU. The goal of sustainable carriage could be achieved if the steadily growing road carriage within the Union could be replaced by more environmentally friendly multimodal transport involving rail and sea carriage. One way to make this happen, as suggested by the European Commission, is to provide the transport industry with a harmonised liability regime for European multimodal transport. By doing so, one obstacle to increased use of multimodal transport arrangements in the shape of the unpredictable legal situation of the parties to a contract of carriage, would be removed. The latter problem, identified as the regulatory gap in international transport, has been discussed internationally for decades, but with no solution so far.

This book outlines and analyses the common transport policy on multimodal sustainable carriage of goods and its impact on the private law regimes governing it. The different proposals for an EU regime on multimodal contracts of carriage will be discussed in this context. One of the questions addressed is the competence of the EU in the area of international transport, which previously was left to the Member States in different international collaboration.

Despite the fact that environmental protection should be integrated in all EU activities, its impact is more of a political than a legal question. Economic research shows that efforts by the EU towards a harmonised liability regime are not likely to be very effective as regards the desired modal shift. This book accordingly argues that the EU Commission should rethink its strategy and not rely upon the mere existence of a harmonised liability regime to reach its goal of sustainable carriage of goods. However, as much work has been allocated to drafting a liability regime, and as there is a call for it on an international level, the Commission should strive to integrate environmental issues into the existing proposed liability regimes. This could be done either within the framework of a regional liability regime for the EU, or within the framework of, for example, the proposed Rotterdam Rules.

This book advocates that the legal entities responsible for organising transport, the so-called freight integrators, should have a duty to inform their customers about the environmental impact of a certain assignment. Neither shippers nor freight integrators can take an informed decision on the choice of route and modes of transport without this information. Work on gathering the environmental footprints of transport should thus continue and the information should be integrated in the sustainable public procurement program of the EU.

The writing of this book took place within the framework of an interdisciplinary research project, The InterTran Project, running in Helsinki, Finland, between 2010 and 2014. The research project was financed by the Scandinavian Institute of Maritime Law and the Academy of Finland. I would like to express my gratitude to both contributors for making the project possible.

Moreover, my colleagues and friends, who have contributed in different ways, through endless discussions, joint papers, presentations and so forth, deserve to be mentioned. I would like to start with Professor Erik Røsæg at the Scandinavian Institute of Maritime Law, University of Oslo, and Professor Lena Sisula-Tulokas, University of Helsinki, who have both supported this project by believing in its idea and accordingly supported it whenever needed. Furthermore, my colleagues in the research project should be mentioned: Dr Anu Bask and Dr Mervi Rajahonka from Aalto University School of Economics have had to learn that lawyers are not as organised as they used to believe. Nevertheless, we have learned to overcome disciplinary cultural gaps and had mutual benefit from our collaboration. In addition, Professor Erkki Hämäläinen and doctoral students Pinja Raitasuo and Elise *Luovula* deserve to be mentioned.

In addition, I would like to thank our student members, Katja Heikkinen, Jenni Hirsto, Binling Zhou and Lotta Laukkanen for participating in the research project and for helping out in all questions related to transport liability, transport documents or EU law. Their joint expertise has been of great assistance. Thank you, Jenni, also for helping out with the more practical work related to this book. Similarly Jan Aminoff and Lalli Castren, both members of the research group, should be thanked. Jan has contributed with his lifelong experience as a transport lawyer and always made sure that our theories and approaches were not too academic. Lalli did a fine job writing his doctoral thesis on the unbreakable liability limit in air law.

The research project was administered by the Institute of International Economic Law, KATTI, at the University of Helsinki. KATTI's director, Professor Pia Letto-Vanamo, together with Secretary Anna-Maija Ekström and various excellent research assistants, could not have provided a better environment for research. I would also like to thank Christopher Goddard for, in a quick and professional way, turning the text into readable English.

Finally, I would like to thank my husband, Professor and Chancellor of the University of Helsinki, Thomas Wilhelmsson, for always encouraging me to continue writing, even when I was of the opinion that I should rather stay at home and take care of the family.

Helsinki, 30 April 2015
Ellen Eftestøl-Wilhelmsson

Part I

Introduction

1 What this book is all about

1.1 Problems discussed

This work discusses the rapidly developing European transport policy on *sustainable freight* and connected efforts initiated by the European Commission (the Commission) on greening transport by means of *contract law*. Greening transport has been a central goal of the European Union (EU) for decades. The main problem has been that far too much carriage of goods within the EU is performed unimodally: by *road carriage* alone.[1] This has caused severe problems, particularly in central Europe where both trade and the environment are suffering from an ineffective transport industry with the increasing problems of congestion and pollution. Hence, a goal for the EU is a *modal shift* in transport from mainly road-based to a form of transport in which more environmentally friendly modes such as rail, inland waterways and seaborne transport are integrated into one transport chain. According to the Commission, the aim is to 'disconnect mobility from its adverse effects. This means, above all, promoting co-modality, i.e. optimally combining various modes of transport within the same transport chain, which is the solution for the future in the case of freight.'[2] In other words, promoting multimodal carriage is a core target of the Common Transport Policy (CTP). In order to implement this goal, intervention on a governmental level has been recognised as necessary. According to the Commission, the industry itself cannot solve the problem. In fact, a business as usual scenario would probably lead to a near doubling of road transport of both passengers and freight.[3] However, it has been the policy of the Commission that governmental intervention

1 Road transport is estimated to grow by around 30 per cent by 2030 and by over 80 per cent by 2050. Road transport will accordingly maintain its dominant role in the freight business, with congestion costs projected to increase by about 50 per cent by 2050. This development is not sustainable and the EU Commission is taking action to hamper it. Commission, White Paper 'Roadmap to a Single European Transport Area – Towards a competitive and resource efficient transport' COM (2011) 144 final at 6.

2 Available online at http://ec.europa.eu/transport/themes/sustainable/index_en.htm (accessed 26 January 2015).

3 Commission, White Paper, 'The future development of the common transport policy – a global approach to the construction of a community framework for sustainable mobility' COM (92) 494 final at 28.

should not be in a form of mandatory objectives; quite the opposite, the idea has been to facilitate growth in environmentally friendly multimodal carriage of goods by making the multimodal transport alternative more attractive to the industry.[4] The idea is to encourage the parties to make environmentally friendly, multimodal contracts of carriage, instead of unimodal polluting contracts of carriage by road.

Providing the industry with a *harmonised (contractual) legal regime* is understood by the Commission as one way to smooth the way for the desired modal shift. In other words, the Commission is not intending to interfere directly with the contractual responsibilities of the parties, but merely to facilitate sustainable carriage of goods by reducing legal uncertainty in the contractual position of the parties. Hence, this use of contract law as a tool to control European transport flows forms an important part of this book. A harmonised legal instrument on international multimodal carriage will, according to the Commission, enhance the use of this form of transport. Clearly, such an instrument is lacking on the international level: the international transport community has so far failed to agree on an international legal regime for multimodal carriage. For this reason, a European regional legal framework is an alternative that could also be used as a model for an international solution.

However, economic research indicates that providing the industry with a harmonised liability regime is not a very effective way of enhancing multimodal carriage. The transaction costs related to legal uncertainty are insignificant. Removing them will therefore not have an impact on the modal choice of the parties in the transport industry. In other words, although an international or regional multimodal regime will benefit the industry, it will not necessarily lead to the desired modal shift. It would therefore be feasible if the Commission did not limit its efforts to impose a harmonised liability regime (and an electronic transport document) when discussing a European legal framework for multimodal transport. Hence, other ways of supporting a shift in transport flows by means of contract law should also be discussed. One way of using contract law as a tool to promote sustainable carriage of goods could be to link sustainability to the contractual duties of transport organisers. Accordingly, this study discusses the role of service providers as regards the desired modal shift and advocates that service providers should have a duty to establish how a certain assignment can be carried out in the most environmentally friendly manner, as well as an obligation to inform customers of such an option. Some service providers already perform this service without any contractual duty to do so. These service providers have been classified as 'freight integrators'. A freight integrator is defined as an entity

4 A question to be asked is whether this policy is in line with the policy laid down in The Treaty on the Functioning of the European Union (TFEU), Art. 11, which points out that environmental protection must be integrated in both defining and implementing Union policies and activities, in particular with a view to promoting sustainable development. See below in Chapter 8.

that needs to be able to 'combine the specific strengths of each mode at European and world level to offer their clients and consequently, society at large, the best service in terms of efficiency, price and environmental impact in the broadest sense (economic, ecological, energy etc.)'.[5]

This book advocates that all transport organisers operating in the EU should have this knowledge.[6] A duty to inform clients of the most cost-efficient and environmentally friendly transport alternative could easily be included in the contractual duties of a transport organiser without introducing mandatory objectives as regards choice of transport means, and would thus be in line with the overall ambition of the Commission, that is to facilitate a change in transport flows without mandatory requirements in choice of transport routes or means. On a general level, the issue turns into a question of the role of contract law; is contract law changing from being a tool merely governing the interests of the parties to becoming a tool where external interests are also promoted or taken into account? The question is simple: can contract law be used as a tool to promote environmental protection? If so, how should this be done? Do we need to restructure the idea of what contracts are all about, or could we instead – as advocated below in Part III – simply state that contract law already provides the necessary tools. Environmental issues can easily be integrated in the system through interpretation of the definition of due care. Both the duty of loyalty and due care can be expanded to include external interests such as protection of the environment.

In addition to contractual issues that arise, the book will also examine *the role of the EU as a new player in the international discussion* on contractual legal transport regimes. Transport law is by tradition governed by sovereign states in close cooperation with the industry. Because of the international character of transport, both the industry and states themselves have cooperated in various international forums to create internationally harmonised solutions. The contracts used in international carriage of goods are highly regulated and standardised, through both international conventions and standard documents. Compared to other business-to-business contracts the contracts used in the transport industry are to a considerable extent governed by mandatory law, which, as mentioned, is created in international cooperation with all stakeholders involved. In other words, if the EU decides on a regional instrument for multimodal contracts of carriage, including a sea leg, this will have big impact on the international regulatory situation. Accordingly, the political interest in the question of governing European multimodal contracts of carriage is huge. Equally, the reactions to the different proposals must be understood in this context.

Entry into the area of transport contract law is, however, not only a political issue: complicated legal issues also arise. Transport has been part of EU

5 European transport policy for 2010: time to decide. COM (2001) 370 p. 47.
6 See Part III: Contract law as a tool to promote sustainable carriage of goods.

competences since the Treaty of Rome.[7] However, the EU did not make much use of its competence at the beginning, because the Member States wanted to keep control over the area. It was only after a ruling from the European Court of Justice in 1985[8] that the EU started to develop a CTP. The early focus was on establishing a free transport market, but starting from the 1990s, *sustainable carriage of goods* has been a core issue for the Union. As explained above, it was this interest that brought the EU into the area of multimodal transport law, and into the area of contract law. Transport has so far *not* been part of the effort towards a *European contract law*. The Commission, while recognising that differences between national contract laws are among the main barriers that hinder cross-border trade, has lately only taken initiatives within the area of sales law, insurance contract law and cloud computing contracts in business-to-business contracts.[9] The legislative efforts of the EU have mainly concentrated on consumer contracts. It is debatable whether the Union has *competence* to govern business-to-business contracts. As regards transport contracts, however, the competence question is not problematic. It is fairly clear that the EU has *internal* competence in the area of contracts of carriage of goods. Whether or not the EU has *external* competence in this area (competence to make agreements with third parties) is, however, more complicated. This question will arise if the EU enters into the area of transport law by, for example, ratifying the United Nations Convention on Contracts for the International Carriage of Goods Wholly or Partly by Sea (The Rotterdam Rules),[10] as many of the Member States are already bound by conventions that involve third parties that are not members of the EU. Questions of EU competence in the area of transport law will, accordingly, be outlined in this book but without going into depth about the complex area of EU external relations.

The capacity of the EU is, however, not only restricted by competence questions. If Member States have obligations under international or bilateral conventions that could collide with EU law, problems might arise. These problems are connected to the different unimodal transport conventions to which one or more Member States belong. Moreover, these conventions might, to a certain

7 The Treaty of Rome, officially the Treaty establishing the European Economic Community (TEEC), is an international agreement that led to the founding of the European Economic Community (EEC) on 1 January 1958. It was signed on 25 March 1957 by Belgium, France, Italy, Luxembourg, the Netherlands and West Germany.

8 The Court of Justice of the European Union (CJEU) is the institution of the EU that encompasses the whole judiciary. It consists of two major courts and a specialised court: the Court of Justice, informally known as European Court of Justice (ECJ), the General Court (formerly the Court of First Instance) and the Civil Service Tribunal, a specialised court created in 2004; see Art. 19 Treaty of the European Union (TEU). In the following, the abbreviation CJEU will be used for the Court of Justice.

9 Available online at http://ec.europa.eu/justice/contract/index_en.htm (accessed 27 January 2105).

10 The Convention was adopted by the General Assembly 67th plenary meeting on 11 December 2008 but is not yet in force. See below in in Chapter 2 (2.2) and Chapter 6 (6.3).

extent, apply to multimodal contracts of carriage. Particular problems are related to conventions entered into before a country became a member of the EU. How a conflict between existing convention obligations and new EU legislation should be handled is hence also discussed.

1.2 What is discussed where?

This book consists of three parts. Part I – Introduction – in Chapter 1 introduces the topics discussed in the following chapters, starting with Chapter 2, which contains an overview of the present legal context as regards international multimodal contracts of carriage in Europe. Whether the EU has competence to act in the area of transport law is thereafter analysed in Chapter 3. The main issue is the *internal competence* of the EU. As will be outlined, the EU has internal competence to legislate in the area of international transport – which means that the Union has competence to govern multimodal transport liability by directives or regulations. A more complicated question, however, is whether the EU also has *external competence* in the area, and what the consequences are if the EU makes use of this competence. This problem will be briefly discussed in relation to EU competence to enter into international conventions, such as the Rotterdam Rules, or to set up a new EU convention on multimodal transport

In Part II, The common transport policy, the development of the CTP on sustainable carriage of goods is presented in Chapter 4, followed by Chapter 5, which reviews what the Commission has been doing (by means of contract law) to provide a modal shift where environmentally friendly multimodal carriage replaces some of the carriage that today is undertaken by road. The main focus of the CTP has been to provide the multimodal transport industry with a legal regime that is predictable and easy to operate. The greater part of the discussion has been on whether or not the EU should go for a regional harmonised liability regime for multimodal carriage of cargo and, if so, how such a liability regime should be framed. This discussion is parallel to the international discussion on the same issue. The question of whether or not the Rotterdam Rules provide a solution for the EU is, accordingly, raised and analysed. Additionally, the idea of providing the industry with a European electronic transport document has been on the agenda. A major problem in all these relations seems to be the connection between a new multimodal legal instrument and existing unimodal conventions, which all to a certain degree also apply to multimodal carriage. Ways to manage this problem of scope is discussed in Chapter 6.

One could, however, raise the question about how effective a harmonised liability regime is, as regards the goal of increased multimodal carriage of goods. This question is addressed in Chapter 7, which introduces the reader to economic research showing that the friction costs related to an unpredictable liability regime are insignificant. A harmonised liability regime will probably have no impact on choice of transport modes.

Hence, other ways to promote multimodal carriage must be addressed. This is done in Part III – Contract law as a tool to promote sustainable carriage of goods – which discusses whether contract law could provide more than merely an instrument to smooth the way for the use of such carriage. This is partly a question whether (and how) the principle of sustainability in Article 11 of the Treaty on the Functioning of the European Union (TFEU) should be integrated in the contractual framework of a contract of carriage. That question is addressed in Chapter 8, which also discusses whether the integration principle is viable in the proposed EU contractual provisions such as the Draft Common Frame of Reference (DCFR) and the proposed EU regulation on international sales contracts, as well as in the different proposals for an EU legal regime on multimodal transport.

Chapter 9 then examines how the integration principle could be integrated into the contractual framework for multimodal contracts of carriage without coming into conflict with existing unimodal regimes. The chapter presents a group of transport providers that, on a voluntary basis, operates the business idea of providing environmental friendly contracts of carriage. The group is identified by the Commission as so-called transport integrators. These are freight forwarders or carriers, which focus on green logistics. A freight integrator is hence defined as: 'an entity which "needs to be able to combine the specific strengths of each mode at European and world level to be able to offer their clients and consequently, society at large, the best service in terms of efficiency, price and environmental impact in the broadest sense (economical, ecological, energy etc.)"'.[11] As the group exists, the question is how to increase its influence and its business ideas within the Union.

The study is summarised and conclusions presented in Chapter 10. The main conclusion is that the present approach is not efficient as regards the goal of sustainable carriage of goods. Nevertheless, contract law provides possibilities not discussed by the Commission. The EU should introduce a duty for transport integrators to offer sustainable carriage and, in particular, to *inform* customers of this possibility. This duty would not conflict with existing transport law and it would be in line with the environmental initiatives of the EU in other areas, such as public procurement. For that reason, this study concludes by suggesting that the EU impose a duty on service providers in the freight industry – that is the freight integrators – to inform customers of the most sustainable way of carrying a specific consignment. This would give shippers a chance to make their choice on an informed basis, without forcing the sustainable solution on shippers, that is by making the more environmentally friendly alternative mandatory, which, of course, is also an alternative. With increased visibility of the issue, the hope is that market mechanisms will force parties to choose the most environmentally friendly transport alternative. A duty to inform would also give the industry a chance to smoothly adapt to new transport patterns.

11 European transport policy for 2010: time to decide. COM (2001) 370 p. 47.

At present there is no such duty on European freight integrators. Indeed, there is no legally accepted, common definition of the term freight integrator. The definition cited above merely reflects the political idea behind the harmonisation project – to highlight environmental issues and develop a shift in existing transport patterns. The vision of the Commission is that environmental friendly carriage could be achieved by introducing a harmonised liability regime for European multimodal contracts of carriage and by doing so filling the legal gap that today hampers the full use of multimodal carriage of goods.[12]

12 See Part II on the CTP for more on the policy behind European efforts.

2 The present legal context

2.1 No international multimodal convention

The idea of introducing a harmonised regional legal regime for European multimodal carriage of goods stemmed from the fact that the multimodal industry suffers from a severe regulatory gap. At present, no harmonised legal regime is applicable to international European multimodal contracts of carriage either on a European or on an international level. Indeed, quite the reverse, the legal situation is fragmented and incomplete. The problem has been heavily discussed in the legal literature at the international level ever since the so-called container revolution, which took place in the 1950s.[1] The legal discussion initially concentrated on the question of how to apply existing unimodal legal rules to containerised carriage, which was normally multimodal.[2] This will not be analysed further here, except for an illustration of the problem with reference to certain well-known European cases.[3] An updated analysis of the applicability of unimodal legal regimes to multimodal contracts of carriage is given by Marian Hoeks in the latest book on the topic: *Multimodal Transport Law – The Law Applicable to the Multimodal Contract for the Carriage of Goods.*[4]

The discussion on a harmonised liability regime for multimodal contracts of cargo is not new. The continuing regulatory gap in international multimodal transport has led to an unclear and unpredictable legal situation because the issue is, to a certain extent, dealt with regionally or domestically.[5] However, the

1 Angus, W., 'Legal Implications of "The Container Revolution" in International Carriage of Goods', *McGill Law Journal*, 1968, Volume 14, pp. 395–429 at p. 422.

2 Harllee, J., Nemirow, S. and Jerome, B., 'Current Regulation and Modern Transportation Schemes', *The Transportation Law Journal*, 1969, Volume 1, pp. 39–50.

3 The famous English quantum case will be outlined below in Chapter 6 (at 6.2), together with some other European cases discussing the applicability of unimodal transport law to multimodal contracts of carriage. The perspective in the discussion is the role of the transport document.

4 Hoeks, M., *Multimodal Transport Law – The Law Applicable to the Multimodal Contract for the Carriage of Goods*, Kluwer Law International, 2010.

5 Such a legal regime exists in the Andean Community. See Nicolás Martínez Devia, *The Multimodal Transport System in the Andean Community: An Analysis from a Legal Perspective*, Erasmus Universiteit, 2008.

increasing tendency towards unilateral and regional solutions has not helped the situation, if viewed from an international perspective.[6] Swedish professor Jan Ramberg has been a strong advocate of an international solution for multimodal carriage. As long ago as 1973 he introduced the idea of moving harmonisation of the laws applicable to multimodal contracts of cargo away from the mode of transport in use and instead focusing on the contractual promise to carry a certain assignment. In this way, liability would relate to (breach of) the promise to transport a consignment, rather than to the means of conveyance.[7] According to Ramberg, multimodal contracts of carriage need a radical approach, such as creating a totally new regime based on the United Nations Convention on Contracts for the International Sale of Goods (CISG 1980). Jan Ramberg has furthermore suggested that an EU regime for multimodal contracts of carriage should apply to all third party logistics (3PL) service providers. Liability should be the same type of liability as under the CISG and the parties should be allowed to opt out of the Convention wholly or in part.[8] As we shall see, since 2005, Ramberg's views have heavily influenced the EU proposal for a legal regime on multimodal contracts.[9]

Environmental protection has by tradition not been part of the legal discussion on liability regimes. However, at the beginning of the twenty-first century, *environmental issues* came to the fore in the academic discussion on multimodal carriage. Environmental liability (the polluter pays principle) was recognised as an important international policy tool.[10] Nevertheless, market demand for green freight was at the time almost invisible. Consequently, scholars proposed that political action be taken.[11] Since then, the common transport policy (CTP) of the EU has been a subject for research. An historical analysis shows that environmental protection became part of the CTP with the Commission's 1992 White Paper,[12] The Future Development of the Common Transport Policy,[13] which is outlined below in 4.1.

6 For a critical view on the regionalisation of maritime law, see Myrburgh, P., 'Uniformity or Unilateralism in the Law of Carriage of Goods by Sea?' *Victoria University of Wellington Law Review*, 2000, Volume 31, pp. 355–382.

7 Ramberg, J., 'The Law of Carriage of Goods – Attempts of Harmonization', *Scandinavian Studies in Law*, 1973, Volume 17, pp. 211–252 at p. 252.

8 Ramberg, J., 'The Future Law of Transport Operators and Service Providers', *Scandinavian Studies in Law*, 2004 Volume 46, pp. 135–151 at pp. 150–151.

9 More below in Chapter 5 (at 5.1).

10 Brunnee, J., 'Of Sense and Sensibility: Reflections on International Liability Regimes as Tools for Environmental Protection', *International and Comparative Law Quarterly*, 2004, Volume 53, pp. 351–368.

11 Corbett, J., 'The Role of International policy in Mitigating Global Shipping Emissions', *Brown Journal of World Affairs*, 2010, Volume XVI, Issue II, pp. 143–154.

12 Schmidt, M. and Giorgi, L., 'Successes, Failures and Prospects for the Common Transport Policy', *Innovation*, 2001 ,Volume 14, Issue 4, pp. 293–313.

13 White Paper, The Future Development of the Common Transport Policy, A global approach to the construction of a Community framework for sustainable mobility COM (92) 494 Final.

It seems, however, that the connection between the environmental perspective and the contractual rules is hard to find, both in the present legal regimes and in the proposals for a harmonised liability regime suggested by different expert groups appointed by the Commission.[14] To connect environmental protection and contractual rules is, however, not an impossible task. The combination of environmental protection and liability regimes is not at all difficult and can be achieved by simple contractual tools (see Chapter 10).

2.2 Different unimodal liability conventions

Generally, in international transport law, the legal position of the parties to a contract of carriage is subject to a harmonised liability regime. If the cargo is damaged, lost or delayed, the liability of the carrier is mandatorily governed by national laws implementing international transport conventions. In some jurisdictions the conventions might even apply directly. This is also the situation in the European Union (EU), where contracts of carriage have by tradition been subject to the jurisdiction of the individual Member States. To date, the EU as an entity has no legislation on contracts of carriage of cargo, although it is a party to several transport conventions.[15]

Due to extensive harmonisation through international conventions, the legal position of the parties to a unimodal contract of carriage is relatively clear, because each mode of transport is subject to a particular set of rules.[16] International contracts of carriage by sea are, to a large extent, covered by the Hague[17] or the Hague-Visby Rules,[18] which provide that the contract is covered by a bill of lading.[19] Some states have also implemented the Hamburg Rules, despite not

14 Proposed liability regimes are analysed in Chapter 5 (at 5.1).

15 See Chapter 3 on the relationship between the EU and its Member States as regards transport law.

16 Nevertheless, it is a fact that the even the unimodal conventions are, for different reasons, subject to constant criticism for not providing a 'clear and predictable' system on an international level. See for example Tetley, W., 'Uniformity of International Private Maritime Law – The Pros, Cons, and Alternatives to International Conventions – How to Adopt an International Convention', *International Maritime Law*, 2000, Volume 24, pp. 775–856.

17 International Convention for the Unification of Certain Rules of Law relating to Bills of Lading (the 'Hague Rules'), and Protocol of Signature (Brussels, 25 August 1924).

18 The Hague-Visby Rules – The Hague Rules as Amended by the Brussels Protocol 1968: The Hague-Visby Rules, Art. II: 'Subject to the provisions of Article VI, under every contract of carriage of goods by sea the carrier, in relation to the loading, handling, stowage, carriage, custody, care and discharge of such goods, shall be subject to the responsibilities and liabilities and entitled to the rights and immunities hereinafter set forth.'

19 The Hague Rules, Art. 1(b): '"Contract of carriage" applies only to contracts of carriage covered by a bill of lading or any similar document of title, in so far as such document relates to the carriage of goods by sea, including any bill of lading or any similar document as aforesaid issued under or pursuant to a charter party from the moment at which such bill of lading or similar document of title regulates the relations between a carrier and a holder of the same.'

being recognised by the leading maritime nations.[20] Additionally, hybrid systems exist, for example in the Scandinavian countries where the codes comply with the Hamburg Rules, given that the chosen Hamburg solution is not inconsistent with Hague-Visby solutions.[21] International carriage by air is governed either by the Warsaw Convention[22] or the Montreal Convention[23] while the Convention on Contract of International Carriage of Goods by Rail (CIM) – Appendix B to Convention concerning International Carriage by Rail (COTIF), applies to international contracts of carriage of goods by rail in the EU, Asia and North-Africa.[24] In Europe (and in some connecting jurisdictions) the Convention on the Contract for the International Carriage of Goods by Road (CMR Convention) applies to international contracts of carriage of goods by road[25] and the Budapest convention on the contract for the carriage of goods by inland waterways (CMNI Convention) applies to international contracts of carriage of goods by inland waterways.[26]

Although the liability schemes set out in the conventions are arguably not fair and balanced and to a large degree are beneficial to the carrier,[27] the fact remains that the legal position of the parties is relatively clear and predictable once the applicable set of rules is established. Doing so in international cases is often a question of deciding the right forum. This is particularly true as regards the most important issue: the scope of damages in the case of damaged or lost cargo where liability is limited, unless the parties have clearly agreed otherwise. The legal barriers related to unimodal contracts of carriage of cargo are accordingly minor, although business is international.

However, in multimodal contracts of carriage, the situation is quite the opposite: A multimodal contract of carriage is normally defined as a contract of carriage which consists of two or more different modes of transport. The definition is based on the one in the United Nations Convention on International

20 United Nations Convention on the Carriage of Goods by Sea (The Hamburg Rules) Hamburg, 30 March 1978, Art. 1, the Hamburg Rules, Art. 2.

21 On the Scandinavian compromise, see Falkanger, T., Bull, H.J. and Brautaset, J., *Scandinavian Maritime Law. The Norwegian Perspective*, 3rd edn, Oslo, 2011, p. 281–282.

22 Convention for the Unification of Certain Rules Relating to International Carriage by Air, signed at Warsaw on 12 October 1929 – Warsaw Convention 1929.

23 Convention for the Unification of Certain Rules for International Carriage by Air – Montreal, signed at Montreal on 28 May 1999.

24 Appendix B to the Convention concerning International Carriage by Rail (COTIF) of 9 June 1999 Uniform Rules Concerning the Contract of International Carriage of Goods by Rail (CIM) Applicable with effect from 1 July 2006.

25 The Convention on the Contract for the International Carriage of Goods by Road (CMR), signed at Geneva, 19 May 1956.

26 Budapest Convention on the Contract for the Carriage of Goods by Inland Waterways (CMNI), Budapest, 25 September–3 October 2000: the CMNI. Art. 1, 'Definitions, In this Convention, 1. "Contract of carriage" means any contract, of any kind, whereby a carrier undertakes against payment of freight to carry goods by inland waterways'.

27 Ramberg, J., 'The Law of Carriage of Goods – Attempts of Harmonization', *Scandinavian Studies in Law*, 1973, Volume 17, pp. 211–252 at p. 252.

Multimodal Transport of Goods (Geneva, 24 May 1980) (the MT convention), despite the fact that the convention never entered into force. According to Article 1 of the multimodal convention: '"International multimodal transport" means the carriage of goods by at least two different modes of transport on the basis of a multimodal transport contract from a place in one country at which the goods are taken in charge by the multimodal transport operator to a place designated for delivery situated in a different country. The operations of pick-up and delivery of goods carried out in the performance of a unimodal transport contract, as defined in such contract, shall not be considered as international multimodal transport.'

With no applicable international legal framework, the legal position of the parties to such a multimodal contract is far from predictable. One solution to the multimodal problem has been to apply the unimodal legal framework to multimodal contracts of carriage. This can be done either directly or by interpretation. However, there is no international coherence as regards this practice. Whether or not, and on what conditions, the unimodal conventions apply, is a very unclear question and the answer varies in different jurisdictions.[28] In other words, no predictability is available as regards the contractual position of the parties to an international multimodal contract of carriage, either in the EU or internationally. In the EU, the Commission has identified the situation as a bottleneck that is preventing the parties to such contracts from choosing a multimodal transport alternative. In particular, unpredictability as regards the liability of the carrier is recognised as a transaction cost preventing the parties from choosing multimodal transport.[29] On an international level, the situation has been described as a 'legal Tower of Babel',[30] which is of course not satisfactory from the standpoint of either the transport customer or the transport operator. Accordingly, a harmonised global legal regime for multimodal transport is not a new request invented by the European Commission; the question has been under discussion for decades, ever since the so-called container revolution started more than 50 years ago. The question has not only been of academic interest, but different international forums have also addressed the problem.

2.3 Attempts to harmonise the law applicable to multimodal transport

Failed conventions

The first attempt to create an international binding legal framework was made by the International Institute for the Unification of Private Law (UNIDROIT),

28 More on this in Chapter 6.

29 More on this in Chapter 3.

30 Dempsey, P., 'The Law of Intermodal Transportation: What It Was, What It Is, What It Should Be', *Transportation Law Journal*, 2000, Volume 27, pp. 367–417 at p. 410.

which presented the Draft Convention on the International Combined Transport of Goods in 1965. This was followed by the Draft Convention on Combined Transport, the so-called Tokyo Rules, drafted by the Comité Maritime International (CMI) in 1969. The drafts differed to a large degree. The first draft was based on the CMR while the latter was based on the maritime liability regime of the Hague Rules and covered only multimodal carriage with a sea leg. These two drafts were combined into a single draft convention by the Inland Transport Committee of the UN Economic Commission for Europe (UN/ECE), the so-called Rome Draft of 1970. During 1970 to 1971, this draft was modified by the UN/ECE in cooperation with the Intergovernmental Consultative Organisation. The work resulted in the Draft Convention on the International Combined Transport of Goods, the so-called TCM draft,[31] which was never developed further.[32]

However, the United Nations Conference on Trade and Development (UNCTAD) followed up the work and eventually prepared a draft convention that led to the United Nations Convention on International Multimodal Transport of Goods (the MT convention) of 1980.[33] Unfortunately, this attempt also failed and the MT convention never entered into force.[34] The close connection between the MT convention and the Hamburg Rules,[35] which also never became an international success, despite being in force, explains the failure of the MT convention.[36] It is, however, not quite fair to characterise the MT convention as a failure. It has had a remarkable impact on legal thinking as regards multimodal contracts of carriage. Most important is that the convention seems to have achieved a harmonised definition of what constitutes multimodal carriage and multimodal contracts of carriage. The MT convention was designed to apply to

31 TCM is the French acronym for Transport Combiné de Marchandises.

32 A further description of these previous attempts to achieve uniformity is given in the report by UNCTAD, 'Implementation of Multimodal Transport Rules', UNCTAD/SDTE/TBL/2, 25 June 2001 at 16.

33 Geneva, 24 May 1980.

34 Available online at http://www.uncitral.org/uncitral/en/uncitral_texts/sale_goods/1980CISG_status.html (accessed 24 February 2015).

35 Both the MT convention as well as the Hamburg Rules have a broad scope of application, and are not restricted to the cargo being loaded on a vessel or other mode of transport. According to the two conventions, the MTO/carrier is responsible for the cargo when in its custody. Furthermore the MT convention and the Hamburg Rules apply to transport, while the Hague-Visby rules only apply if a bill of lading is issued. Additionally, the core area of the conventions contains distinct differences. In the 'new conventions' liability covers a broader range of areas (e.g. carriage of live animals) and the basis of liability varies. Under the Hague-Visby Rules the carrier must exercise due diligence to make the ship seaworthy, with many exceptions, whereas under the MT convention and the Hamburg Rules the MTO/carrier will be liable unless it can prove otherwise. For more on the differences between the conventions see Masud, R., 'The Emerging Legal Regime for Multimodal Transport', *Int'l Business Law Journal*, 1992, Volume 7, p. 825–834.

36 Available online at http://www.uncitral.org/uncitral/en/uncitral_texts/transport_goods/Hamburg_status.html (accessed 24 February 2015).

all contracts of multimodal transport between places in two states.[37] International multimodal transport was defined as 'carriage of goods by at least two different modes of transport on the basis of a multimodal transport contract from a place in one country at which the goods are taken in charge by the multimodal transport operator to a place designated for delivery situated in another country'.[38] This definition is commonly used today. See for example the UN/ECE list of Terminology on Combined Transport, where multimodal transport is defined as: 'Carriage of Goods by two or more modes of transport.'[39]

According to the MT convention, a multimodal transport contract, which is concluded by a multimodal transport operator (MTO), means a contract whereby a MTO undertakes, against payment of freight, to perform or to procure performance of international multimodal transport.[40] The convention was, in other words, designed not only to govern the task of a traditional carrier to perform transport, but also that of freight forwarders and other entities involved in organising carriage.[41]

As regards the liability system, the MT convention offered a compromise between the so-called network and harmonised liability systems. Whereas mode-based liability applies under a network liability system, a harmonised system applies the same liability throughout the carriage. The MT convention applied a harmonised liability system, with an exemption for liability limits in the case of localised damages. If damage is localised, the limits of liability are to be determined by reference to the applicable international convention or mandatory national law that sets a higher liability limit than that of the convention.[42] This solution is known as the modified network system.[43] The limitation limits were set at 920 Special Drawing Rights (SDR) per unit or 2.75 SDR per kilo, whichever was the higher.[44] For multimodal contracts of carriage without a sea or inland waterway leg the liability limit should however, be equal to the CMR liability of 8.33 SDR per kilogram gross weight.[45] The limitations on liability resulting from delay should, according to Article 18(4) the MT convention, be calculated by reference to the freight rate. In the case of concurrent causes, the MT convention, in Article 17, prescribes that the MTO is liable only to the extent that loss, damage or delay in delivery is attributable to acts or omissions of the MTO or anyone it is responsible for. The MTO would have the burden of proof.

37 MT convention, Art. 2.

38 MT convention, Art. 1.1.

39 Terminology on Combined Transport, prepared by the UN/ECE, the European Conference of Ministers of Transport (ECMT) and the European Commission, United Nations, New York and Geneva, 2001, at 1.0.

40 MT convention, Art. 1.3.

41 This was also proposed by the 2005 expert group assisting the Commission in the search for a EU regime on multimodal contracts of carriage, see Chapter 5 (at 5.1).

42 MT convention, Art. 19.

43 More on this in Chapters 4 and 6.

44 MT convention, Art. 18.1.

45 MT convention, Art. 18.3.

The MT convention has had a great impact on legislation in the area of multimodal transport by serving as a model for several standard documents in use, as well as for both regional and national legislation on multimodal contracts of carriage.

UNCTAD/ICC rules for multimodal transport documents

The most widespread set of soft law rules, based on the MT convention, is ICC (International Chamber of Commerce) publication No. 418, the UNCTAD/ICC rules.[46] The UNCTAD/ICC rules is a set of soft law rules that apply on an opt-in basis: if the parties have agreed that the rules will apply, then they will apply and, furthermore, they will supersede any additional contractual term in conflict with them.[47] However, because the rules are contractual by nature, they will only take effect if not contrary to mandatory provisions of international conventions or national law applicable to international multimodal contracts of carriage. This is explicitly stated in Article 13 of the UNCTAD/ICC.

The UNCTAD/ICC rules were prepared, at the request of the UNCTAD Committee on Shipping, by a joint working group consisting of members from the UNCTAD secretariat and the ICC. The instruction to the group was that the rules should be based on the Hague and the Hague-Visby Rules, as well as on existing standard documents such as the International Federation of Freight Forwarders Associations (FIATA) Bill of Lading (FBL) and the ICC Uniform Rules for Combined Transport Documents.[48] The UNCTAD/ICC rules were finalised in 1991 and entered into force on 1 January 1992. They have been incorporated into the FIATA FBL 1992 and the MULTIDOC 95 prepared by the Baltic and International Maritime Council (BIMCO).

Although inspired by the MT convention, the rules apply a slightly different liability system. First of all, the UNCTAD/ICC rules only apply to multimodal transport contracts where a MTO has undertaken the obligation to perform carriage, or is actually doing so.[49] The legal position of entities merely involved in organising carriage, such as freight forwarders, is not governed by the rules. Furthermore, the UNCTAD/ICC rules do not apply to delay, unless the consignor has made a declaration of interest in timely delivery that has been signed by the multimodal transport organiser.[50] And, finally, damage, loss or delay related to navigational errors and fire are exempted in the case of carriage by sea or inland waterways. This, however, does not apply to initial unseaworthiness.[51]

46 The rules are published in ICC publication No. 418, and are also available online at http://unctad.org/en/PublicationsLibrary/tradewp4inf.117_corr.1_en.pdf (accessed 24 February 2015).

47 UNCTAD/ICC rules, Art. 1.

48 UNCTAD/ICC, Introduction.

49 UNCTAD/ICC rules, Arts 2.1 and 2.2.

50 UNCTAD/ICC rule, Art. 5.1.

51 UNCTAD/ICC rules, Art. 5.4.

Despite the latter exception, the differences between the MT convention and the UNCTAD/ICC rules are clearly attributable to the fact that the UNCTAD/ICC rules were drafted to correspond with the maritime conventions. This divergence between the maritime system and other land-based solutions seems to be a core explanation for the slow progress in finding a joint international solution to the multimodal problem. So far, the maritime lobbyists appear to have been the more influential than lobbyists from other transport sectors in the international arena. However, as will be outlined below, in particular in Chapters 4 and 6, the conflict between land-based systems and maritime systems is still on the political agenda. National interests related to the different industries are a driving factor.

Political and economic divergences seem to be the main hindrance to a new legal regime for multimodal transport.[52] This was already visible during the negotiations on the failed 1980 MT convention. The representatives from the US delegation to the UN Conference on the Convention, William Driscoll and Paul B. Larsen, claimed that the proposed MT Convention represented 'a distinct departure from the earlier transportation liability conventions . . . which were basically legal and technical documents'. The proposed multimodal convention was, to the contrary, 'an integral part of a long-term strategy on the part of the developing countries to realize maximum economic benefits from the international transport sector'.[53] As will be outlined below, the tension related to the political and economic interests involved have not eased in the nearly 40 years that have passed. Even today, when the international transport community is discussing a regime that should (partly) apply to multimodal contracts of carriage, the political divergences are strong, and what Driscoll and Larsen expressed about the MT convention in 1982 – 'It is an accepted fact that the Convention is not likely to come into force in the near future'[54] – also relates to the present discussion.

The pending Rotterdam Rules

On 11 December 2008 the United Nations Commission for International Trade Law (UNCITRAL) General Assembly adopted the United Nations Convention on Contracts for the International Carriage of Goods Wholly or Partly by Sea. The Convention was signed on 29 September 2009 in Rotterdam, and is therefore called the Rotterdam Rules. If the Rotterdam Rules become an international success, the absence of an international legal framework for multimodal contracts of carriage will no longer fully apply. How this will affect the EU discussion

52 More on this below in Part II.

53 Driscoll, W. and Larsen B., 'The Convention on International Multimodal Transport of Goods', *Tulane Law Review*, 1982, Volume 5, pp. 193–280 at p. 195. Driscoll and Larsen were respectively Chairman and Vice Chairman of the United States Delegation to the 1980 United Nations Conference on a Convention on International Multimodal Transport of Goods. The article reflects their personal views.

54 Op. cit., note 53, at p. 195.

remains to be seen, but it might put an end to the EU attempt.[55] So far, the following Member States have signed the Convention: Denmark, France, Greece, Luxembourg, the Netherlands, Poland, Spain and Sweden. From an international point of view it is interesting that the United States has signed but China has not, and from a Nordic perspective there may be split in traditional Nordic transport law cooperation: Denmark, Norway and Sweden have signed, but Finland and Iceland have not. However, as of 1 May 2015, Spain is the only EU Member State that has ratified the Convention.[56]

The Rotterdam Rules are a result of intergovernmental negotiations that took place during the period from 2002 to 2009. The negotiations were held by UNICITRAL and its Working Group III 2002–2008: Transport Law.[57] The preparatory work and a preliminary draft of the rules were presented by the CMI.[58] Generally speaking, the Rotterdam Rules represent an intervention in international transport regimes. It is not only a liability convention, but also a modern convention governing almost the whole contractual relationship between the parties to a multimodal contract with a sea leg.[59] If it succeeds it will be the first international convention governing international multimodal transport. Numerous articles and several books have been published on different questions related to the Rotterdam Rules. Some are gathered online by UNCITRAL.[60]

As regards multimodal carrier liability, the Rotterdam Rules apply a network liability system with a fallback clause, which has been defined as a modified or limited network system.[61] In a limited or modified network system the great majority of the rules are uniform, whereas a few vary according to the rules applicable to the individual transport legs. In the Rotterdam Rules, the specific rules on carrier liability are subject to a network system:[62] according to Article 26,

55 More on this in Chapter 5 (at 5.2).

56 For the convention to enter into force, 20 states must ratify it. As at 1 May 2015, in addition to Spain, which was the first country to ratify it in 2011, only Togo and Congo have ratified the convention. Available online at http://www.uncitral.org/uncitral/en/uncitral_texts/transport_goods/rotterdam_status.html (accessed 26 February 2015).

57 Available online at http://www.uncitral.org/uncitral/en/commission/working_groups/3Transport.html (accessed 26 February 2015). The background to the Rules is described by several authors, see e.g. Diamond, A., 'The Rotterdam Rules', *Lloyd's Maritime and Commercial Law Quarterly*, 2009, Part 4, pp. 445–536.

58 Available online at http://www.rotterdamrules2009.com/cms/index.php?page=general-information (accessed 26 February 2015).

59 von Ziegler, A, ' Liability of the Carrier for Loss, Damage or Delay', in von Ziegler, A., Schelin, J. and Zunarelli, S. (eds), *The Rotterdam Rules 2008*, Kluwer, 2010, pp. 93–132 at pp. 94–95.

60 Available online at https://www.zotero.org/groups/bibliography_of_recent_writings_related_to_the_work_of_uncitral/items/collectionKey/K7J78DUJ (accessed 26 February 2015).

61 On the terminology see, De Witt, R., 'Multimodal Transport', *Lloyd's Shipping Law Library*, London/Hong Kong, 1995, pp. 138–143.

62 Haak, K.F., 'Carriage Preceding or Subsequent to Sea Carriage under the Rotterdam Rules', *European Journal of Commercial Contract Law*, 2010, Volume 1/2, pp. 63–71.

provisions in mandatory international unimodal conventions regulating non-maritime legs and dealing with the *carrier's liability, limitation of liability and time for suit*, will, in certain conditions, prevail over provisions in the Rotterdam Rules governing the same. The situation has also been described as being a result of the *lex specialis* principle.[63] Another way of addressing this is to see the liability rules of inland carriage conventions as *integrated parts* of the framework of the Rotterdam Rules.[64]

The network liability system of Article 26 is one of the most challenged provisions of the Rotterdam Rules. It has, for example, been accused of being *too expansive* as it expands its scope to include land legs (also *national* land legs) in combination with short sea legs, and furthermore because it does not include environmental concerns and does not comply with European needs.[65] On the other hand, the network system of the Rotterdam Rules has also been criticised for being *too narrow*; the inclusion of other legs should not be restricted to the liability system, but should include all parts of the Convention.[66] Professor Diamond therefore calls for a complete revision of the rules on applicability and conflict of conventions.[67] This is supported by Mahin Faghfouri, presenting his own view, but nevertheless representing the International Multimodal Transport Association. Faghfouri states in his conclusions that the Rotterdam Rules do not reflect 'the objective of a multimodal regime establishing one set of liability rules to cover the entire multimodal movement of goods under the responsibility of one operator', which according to Faghfouri is what the multimodal industry urgently needs.[68] Using the same words as the EU Commission, he calls for a 'simple, transparent and predictable legal framework' for multimodal contracts of carriage.[69] Until such a system is agreed, Faghfouri predicts that the present legal situation will continue.[70]

63 In relation to this, see Rasmussen, U., 'Additional Provisions Relating to Particular Stages of Carriage', in von Ziegler, A., Schelin, J. and Zunarelli, S. (eds), *The Rotterdam Rules 2008*, Kluwer, 2010, pp. 93–132 at p. 144.

64 In relation to this, see van der Ziel, G.J., *Multimodal Aspects of the Rotterdam Rules, CMI Yearbook, Part II*, 2009, at p. 301. See also Haak, K.F., 'Carriage Preceding or Subsequent to Sea Carriage under the Rotterdam Rules', *European Journal of Commercial Contract Law*, 2010, Volume 1/2, pp. 63–71 at p. 65.

65 Røsæg, E., 'The Rotterdam Rules as a Model for Multimodal Transport Law', *European Journal of Commercial contract Law*, 2010 Volume 1/2, pp. 94–97 at p. 97. However, the author also states that 'although the Rotterdam Rules are not regarded as the best set of rules for multimodal transport, it might still be the best we could hope for'. l.c.

66 Hancock, C., 'Multimodal Transport and the New UN Convention on the Carriage of Goods', *The Journal of International Maritime Law*, 2008 Volume 14, pp. 484–495 at pp. 491–492 and p. 495.

67 Diamond, A., 'The Next Sea Carriage Convention?' *Lloyd's Maritime and Commercial Law Quarterly*, 2008, Part 1, pp. 135–187 at p. 187.

68 Faghfouri, M., 'International Regulation of Liability for Multimodal Transport – in Search of Uniformity', *WMU Journal of Maritime Affairs*, Volume 5, Issue 1, pp. 95–114 at p. 113–114.

69 Op. cit., at p. 114. More on this in Chapter 5 (at 5.2).

70 L.C.

If the liability system of the Rotterdam Rules applies, which will normally be the case for loss, damage or delay attributable to the sea leg of a multimodal voyage, then the liability provisions in Chapter 5 of the Rotterdam Rules will apply. Carrier liability under the Rotterdam Rules is contractual and must accordingly be considered in the light of the provisions on the basic obligations of the carrier (Chapter 4 of the Rules). If the claimant can prove that the carrier is in breach of contract, the latter will be liable, unless able to prove otherwise, Article 17(2). The carrier will also be relieved of liability if it can prove that some of the alternatives under Article 17(3) apply. Liability will be calculated by reference to the value of goods (Article 22) and may be limited under Article 59. According to Article 59, liability might be limited to 875 SDR per unit or 3 SDR per kilo. This is a slight increase in liability compared to the present maritime conventions, such as the Hague-Visby and Inland Waterways conventions where the liability is 2.5 SDR per kilo, and 666.67 per unit, but far less than the liability limit in the other unimodal conventions.[71] The highest liability limit applies in air transport with 19 SDR per kilo,[72] followed by rail at 17 SDR per kilo[73] and road transport where 8.33 SDR per kilo applies.[74] As the liability limits are widely applicable, with the exception of situations of gross neglect or wilful misconduct, the liability of the carrier will vary considerably depending on which liability system is adopted. It should, however, be noted that according to all conventions, except the CMR, the carrier can by agreement accept a higher liability.

In relation to discussion on the Rotterdam Rules, the question whether mandatory rules on carriage of goods are at all desirable has been raised again. Although the intent behind the Rotterdam Rules was to promote trade and economic development, it has been argued that none of this has been achieved.[75] However, unlike previous negotiations, the atmosphere during the Rotterdam Rules negotiations was found to be one of cooperation rather than political confrontation.[76] Nevertheless, the Rules have been subject to massive criticism, perhaps more from an academic perspective than from the industry itself. Many stakeholders and scholars find the convention complicated and therefore do not advocate ratification of the Rules. The terminology is considered to be unclear. For example, the wording 'performing party' and 'maritime performing party' should be changed and the familiar terms 'subcontractors' and 'agents' should

71 Hague-Visby Rules Art. IV.5(a) and Art. 20 CMNI.

72 The Montreal Convention, Art. 22, sets the limit at 17 SDR, but according to Art. 24, the limit should be reviewed every fifth year. The International Civil Aviation Organization (ICAO) raised the limit to 19 SDR with effect from 30 September 2009.

73 CIM, Art. 30.2.

74 CMR, Art. 23.3.

75 Aguirre, C., 'The Rotterdam Rules from the Perspective of a Country that Is a Consumer of Shipping Services', *Uniform Law Review*, 2009, Volume 14, pp. 869–884.

76 Faria, J., 'Uniform Law and Functional Equivalence: Diverting Paths or Stops Along the Same Road? Thoughts on a New International Regime for Transport Documents', *Elon Law Review*, 2011 Volume 2, Issue 1, pp. 1–37.

be used throughout the Rotterdam Rules.[77] In some areas, however, such as the obligation of the carrier, the Rotterdam Rules have retained the language of the maritime conventions such as the Hague Rules and the Hague-Visby Rules and might thus benefit from the existing body of case law[78] although the duties of the carrier in some areas have been extended.[79] The Rotterdam Rules are mainly a maritime convention, and the maritime industry in particular has been positive towards those Rules.[80]

In a multimodal context, however, the main concern has been the relationship between the Rotterdam Rules and existing unimodal conventions. From a European perspective, the convention on international road carriage, CMR, has been pointed out as the most problematic convention.[81] This is mainly because the CMR in some jurisdictions also applies to the road leg of a multimodal contract of carriage, which is then considered a mixed contract of carriage.[82] From a US perspective the famous *Kirby* case abolished the mixed contract approach;[83] today an inland carrier might also be protected by the maritime legal regime under certain conditions. Because of its *network system* the Rotterdam Rules would change the new US doctrine.[84] The future of the Convention from a US perspective is, however, still open and this is a fact that hinders the success of the Rotterdam Rules, as US ratification is considered crucial for the future of the Rules.[85]

The Rotterdam Rules are also criticised for not identifying the person liable for cargo damage. The provision on 'identity of the carrier' in Article 32 is,

77 Atamer, K., 'Construction Problems in the Rotterdam Rules regarding the Performing and Maritime Performing Parties', *Journal of Maritime Law & Commerce*, 2010, Volume 41, Issue 4, pp. 469–497.

78 Nikaki, T., 'The Carrier's Duties Under the Rotterdam Rules: Better the Devil You Know?' *Tulane Maritime Law Journal*, 2010, Volume 35, Issue 1, pp. 1–44.

79 Nikaki, T., 'The Fundamental Duties of the Carrier under the Rotterdam Rules', *The Journal of International Maritime Law*, 2008, Volume 14, p. 512–523.

80 E.g. BIMCO favours the Rotterdam Rules. Available online at https://www.bimco.org/About/Viewpoint/13_Rotterdam_Rules.aspx (accessed 2 March 2015).

81 Clarke, M., 'A Conflict of Conventions: The UNCITRAL/CMI Draft Transport Instrument on Your Doorstep', *The Journal of International Maritime Law*, 2003, Volume 9, pp. 28–39, and Legros, C., 'Relations Between the Rotterdam Rules and the Convention on the Carriage of Goods by Road', *Tulane Maritime Law Journal*, 2012, Volume 36, pp. 725–740. More on this Chapter 6 (at 6.2).

82 See e.g. the English *Quantum* case discussed in Chapter 6 (at 6.2).

83 *Norfolk Southern Ry. v James N. Kirby, Pty Ltd.*, 543 U.S. 14 (2004). The *Kirby* case is described in Chapter 6 (at 6.2).

84 Crowley, M., 'The Limited Scope of the Cargo Liability Regime Covering Carriage of Goods by Sea: The Multimodal Problem', *Tulane Law Review*, 2005, Volume 79, pp. 1461–1504.

85 This is clearly stated by Chester D. Hopper who claims that the wait and see attitude as regards the Rotterdam Rules is easily traced to the fact that the maritime world does not need another maritime treaty that the United States has not ratified. See Hooper, C., 'Ratification of the Rotterdam Rules and their Implications for International Shipping', p. 1. Available online at http://www.skuld.com/documents/library/beacon/beacon_2_2012_rotterdam_rules.pdf (accessed 2 March 2015).

for example, criticised for not being precise enough.[86] Additionally, even the procedural part of the Convention is considered difficult and as not providing the simple and straightforward regime which the industry is in need of.[87] However, the incompleteness can be explained: according to its supporters, it is not the Convention per se that is complicated; it is rather the issues that are intricate.[88]

It has been argued that the Rotterdam Rules would fulfil the need of the industry today,[89] but also that the scope of the Rules is too narrow – an international multimodal convention should be based on all transport conventions, not only maritime conventions.[90] In the end, it seemingly boils down to politics. As pointed out by Professor Tetley, all attempts at international harmonisation must recognise the existing diversity of social purpose and manner, as well as style, or they will fail.[91] In an area of business where different interests are at stake, the harmonising process is a delicate matter of balance and compromise. However, the whole idea of harmonisation through conventions has been questioned and soft law solutions have been proposed as an alternative, and a model law, restatements, standard form agreements, standard clauses and terms and the modern *lex mercatoria/maritimia* have been suggested as methods to increase legal uniformity.[92]

The international problem has been, as stated by Bonell, that 'the real trouble' begins when conventions are implemented in national law and become subject to interpretation by national lawyers.[93] This point is also recognised by Berlingieri, who nevertheless finds that adoption of conventions in their original text contributes to uniformity, though this cannot by itself ensure uniformity.[94] The theoretical

86 Zunarelli, S., 'The Carrier and the Maritime Performing Party in the Rotterdam Rules', *Uniform Law Review*, 2009, Volume 14, pp. 1011–1023.

87 Lamont-Black, S., 'Claiming Damages in Multimodal Transport: A Need for Harmonisation', *Tulane Maritime Law Journal*, 2012, Volume 36, pp. 707–724. Lamont-Black shows how the process of making a claim for damages is made unnecessarily complicated under the Rotterdam Rules, p. 723–724.

88 Fujiati, T., 'The Comprehensive Coverage of the new Convention: Performing Parties and the Multimodal Implications', *Texas International Law Journal*, 2009, Volume 44, pp. 349–373. Berlingieri, F., 'Revisiting the Rotterdam Rules', *Lloyd's Maritime and Commercial Law Quarterly*, 2010, Volume 6, p. 583–639.

89 Beare, S., 'Liability Regimes: Where We Are, How We Got There and Where We Are Going', *Lloyd's Maritime and Commercial Law Quarterly*, 2002, Volume 3, pp. 306–315.

90 Alcántara, J.M., 'The New Regime and Multimodal Transport', *Lloyd's Maritime and Commercial Law Quarterly*, 2002, Part 3, pp. 339–404.

91 Tetley, W., 'Uniformity of International Private Maritime Law – The pros, Cons, and Alternatives to International Conventions – How to Adopt an International Convention', *International Maritime Law*, 2000 Volume 24, pp. 775–856 at p. 823.

92 L.C.

93 Bonell, M., 'International Uniform Law in Practice – Or Where the Real Trouble Begins', *The American Journal of Comparative Law*, 1990, Volume 38, pp. 865–888.

94 Berlingieri, F., 'Uniformity in Maritime Law and Implementation of International Conventions', *Journal of Maritime Law and Commerce*, 1987, Volume 18, Issue 3, pp. 317–350.

problem of 'legal irritants'[95] in national legal systems will not be addressed further here, but is a reminder of the problems connected to harmonisation through international legal instruments.[96] However, it should be emphasised that the problems referred above to a large extent are problems that do not exist in the EU, where the Court of Justice of the European Union plays an important role in the harmonising process.

While waiting for a regional or international solution, two EU Member States, the Netherlands and Germany, have opted for their own national legislation on international multimodal carriage of goods.

2.4 National solutions in the EU

The 1991 Dutch solution – an all-inclusive network system

The Netherlands is a country with a strong maritime tradition. It is host to some of the largest ports in Europe. National rules on multimodal transport were introduced in the Dutch Civil Code (Burgerlijk Wetboek) in 1991.[97] The Dutch Code defines multimodal or combined carriage of goods as 'a contract of carriage of goods whereby the carrier (combined carrier) binds himself towards the consignor, in one and the same carriage, to the effect that the carriage will take place in part by sea, inland waterway, road, rail, air, pipeline or by means of any other mode of transport'.[98] Apart from the fact that the Dutch regulation includes transport partly by pipeline, the definition of multimodal carriage is in line with the traditional perception of multimodal carriage – one contract of carriage performed by more than one mode of transport. Moreover, the defined task of a multimodal carrier is, according to Dutch law, in line with the task of a traditional unimodal carrier. The carrier is to perform the carriage, not to procure it. Dutch law, in other words, draws a strict line between the multimodal carrier and the freight forwarder.[99]

95 The term 'legal irritants' was coined by Gunter Teubner in his famous article: 'Legal Irritants: Good Faith in British Law or How Unifying Law Ends Up in New Differences', *Modern Law Review*, 1998, Volume 61, pp. 11–32. In the article, Teubner highlights the problems that arise when bringing a legal concept from one legal system to another.

96 However, harmonisation through the EU system is more efficient because of the supranational character of the Union. This point will be discussed further in Chapter 10.

97 Book 8, Title 2, Chapter 2, Sections 40–52, entered into force on 1 April 1991. The Dutch rules on multimodal contracts of carriage are available online at http://www.dutchcivillaw.com/civilcodebook088.htm (accessed 4 March 2015).

98 Dutch Civil Code, Book 8, Section 40.

99 The freight forwarder is governed by the Dutch Civil Code, Book 8, Section 60: 'A "freight forwarding contract" is a contract under which one of the parties (the forwarder) has engaged itself towards its counterparty (the principal) to conclude on its behalf one or more contracts of carriage of goods with a carrier in respect of goods which that counterparty has placed at the disposal of the forwarder, or to make on behalf of that counterparty one or more stipulations (clauses) in one or more of such contracts of carriage of goods.'

A multimodal contract is seen as a *mixed contract* subject to an accumulation of regulations.[100] This means that the contract is regarded as the sum total of unimodal contracts and is by no means regarded as *sui generis*.[101] According to Dutch Law, the *contractual carrier* is liable for damage, loss or delay according to the rules of the *unimodal regimes* regulating the mode of transport during which the damage, loss or delay occurred, regardless of its own actual performance, unless it can prove no fault.[102] Liability is, in other words, normal contractual liability based on presumed fault or neglect. The contractual carrier is thus liable regardless of the fact that the carriage might have been outsourced to an independent subcontractor or performed by the carrier's employees.

If none of the specific regimes applies, for example if the carrier cannot provide evidence of where the loss occurred, then 'liability is determined according to the rules of law applicable to the part or parts of the transport where that event may have occurred and from which results the highest amount of damages'.[103]

The 1998 German CMR-based solution

In Germany, transport law was hugely reformed in 1998. The old Commercial Code (Handelsgesetzbuch (HGB)) §§ 407–472 was replaced by new provisions on contracts of carriage, contracts of forwarding and contracts of warehousing.[104] Sea transport was not included in the reform, as contracts of sea carriage were already regulated by the HGB. However, multimodal contracts with a sea leg were included. The German law commission set up in 1992 had clear instructions to work out a report and a draft law to modernise and unify the field of transport law by making it simpler and less mandatory, and adapting it as far as possible to the international rules of transport, mainly the 1956 CMR.[105] The new German regime is, to a large degree, based upon the CMR Convention, with one deviation: except for the provisions on liability limitation, the regime provides an *opt-out solution* and is therefore entirely subject to contractual modifications by the parties. The regime applies to national contracts of carriage, and – in the absence

100 Hoeks, M., *Multimodal Transport Law – The Law Applicable to the Multimodal Contract for the Carriage of Goods*, Kluwer Law International, 2010, at 10.4.1.

101 *Sui generis* is a Latin phrase meaning 'of its own kind or class' and hence unique in its characteristics. *Sui generis* could also describe something as being the only one of its kind, or peculiar. *Black's Law Dictionary*, 6th edn, West Publishing, 1990. More on this in Chapter 6.

102 Dutch Civil Code, Book 8, Section 41.

103 Dutch Civil Code, Book 8, Section 43.

104 The new law was adopted on 25 June 1998.

105 Herber, R., 'The New German Transport Legislation', *European Transport Law*, 1998, Volume XXXIII, No 5., pp. 591–606 at p. 593.

of binding international conventions – to international transport if governed by German law.[106]

The main principle is that multimodal contracts of carriage are subject to the German transport law system as laid down in HGB §§ 407–472. According to this, a contract of carriage is purely consensual and does not depend on any formality, including the issuance of a consignment note, which is only regarded as proof of the contract.[107] A negotiable transport document might, however, be issued: this is regulated in HGB §§ 444 *et seq*. Furthermore, the German law is not mandatory like the CMR. However, this does not fully apply to the liability rules, which have a limited mandatory character in some cases.

First of all, the basis of liability cannot be modified by any of the parties by general conditions. Individual stipulations, on the other hand, are allowed.[108] The borderline between what are considered general conditions and what are individual stipulations might be hard to draw. As it is the carrier that normally introduces general conditions into the contract of carriage, it is the carrier that must prove that the contract was individually negotiated.[109] The intention of the rule is to protect the weaker party, which in this context is the cargo owner or the sender. The special rules protecting a sender who is a consumer are another peculiarity introduced in German legislation. In such a case, the rules on liability are completely binding.[110]

The provisions on liability can be found in HGB §§ 425–439 and are mainly built on the CMR solution. Accordingly, the carrier is liable for damage, loss or delay unless it can prove that the damage, loss or delay was caused by circumstances the carrier could not avoid, or was unable to prevent.[111] However, the German legislation has clarified that the carrier must in any case prove that it has exercised the utmost diligence. Regarding the amount of liability, *limitations* regarding loss or damage are the same as under the CMR, that is 8.33 SDR, except liability for delay, which is set at three times the freight (and three times the CMR solution).[112] In line with other international regimes, however, German law acknowledges the parties' right to derogate from the limitation rules (and here also by general conditions), though restricted to a range of between 2 SDR and 40 SDR.[113] The German code has a particular provision on limitation of economic loss caused otherwise than by loss of or damage to the goods, or by delay. This kind of economic loss can be a result of side obligations of the

106 Op. cit., at p. 605.
107 HGB §§ 407–408, see: Herber, p. 595.
108 HGB § 449.
109 Herber, op. cit., note 105, p. 597.
110 HGB §§ 451 and Herber, p. 599.
111 Herber, p. 593.
112 HGB §§ 431(1)
113 HBG §§ 449(2)1.

contract of carriage not covered by the scope of application of the code. And, according to § 437, the actual carrier is also liable along with the contractual carrier. All persons liable under the contract of carriage – carrier, actual carrier, sender, agents and employees – might lose their right to limit their liability in case of intent or severe fault.

Regarding liability in *multimodal contracts of carriage*, the regime applies to these contracts as far as concealed damages are concerned.[114] However, a party that is able to prove that loss of or damage to the cargo or the circumstances causing delay were caused by a specific part of the voyage subject to mandatory rules different from the German transport liability regime may invoke the rules of that other regime. This is in line with the network principle.[115] Furthermore, although the parties are allowed to agree that even in cases where the place of damage is known (localised damage), the liability system of the HGB will apply, this is not possible if there is a conflict with mandatory international conventions.[116]

2.5 No rules on environmental matters

Interestingly enough, none of the proposed international legal frameworks on multimodal carriage, nor any of the two European national legal regimes, mention environmental issues either as the rationale behind the proposed rules or in relation to the contractual obligations of the parties. Both the international discussion and the national discussion in Germany and the Netherlands have been focusing on the needs of the industry and the benefits of harmonised contractual rules.

As will be outlined in Chapter 4, the EU Commission's effort towards a harmonised liability regime is justified by environmental considerations and therefore pioneering. After the Lisbon Treaty,[117] environmental issues should permeate all EU policy, including transport policy. In the following chapters we will have a closer look at the CTP and its focus on sustainability. First,

114 HGB, §§ 452a.

115 HGB, §§ 452a.

116 This is not always clear, as pointed out by Herber, op. cit., note 105, p. 601, e.g. in maritime law a bill of lading is necessary to make the Hague or Hague-Visby Rules binding. As the test in a multimodal case is 'hypothetical' it is not always easy to know whether a bill of lading would have been issued or not.

117 The Treaty of Lisbon (initially known as the Reform Treaty) is an international agreement that amends the two treaties that form the constitutional basis of the EU. The Treaty of Lisbon was signed by the EU Member States on 13 December 2007, and entered into force on 1 December 2009. It amends the Maastricht Treaty (1993), which also is known as the Treaty on European Union, and the Treaty of Rome (1958), which also is known as the Treaty Establishing the European Community (TEEC). In Lisbon, the Treaty of Rome was renamed the Treaty on the Functioning of the European Union (TFEU). More on the EU legal framework in Chapter 3.

however, the question of Union competences in the area of transport law will be addressed. In the general discussion of EU competences in the area of contract law,[118] it is clear that EU has competence to govern contracts of carriage. However, the Union has not taken advantage of this competence; quite the reverse, the EU has restricted its activity in business-to-business transport contracts. In this context, discussion of a regional liability regime for European multimodal carriage of goods is innovative and represents a new step by the EU into what has previously been an area within the competences of the Member States.

118 See e.g. Weatherill, S., 'European Private Law and the Constitutional Dimension', in F. Cafaggi (ed.), *The Institutional Framework of European Private Law*, Oxford University Press, 2006, pp. 79–106.

3 EU competence in the area of international transport

3.1 Internal competence

Established by the Treaty of Rome

The legal base for a common transport policy (CTP) was established in 1957 by the Treaty of Rome,[1] which recognised transport as an essential prerequisite for a common market. Accordingly, the Community was given competence to develop a common policy in the sphere of transport. Article 3 listed the activities of the Community, which included: 'the inauguration of a common transport policy'.[2] Transport, being one of three policies, was accordingly assigned its own title.[3] However, competence was restricted to the area of *rail, road and inland waterways*.[4] The Council of the European Union could decide whether and to what extent and by what procedure appropriate provisions *might* be laid down for sea and air transport. However, such decisions could only be made unanimously.[5]

1 The Treaty of Rome, signed in Rome on 25 March 1957, established the European Economic Community (EEC).

2 Treaty of Rome, Article 3: 'For the purposes set out in the preceding Article, the activities of the Community shall include, under the conditions and with the timing provided for in this Treaty: . . . (e) the inauguration of a common transport policy.'

3 Title IV TRANSPORT, e.g. Arts 74 and 75(a):

'ARTICLE 74

The objectives of this Treaty shall, in matters governed by this Title, be pursued by Member States within the framework of a common transport policy.

ARTICLE 75

1 For the purpose of implementing Article 74, and taking into account the distinctive features of transport, the Council shall, acting unanimously until the end of the second stage and by a qualified majority thereafter, lay down, on a proposal from the Commission and after consulting the Economic and Social Committee and the Assembly [European Parliament]:

(a) common rules applicable to international transport to or from the territory of a Member State or passing across the territory of one or more Member States;
(b) the conditions under which non-resident carriers may operate transport services within a Member State;
(c) any other appropriate provisions.'

4 Treaty of Rome, Art. 84(1).

5 Treaty of Rome, Art. 84(2).

Thus, from the very beginning, sea and air transport were left out of the area of Community competence.

Economic integration was nevertheless expected to lead to growth in transport. The transport sector was therefore anticipated to become one of the 'major motors of economic integration'.[6] Despite the Treaty instruction and general expectations, progress in the area of transport was very slow to start with, from a Community perspective. A common transport policy did not emerge until the European Court of Justice[7] intervened in 1985 and, in a landmark decision, *Parliament v Council*,[8] ruled that the Council had failed to develop a common transport policy. Court intervention was followed by an amendment to the Treaty of Rome in 1986 by The European Single Act.[9] As the first major revision of the Treaty of Rome, this provided the Community with extended competence in the area of transport. After the revision, the decision to act in the area of sea and air transport could be taken 'by a qualified majority'.[10] This rule has been kept.

Following the entry into force of the Treaty of Lisbon, the competence of the European Union (EU) is governed by the Treaty on European Union (the TEU) and the Treaty on the Functioning of the European Union (the TFEU).[11] These treaties represent the foundations of the European Union and carry the same legal weight.[12] Today, EU competence in transport by rail, road and inland waterways is governed by TFEU, Article 100(1), while transport by sea and air is governed by Article 100(2). The difference between the first and second paragraphs is that the provisions of TFEU Title VI on transport 'shall' apply to transport by road, rail and inland waterways while, according to Article 100(2), the European Parliament and the Council 'may lay down appropriate provisions' for sea and air transport. Even though the Parliament and Council need not legislate in the area of sea and air transport, they can do so. Therefore, the difference in wording has no impact on the question of competence as in whether the EU can act or not.[13] We should also note that the procedural requirements for enacting legislation are the same for all modes of transport: appropriate provisions should

6 Smith, D., 'The European Union's Commitment to Sustainable Development: Is the Commitment Symbolic or Substantive in the Context of Transport Policy?' *Colo. J. Int'l Envtl. & Pol'y*, 2002, Volume 13, pp. 242–331 at p. 271.

7 Now The Court of Justice (CJEU).

8 *European Parliament v Council of the European Communities* C-13/183 [1985] ECR.

9 The Single European Act, Luxembourg, 17 February 1986.

10 Op. cit., note 9, Art. 16(5). The new version of Art. 84(2) is accordingly: 'The Council may, acting by a qualified majority, decide whether, to what extent and by what procedure appropriate provisions may be laid down for sea and air transport.'

11 Consolidated versions of the TEU as amended by the Treaty of Lisbon, and the TFEU are published in OJ C 83, 30.3.2010, 1.

12 Art. 1(2) TFEU.

13 The Lisbon Treaty here accords with the EC Treaty Art. 80 and previous case law from the CJEU, such as the French merchant seamen case: *Commission v French Republic*, C-167/73, [1974] ECR 359 and the Open Skies judgment, *Commission v Germany*, C-476/98 [2002] ECR I-9885.

or may be laid down to be accomplished in accordance with ordinary legislative procedures, after consulting the Economic and Social Committee and the Committee of the Regions.[14] The difference is rather that the EU has no duty to act in the area of sea and air carriage, whereas it probably is obliged to do so in the other legislative areas. However, its competence is restricted by certain fundamental principles of EU law.

Limited by certain fundamental principles of EU law

The EU replaces and succeeds the previous European Community and possesses legal personality.[15] In accordance with the *principle of conferral* established in Article 5 of the TEU, EU competences are conferred on it by its Member States. The Union has no competence as of right, which means that unless the treaties contain explicit agreement to the contrary, areas of policy remain within the sphere of Member State competence and outside the competence of the EU.[16] This was also the case earlier, but the rule was stated explicitly for the first time in the failed Treaty establishing a Constitution for Europe[17] and was then carried over into its replacement, the Treaty of Lisbon.

According to the TFEU, the competence of the EU can be either exclusive or shared.[18] In the area of transport, the EU has been granted shared competence.[19] Shared competence means that both the EU and the Member States may *legislate* and *adopt legally binding acts* in the relevant area.[20] Clearly, shared competence could lead to conflicts of legally binding norms. For this reason, the mechanism by which competence is shared is governed in the treaties.

With regard to the Member States, their competence to legislate is restricted by the activity of the Union: the Member States may exercise their competence to the extent that the Union has not exercised its competence or to the extent that the Union has decided to cease exercising its competence.[21] If the Member States have conferred competence on the Union, and the Union makes use of its competence, it will be contrary to EU legislation to exercise that competence on a national level.[22]

14 For sea and air transport this follows from Art. 100(2), while for transport by rail, road and inland waterways it follows from Art. 91.1. The ordinary legislative procedure is governed by Art. 294 TFEU.

15 Art. 47 TFEU.

16 Art. 5(1) and (2) TEU.

17 Treaty Establishing a Constitution for Europe Article 1–1, published in OJ C 310, 16.12.2004.

18 Art. 2(1) and (2) TFEU.

19 Art. 4(1)(g) TFEU.

20 Art. 2(2) TFEU.

21 Art. 2(2) TFEU, third and fourth sentences.

22 This was also stated in the so-called ERTA judgment from the CJEU: *Commission of the European Communities v Council of the European Communities, European Agreement on Road Transport* (ERTA), Case 22–70 [1971] ECR 263.

With regard to the EU, even where competence has been conferred in an area, this competence is not unlimited, but is restricted by other principles of EU law. Both the Member States and the Union have a duty of loyal cooperation. This is set out both in case law from the Court of Justice of the European Union (CJEU)[23] and in the Lisbon Treaty. According to Article 4(3) of the TEU, the Union and the Member States shall 'in full mutual respect, assist each other in carrying out tasks which flow from the Treaties'. This duty of cooperation stems from the requirement of unity in the international representation of the Community and is also known as the principle of loyalty.[24] In the area of shared competence, the competences of the Union are additionally limited by *the principles of subsidiarity and proportionality.*[25] According to the principle of subsidiarity, the EU shall act

> only and in so far as the objectives of the proposed action cannot be sufficiently achieved by the Member State, either at central level or at regional and local level, but can rather, by reason of the scale of effects of the proposed action, be better achieved at EU level.[26]

This principle also accords with previous case law from the CJEU to the effect that the EU has competence to legislate if the objective of the proposed action will be better achieved at Community level,[27] and cannot be sufficiently achieved by the Member States individually.[28] The action should also not go beyond what is necessary to achieve the objective pursued.[29] The latter rule accords with the principle of proportionality, which states that the content and form of EU action

23 Case C-25/94, *Commission v Council* [1996] ECR I-1469 para 48: 'It must be remembered that where it is apparent that the subject-matter of an agreement or convention falls partly within the competence of the Community and partly within that of its Member States, it is essential to ensure close cooperation between the Member States and the Community institutions, both in the process of negotiation and conclusion and in the fulfilment of the commitments entered into. That obligation to cooperate flows from the requirement of unity in the international representation of the Community (Ruling 1/78 [1978] ECR 2151, paragraphs 34 to 36, Opinion 2/91 [1993] ECR I-1061, paragraph 36, and Opinion 1/94 [1994] ECR I-5267, paragraph 108). The Community institutions and the Member States must take all necessary steps to ensure the best possible cooperation in that regard (Opinion 2/91, paragraph 38).'

24 See Klamert, M., *The Principle of Loyalty in EU Law*, Oxford, 2014, chapter 4.

25 Art. 5(3) and (4) TEU. More generally on the distribution of powers between the EU and the Member States, see Moens, G. and Trone, J., *Commercial Law of the European Union*, Springer, 2010, at pp. 26–30.

26 Art. 5(3) TEU.

27 Case C-491/01, *The Queen v Secretary of State for Health, ex parte British American Tobacco (Investments) Ltd and Imperial Tobacco Ltd.* at 180.

28 Op. cit., note 27, at 182.

29 Op. cit., note 27, at 184.

should not exceed what is necessary in order to achieve the objectives of the treaties.[30] However, according to the CJEU:

> it should be noted that the Community legislature must be allowed a broad discretion in an area . . ., which involves political, economic and social choices on its part, and in which it is called on to undertake complex assessments. Consequently, the legality of a measure adopted in that area can be affected only if the measure is manifestly inappropriate having regard to the objective which the competent institutions are seeking to pursue.[31]

In other words, the EU has quite a wide authority (cf. 'must be allowed a broad discretion') to decide when it is necessary to pass legislation in an area and will only exceed its powers if the measure is 'manifestly inappropriate' in relation to the objective pursued. So far it is not hard to agree with the Commission in its assumption that a regional liability regime on European multimodal transport would not be contradictory to the principle of subsidiarity.[32] Currently, it seems unlikely that the goal of a harmonised liability regime for multimodal contracts of cargo will be sufficiently achieved by the Member States individually.

However, the Rotterdam Rules might change the picture. If the Rotterdam Rules enter into force and are ratified and implemented by the Member States, the need for a regional European regime on multimodal carrier liability will not be evident. The need for a regional regime on multimodal contracts of carriage all depends on the international success of the Rotterdam Rules. Indeed, if the Rotterdam Rules are accepted by most or all of the Member States, the considerations of the Commission will have to change. Yet, as the Rotterdam Rules only apply to 'wet multimodal contracts of carriage', we might see a split in the discussion, with separate strategies for multimodal transports with and without a sea leg. The EU will still have a problem with multimodal contracts of carriage *without* a sea leg. Here the EU has at least two choices, either to make the Rotterdam Rules also applicable to European multimodal contracts of carriage without a sea leg, or to choose a separate system for these contracts.[33] As will be outlined below, the current policy of the EU is to wait and see how the Rotterdam Rules fare internationally and within the EU.[34]

30 See Art. 5(4) TEU and Joined Cases C-453/03, C-11/04, C-12/04 and C-194/04 *ABNA Ltd and Others v Secretary of State for Health and Others*: 'According to settled case-law, the principle of proportionality, which is one of the general principles of Community law, requires that measures implemented through Community provisions be appropriate for attaining the objective pursued and must not go beyond what is necessary to achieve it' at 68.

31 Op. cit., at 69.

32 Commission Staff Working Document: Accompanying Document to the Communication from the Commission – Freight Transport Logistics Action Plan – Impact Assessment, SEC (2007) 1320 at 2.4.2.

33 These questions are discussed in Chapter 6 (at 6.3).

34 In Chapter 5 (at 5.2).

3.2 External competence – the Rotterdam Rules

A regional legal regime is nevertheless not the only legislative solution for the EU as regards multimodal contracts of carriage. It is not only the Member States, but also the Union as an entity that have the possibility of entering into an international agreement in the area of international multimodal transport liability, for example the Rotterdam Rules. Article 93(1) of the Rotterdam Rules grants the EU, as a regional economic integration organisation, the right to sign, ratify, accept, approve or accede to the Convention and, according to Article 216(1) of the TFEU,[35] the EU has potential competence to enter into such an agreement. Article 216 codifies what has been developed by the CJEU as the *principle of 'parallelism'*: if the Union has an internal competence, it also has an external competence, meaning that the EU has competence to enter into international agreements if it has exercised its internal powers. As outlined above, the EU has internal competence to act in the area of international multimodal transport law and, consequently, also (potential) external competence to enter into an international agreement such as the Rotterdam Rules. However, this requires that the EU has made use of its internal competence. In other words, the EU must first pass a directive or a regulation with similar content as the Rotterdam Rules, and thereafter ratify the Rotterdam Rules on the basis of the doctrine of parallelism – Article 216 of the TFEU.[36]

Whether the EU chooses an internal regime for multimodal contracts of carriage or to accede to the Rotterdam Rules, Article 351 of the TFEU must be considered. Article 351 of the TFEU protects agreements made by Member States before accession to, or the establishment of, the Union. Many of the Member States have already ratified the Hague-Visby Rules (HVR), which govern contracts of carriage by sea covered by a bill of lading. The Rotterdam Rules also apply to such contracts. According to Article 351(1) of the TFEU: 'The rights and obligations arising from agreements concluded before 1 January 1958 or, for acceding States, before the date of their accession, between one or more Member States on the one hand, and one or more third countries on the other, shall not be affected by the provisions of the Treaties.' Indeed, conventions entered into before the time limit prevail over EU law. However, according to Article 351(2), Member States must take all appropriate steps to eliminate incompatibilities. In other words, if the EU accedes to the Rotterdam Rules, the Member States would have to denounce from the Hague-Visby Rules (HVR), as is

35 Art. 216(1): 'The Union may conclude an agreement with one or more third countries or international organizations where the Treaties so provide or where the conclusion of an agreement is necessary in order to achieve, within the framework of the Union's policies, one of the objectives referred to in the Treaties, or is provided for in a legally binding Union act or is likely to affect common rules or alter their scope.'

36 Wouters, J., Coppens, D. and De Meester, B., 'The European Union's External Relations after the Lisbon Treaty', in Griller, S. and Ziller, J. (eds), *The Lisbon Treaty. EU Constitutionalism without a Constitutional Treaty?*, Springer 2008, pp. 144–203 at p. 168.

possible under Article 15 of the Hague-Visby Rules.[37] Additionally, other unimodal conventions, such as the Convention on the Contract for the International Carriage of Goods by Road (CMR), should be considered before the EU accedes to the Rotterdam Rules.[38]

If the EU were to make use of its (potential) competence to sign and ratify the Rotterdam Rules, the Convention would become binding on all EU institutions, as well as on the Member States, and thus form an integral part of EU law.[39] This would lead to the Rotterdam Rules being coherently implemented within the EU, which would be more efficient than implementation by each Member State on a unilateral basis. On the other hand, the method would allow less flexibility to the Member States and might interfere with their national interests.

The EU as a legal entity has, as at 30 April 2015, not taken any steps towards signing or ratifying the Rotterdam Rules. The European Commission did not take part in the negotiations related to the substantive parts of the Convention, because, due to absence of internal legislation, it did not have external competence to enter into a convention on contracts of carriage.[40] Nevertheless, the Rotterdam Rules are potentially an option for the EU as regards the struggle for a European regime on multimodal contracts of carriage.[41]

The only official statement so far on the Rotterdam Rules emerging from an EU institution is a resolution from the European Parliament encouraging the Member States to sign the Convention.[42] Indeed, the Member States have the

37 See Art. 15: 'In the event of one of the contracting States wishing to denounce the present Convention, the denunciation shall be notified in writing to the Belgian Government, which shall immediately communicate a duly certified copy of the notification to all the other States, informing them of the date on which it was received. The denunciation shall only operate in respect of the State which made the notification and on the expiry of one year after the notification has reached the Belgian Government.' Formally, another possibility would be to call for a fresh conference to amend the HVR according to HVR Art. 16. However, this is not a realistic approach due to the lengthy negotiations for the Rotterdam Rules. Art. 16 has the following wording: 'Any one of the contracting States shall have the right to call for a fresh conference with a view to considering possible amendments. A State which would exercise this right should notify its intention to the other States through the Belgian Government, which would make arrangements for convening the Conference.'

38 How this can be done is discussed in Chapter 6 (at 6.3).

39 Art. 216(2) TFEU.

40 On the other hand, in the area of jurisdiction and arbitration, where the EU has internal legislation, the EU Commission was solely negotiating on behalf of the EU, and the Member States did not take part in the negotiations. Sturley, M., 'Jurisdiction Under the Rotterdam Rules', *Uniform Law Review*, 2009, Volume 14, Issue 1/2, p. 1–36 at p. 6.

41 More below in Chapter 6 (at 6.3).

42 European Parliament resolution of 5 May 2010 on strategic goals and recommendations for the EU's maritime transport policy until 2018. See the resolution at 11 where the European Parliament '[c]alls on Member States speedily to sign, ratify and implement the UN Convention on Contracts for the International Carriage of Goods Wholly or Partly by Sea, known as the "Rotterdam Rules", establishing the new maritime liability system'. Available online at http://www.europarl.europa.eu/sides/getDoc.do?pubRef=-//EP//TEXT+TA+P7-TA-2010-0128+0+DOC+XML+V0//EN (accessed 29 April 2015).

right to sign and ratify the Rotterdam Rules.[43] So far, 25 states, including eight EU Member States,[44] have signed the Rotterdam Rules. The Rules are not yet in force.[45] On 19 January 2011, Spain became the first state, both internationally and on a European level, to ratify the Rotterdam Rules. If a Member State enters into an international agreement, the starting point is that this does not affect EU law.[46] Accordingly, ratification of the Rotterdam Rules by a Member State does not make the Rules part of EU law, but instead part of the national law of the ratifying Member State. This implies that if the Rotterdam Rules are ratified by the Member States and not by the EU as an institution, the Rules will not be subject to the principles of EU law, nor will the Court of Justice have jurisdiction to authoritatively interpret them in preliminary rulings. The Court of Justice does, however, have competence to decide on the meaning of the Rotterdam Rules, in the same way as it can decide on the meaning of other parts of the national law of a Member State in order to determine whether there has been a breach of EU law. The CJEU can, in other words, draw the line between EU law and national law. The Member States must interpret their national non-EU law accordingly.[47] As long as the EU does not enact legislation in the area of multimodal transport liability and does not sign up to the Convention, the risk of conflicts with EU law is insignificant.

If, however, the EU chooses to legislate in the area of multimodal transport liability, the picture will change. As mentioned above, the competence of the Member States is restricted by the activity of the EU: the Member States may only exercise their competence to the extent that the Union has not exercised its competence or to the extent that the Union has decided to cease exercising its competence.[48] If the EU decides on a regional multimodal liability regime different from the modified network liability system of the Rotterdam Rules, then the Member States will not be allowed to derogate from this EU law obligation by entering into an agreement with one or several third states, such as by ratifying the Rotterdam Rules.[49] On the other hand, if the EU decides on a European

43 Art. 88(1) and (2) Rotterdam Rules.

44 Of the EU Member States, Denmark, France, Greece, Luxembourg, the Netherlands, Poland, Spain and Switzerland have signed the Rotterdam Rules.

45 Only three states have ratified (Spain, Togo and Congo), whereas 20 ratifications are necessary for entry into force. Available online at http://www.uncitral.org/uncitral/en/uncitral_texts/transport_goods/rotterdam_status.html (accessed 14 November 2014).

46 The several exceptions to this will not be discussed here. See Rosas, A., 'EU Law and International Agreements Concluded by EU Member States, with Particular Emphasis on Maritime Law', in Rak, H. and Wetterstein, P. (eds), *Environmental Liabilities in Ports and Coastal Areas – Focus on Public Authorities and Other Actors*, Turku, 2011, pp. 9–47 at pp. 22–26.

47 Op. cit., at pp. 18–19. This is also true as regards current international unimodal regimes; see more in Chapter 6 (at 6.3).

48 Art. 2(2) TFEU, third and fourth sentences.

49 Rosas, A., 'EU Law and International Agreements Concluded by EU Member States, with Particular Emphasis on Maritime Law', in: Rak, H. and Wetterstein, P., *Environmental Liabilities in Ports and Coastal Areas – focus on Public Authorities and Other Actors*, Turku, 2011, pp. 9–47 at p 19 with a reference to a different view presented by Klabbers, J., *Treaty Conflict and the European Union*, Cambridge University Press, 2009.

regional liability regime in line with the Rotterdam Rules, this will be binding on the Member States and will certainly make harmonising the Rotterdam Rules in Europe more effective.

3.3 Conclusions

The above discussion of the *competence* of the EU as a legal entity to regulate European international multimodal transport shows that the EU has conferred competence to act in the area of international transport law, subject to the restrictions imposed by some fundamental principles of EU law such as those of subsidiarity and proportionality. For the purposes of regulating multimodal transport liability, the most significant limitation on EU competence to act is that it is limited to implementing the CTP. The objective pursued by the relevant legislation (in our context, a regional liability regime for European multimodal transport), must form part of the European policy in question, which in the area of transport is specified in Title VI, Articles 90–100 of the TFEU. According to Article 90 of the TFEU, the objectives of the treaties in the matter of transport should be accomplished within the framework of a CTP. The wording in this respect differs little from what has been agreed since the Treaty of Rome, in which transport had its own title.[50] Currently, the Commission is still exploring what kind of liability system would be best suited for the EU: the modified network liability system of the Rotterdam Rules or a voluntary uniform liability system as proposed by a group of legal experts acting on the instructions of the Commission. The answer to this question is completely dependent on the international success of the Rotterdam Rules.

As regards the Member States, they have conferred on the EU competence to act in the area of international transport law. Although this competence is shared, the Member States' right to legislate is lost as soon as the EU regulates the issue. This is set out in Article 2(2) of the TFEU and follows from the supranational character of EU law. In the area of international multimodal transport liability, any legislation from the EU will, in other words, restrict the sovereignty of the Member States in this area. The CTP as regards multimodal contracts of carriage and sustainability will be outlined in Part II.

50 Treaty of Rome, 1957 Title IV, Art. 74.

Part II

The common transport policy

4 The aim of sustainable transport

4.1 Development of a CTP on sustainable carriage

A slow start

Before the intervention of the Court of Justice and the following amendments to the treaty of Rome, the CTP (common transport policy) was restricted to the stated intention of facilitating international transport between the Member States. The Council of Ministers of Transport supported by the European Conference of Transport Ministers (ECTM) was more a forum for exchanging ideas than a forum for creating European solutions, and transport policy was primarily a matter for nation states.[1] The turning point came in 1985 with a White Paper[2] from the European Commission to the European Council entitled 'Completing the Internal Market'.[3] According to the White Paper, a free market for services, including, transport services, was considered a precondition for economic prosperity.[4] Barriers to a free market consequently needed to be removed. Transport was given high priority and the White Paper specified a list of measures that needed to be adopted in the transport field in order to perfect the transport market.[5] However, the White Paper stated clearly that the measures merely formed part of the CTP. Other measures were also included in the CTP, such as state aid policy, improvements to railway financing, harmonisation in the road

1 Schmidt, M. and Giorgi, L., 'Successes, Failures and Prospects for the Common Transport Policy', *The European Journal of Social Science*, 2001 Volume 14, Issue 4, pp. 293–313 at p. 294.

2 Commission White Papers are documents containing proposals for Community action in a specific area. In some cases they follow a Green Paper published to launch a consultation process at European level. When a White Paper is favourably received by the Council, it can lead to an action programme for the Union in the area concerned. Information available online at http://europa.eu/legislation_summaries/glossary/white_paper_en.htm (accessed 24 March 2014).

3 White Paper from the Commission to the European Council: Completing the Internal Market, COM (85)310.

4 Op. cit., at p. 100.

5 Op. cit., at p. 108–112.

sector and infrastructure planning – all measures of no direct relevance to the internal market but nevertheless an essential part of transport policy.[6] In the late 1980s, transport policy was accordingly concentrating on opening up the market. Between 1985 and 1991, the Commission initiated more than a dozen directives and regulations on transport, mainly related to development of the Community's railways and on the elimination of quantitative restrictions on international goods transported by road and on the establishment of conditions allowing cabotage, as well as on different liberalisation packages related to air transport.[7]

The 1992 White Paper on sustainable mobility

The next milestone in the rather short history of the European CTP was reached in 1992, when *sustainable mobility* was highlighted as a core goal of transport policy in the Union, and when the Commission introduced the idea of using harmonised contractual rules as a tool to promote such development. The starting point for the European project towards sustainable carriage was the 1992 White Paper with the ambitious title of 'The Future Development of the Common Transport Policy: A Global Approach to the Construction of a Community Framework for Sustainable Mobility'.[8] In the White Paper the Commission recognised the need for change and outlined a vision of sustainable mobility. The White Paper followed an earlier Green Paper, where the notion of sustainable mobility was presented for the first time. The Green Paper recognised that transport needed to fulfil social and economic roles, and its harmful effects on the environment should be limited.[9] Sustainable development has not been assigned a particular definition by the European Union (EU). The Union relies upon the definition of sustainable development provided by the World Commission on Environment and Development in 1987, according to which sustainable development 'meets the needs of the present without compromising the ability of future generations to meet their own needs'.[10] In the context of transport, sustainable development meant reducing the negative impacts of the industry. The challenges for the Community were huge. Transport activities had grown

6 Op. cit., at p. 12.

7 Crowley, J., 'Inland Transport in the European Community following 1992', *The Antitrust Bulletin*, 1992, Volume 2, pp. 453–480 at pp. 459–463.

8 White Paper on 'The future development of the common transport policy – A global approach to the construction of a Community framework for sustainable mobility' COM (92) 494 final.

9 Green Paper on 'The Impact of Transport on the Environment. A Community strategy for "sustainable mobility"' COM(92) 46 final at 9: 'This Green Paper provides an assessment of the overall impact of transport on the environment and presents a Common strategy for "sustainable mobility" which should enable transport to fulfil its economic and social role while containing its harmful effects on the environment.'

10 World Commission on Environment and Development, *Our Common Future*, Oxford University Press, 1987, p. 43; see e.g. and available online at http://europa.eu/legislation_summaries/environment/sustainable_development/index_en.htm (accessed 10 March 2015).

by 50 per cent from 1970 to 1990 and road transport accounted for most of that.[11] For this reason, both transport capacity and the environment were suffering.[12] The environmental impact of the accelerating transport industry could be reduced to a few areas such as consumption/gaseous emissions, congestion, land use and carriage of dangerous goods. Regarding the first – energy consumption – road transport was deemed as 'worst in class' by the Commission. Road transport consumed 80 per cent of the total final energy used in the transport sector and contributed to over 75 per cent of the total CO_2 output in the EU.[13] A change of course was crucial. This was accepted by the Commission, which stated that: 'The end of 1992 will mark the beginning of a new departure for the Community's common transport policy (CTP).'[14]

The challenge for the Community's transport system was defined as how to provide, in the most efficient manner, 'the services that are necessary for the continued success for the single market and the mobility of the individual traveller, while continuing to reduce the inefficiencies and imbalances of the system and safeguarding against the harmful effects that increased transport activity generates',[15] An efficient and sustainable transport system was, in other words, seen as an essential prerequisite for the Inner Market and EU competitiveness.

Multimodality as a solution to problems in transport

The White Paper was followed up by several Communications and new White Papers, starting with a Communication from the European Commission in 1997 on Multimodality and Multimodal Freight Transport in the EU.[16] The Communication was based on recognition of the fact that the transport sector had proved incapable of appropriate self-regulation. From 1970 to 1997, European freight transport had increased by about 70 per cent. In the same period, road transport had increased its market share from nearly 50 per cent to 72 per cent.[17] Consequently, transport systems had become a source of environmental and social costs and a business as usual approach was accordingly not feasible.

Promoting multimodality was presented as a solution to these problems, and hence the objective was set to develop a framework for optimal integration of different modes. Through this the Commission wanted to 'enable efficient and cost-effective use of the transport system through seamless, customer-oriented door-to-door services whilst favouring competition between transport

11 COM (92) 494 final at 14.
12 Op. cit., at 20.
13 Op. cit., at pp. 151–152.
14 Op. cit., at p. 1.
15 Op. cit., at p. 92.
16 Communication from the Commission to the Council, the European Parliament, the Economic and Social Committee and the Committee of the Regions – Intermodality and intermodal freight transport in the European Union – A system's approach to freight transport – Strategies and actions to enhance efficiency, services and sustainability, COM (97) 243 final.
17 Op. cit., at p. 3.

operators.'[18] The idea was that integration of modes should take place at different levels: the level of infrastructure and other hardware (e.g. loading units, vehicles, telecommunications), the level of operations and services; and the regulatory level. Integration on the regulatory level meant harmonising the regulatory conditions governing multimodal transport.[19] The regulatory conditions were identified as the need for both *a harmonised legal framework on carrier liability as well as a European single transport document* that should be electronic. In addition, the Commission recognised that by strengthening multimodal transport, a structural change in the transport market would take place. Multimodal operators would be competing with traditional 'unimodal carriers' that specialised in carrying goods on certain modes of transport and this 'new' group could be encouraged to promote sustainable transport.[20] A report on these so-called freight integrators was ordered.[21] However, so far the Commission has not discussed how these tools could be connected in order to promote sustainable carriage more efficiently. Some ideas for how this can be done will be presented in Chapter 10.

4.2 Identified friction costs preventing modal shift

Different levels of friction costs

In the 1997 White Paper, the Commission acknowledged that the transport industry itself was incapable of reforming the transport system. The reason for this was, according to the Commission, that any change of mode in the current modally oriented transport system would involve a change of system, rather than a mere technical transhipment. This change of system created *friction costs*, preventing formation of a competitive multimodal transport chain. Friction costs were defined as *a measurement of the inefficiency of a transport operation*. They are expressed in the form of higher prices, longer journeys, more delays, less punctuality, lower availability of quality services, limitations on the types of goods available, higher risk of damage to cargo and more complex administrative procedures.[22] In order to strengthen the multimodal transport chain, the friction costs would have to be identified and reduced.[23]

The Commission identified friction costs at three levels and suggested a range of actions to reduce these costs. The *first level* of friction costs was linked to *infrastructure*, which was clearly inadequate. In 1997, a comprehensive network of modes, with interconnections between modes, was lacking. This was partly apparent physically – in certain transport corridors, there were no connections between, for example, ports and the rail network. Another problem was that

18 Op. cit., note, at p. 16.
19 L.C.
20 Op. cit., at p. 56.
21 Op. cit., at p. 57.
22 Op. cit., at p. 26.
23 Op. cit., at p. 27.

technical specifications for different modes of transport were regulated differently. A variation of loading unit dimensions could also cause friction costs. Even if the infrastructure could be made to work, the *second level* at which such costs could arise was at the *points of transport between modes.*[24] Road, rail, air and waterborne transport were characterised by dissimilar levels of performance, different working times, etc. This problem was considered particularly valid in relation to *terminals.*

In the Communication, several possible courses of action were mentioned. These were discussed by four action groups: Group A – *Integrated infrastructure and transport means*, Group B – *Interoperable and interconnected operations*, Group C – *Mode-independent services and regulations* and Group D – *Horizontal activities.*[25] The titles of the discussions are not very informative in themselves, but the content is explained in the Communication:

> Groups A, B and D cover possible actions in relation to issues of logistics and competition: As part of the task assigned to *Group A*, Integrated infrastructure and transport means, the Commission pointed out the need for a coherent infrastructure network at a European level. To attain such a goal, a revision of the Guidelines for a trans-European transport network needed to take place.[26] . . . Furthermore, the points of transfer between modes needed to be turned into attractive nodes, providing logistical services.[27] . . . Finally, work on harmonising standards for loading units needed to be initiated by the Commission. In this regard the Commission itself intended to act as a driving force in the relevant standardisation bodies and international organisations.[28] . . . For optimisation of Interoperable and interconnected operations, as discussed by *Group B*, management and control of the new door-to-door transport chain was essential. The Commission therefore planned to conduct a survey of the various actors in the market. Of great importance was the issue of open access to infrastructure for licensed rail operators.[29] . . . More controversial was the proposal on common charging and pricing principles.[30] . . . On the other hand, a revision of Regulation 1107/70 with regard to aid for combined transport, as well as the rules on state aid, would have to be conducted.[31] . . . Cooperation to secure efficient door-to-door transport, such as the coordination of multimodal timetables was, nevertheless, welcomed by the Commission.[32] . . . In respect of the

24 Op. cit., at pp. 35–39.
25 Op. cit., at pp. 45 *et seq.*
26 Op. cit., at p. 49.
27 Op. cit., at pp. 51–53.
28 Op. cit., at p. 55.
29 The work on creating trans-European Rail Freight Freeways has been given priority, COM (97) 243 final at 61.
30 Op. cit., at pp. 62–63.
31 Op. cit., at pp. 66–68.
32 Op. cit., at pp. 69.

> fourth and last action group, Group D – Horizontal activities, the Commission discussed various research projects that would have to take place to carry out the necessary innovations to fulfil the project outlined in the Communication.[33] . . . A European Multimodal Reference Centre for Freight Transport should be established together with National Round Tables where questions on multimodality could be discussed in contrast to the traditional modes.[34]

A whole range of actions was planned to reduce the transport's negative impact on the environment. Only activities that involve contract law will be discussed here. These involve friction costs at the so-called third level.

Legal friction costs

The *third level* of friction costs to be identified by the Commission was linked to the existing *mode-based information transmission system* and other *administrative bottlenecks.* At the time (as indeed is still the case today), each mode of international transport in Europe was regulated by different liability conventions. In addition, special liability regimes existed for national transport in several Member States. The problem of determining where in the transport chain the ultimate responsibility lies for cargo damage, loss or delay, was thus clearly a friction cost in the terminology of the Commission.[35] The uncertainty in relation to the issue of carrier liability was, in other words, considered an obstacle to an efficient European transport chain. Additionally, the fact that transport documents to a large extent were (and still are) paper-based and differ according to different modes was recognised as hampering the competitiveness of multimodal transport.[36] Hence, the challenge for policymakers would be to provide a framework for optimal integration of different transport modes.[37] One important aspect was information and management systems in door-to-door-transport. An intermodal real-time electronic information and transaction system should thus be provided, with harmonised communication standards, procedures and transport documents as part of it.[38] In other words, a harmonised contractual framework is needed to support upgrading and modernization of the European transport industry. A dialogue should be started with the relevant parties, with the objective being to reach agreement on a harmonised liability regime for European Multimodal Carriage of Goods.[39]

33 Op. cit., at pp. 83–87.
34 Op. cit., at p. 92.
35 Op. cit., at p. 41.
36 Op. cit., at p. 42. In addition, the rules on customs transit operations differ according to mode. As this work concentrates on private law tools, the question of customs will be left out.
37 Op. cit., at p. 45.
38 Op. cit., at p. 73.
39 Op. cit., at p. 80.

Regarding the features of a European regional legal regime, the 1997 Communication said:

The intermodal operators should be able to offer their customers a clear set of transparent liability conditions and procedures for any cargo that is damaged or lost in its journey. From the end-user's point of view, the liability rules should not be mode-specific and should not distinguish between national and international transport. In addition to covering the actual transport of goods, these rules will also cover the damage or loss that may result from the performance of a value added logistics activity in the intermodal chain, for example warehousing or product customisation at the nodal point. Action: Promotion of voluntary intermodal liability regime.[40]

The Commission had thus spelt out the requirement for a transparent, uniform liability regime, with opt-out, applicable both to national and international European multimodal transport. The approach was radical compared to previous international attempts, and would be modified after consultations with stakeholders.[41] It is worth keeping in mind that the Commission, at this stage, wanted to keep the discussions on an international legal instrument alive. In this respect, the 1997 Communication was addressing the reopening of the MT convention (United Nations Convention on International Multimodal Transport of Goods);[42] but that never took place. Today, almost two decades later, the Commission is still waiting for a possible international solution. This time the question is whether the Rotterdam Rules can solve the European problem.[43]

4.3 Current status of the CTP

The 1992 White paper on the future development of the CTP can certainly be truly identified as the beginning of a new departure for the Community's CTP, as expressed by the Commission.[44] A range of projects and ideas has been launched in order to promote the idea of an efficient and sustainable transport sector. Still, most EU legislation on transport has so far been related to market access and competition as well as safety aspects.

The EU has, for example, developed a framework of rules for ***road transport*** with a focus on road safety and social protection of road transport workers, in addition to harmonising conditions of competition, or building an inner market for international road transport.[45] Three regulations, the so-called road package

40 Op. cit., at p. 81.

41 More on this in Chapter 5 where contractual issues are outlined and discussed.

42 Op. cit., at 82.

43 See Chapter 5 (at 5.2).

44 Green Paper on 'The Impact of Transport on the Environment. A Community strategy for "sustainable mobility"', COM (92) 46 final at 1.

45 Rules on driving time and rest periods have been agreed (Regulation 561/2006) and supplemented by rules on the maximum working time (Directive 2002/15). Enforcement of these rules is also progressively harmonised, in particular through the digital tachograph regulation (Regulation 3821/85) and a directive on minimum levels of controls (Directive 2006/22).

legislation, establish European rules for access to the profession of transport operators and more efficiently regulate the market for the international carriage of goods and passengers.[46] Heavy goods vehicles, including buses and coaches, transporting goods in Europe must comply with certain rules on weights and dimensions for road safety reasons and to avoid damage to roads, bridges and tunnels. Directive 96/53/EC ensures that Member States cannot restrict vehicles that comply with these limits from performing international transport operations within their territories.

Air transport has traditionally been a highly regulated industry, dominated by national flag carriers and state-owned airports. However, the internal market has removed all commercial restrictions for airlines flying within the EU, such as restrictions on routes, the number of flights or setting fares. Today all EU airlines may operate air services on any route within the EU.[47]

In the *maritime sector* an internal market was also created rather early, starting with a regulation from 1986 applying the principle of freedom to provide services to maritime transport between Member States and between Member States and third countries.[48] The maritime sector is important for the EU. Almost 90 per cent of the EU external freight trade and 40 per cent of the internal freight trade are seaborne.[49] Furthermore, the European Commission has defined its objective as protecting Europe with very strict safety rules preventing sub-standard shipping, reducing the risk of serious maritime accidents and minimising the environmental impact of maritime transport. As regards the latter, the sulphur directive is probably the most discussed instrument so far.[50]

The above-mentioned 1986 Regulation on freedom to provide services to maritime transport also applies to *inland waterways*, which offer an environmentally friendly transport alternative. According to recent studies, the total external costs of inland navigation (in terms of accidents, congestion, noise emissions, air pollution and other environmental impacts) are seven times lower than those of road transport.[51] The Commission is hence working on integrating inland

46 Regulation (EC) No 1071/2009 on admission to, and the pursuit of, the occupation of road transport operator, Regulation (EC) No 1072/2009 on common rules for access to the international road haulage market and Regulation 1073/2009 common rules for access to the international market for coach and bus services.

47 Available online at http://ec.europa.eu/transport/modes/air/internal_market/index_en.htm (accessed 15 March 2015).

48 Council Regulation (EEC) No 4055/86 of 22 December 1986, applying the principle of freedom to provide services to maritime transport between Member States and between Member States and third countries

49 See the home page of the European Commission on transport. Available online at http://ec.europa.eu/transport/modes/maritime/index_en.htm (accessed 15 March 2015).

50 Directive 2012/33/EU amending Council Directive 1999/32/EC as regards the sulphur content of marine fuels. Available online at http://ec.europa.eu/environment/air/transport/ships.htm (accessed 15 March 2015).

51 See the home page of the European Commission on transport. Available online at http://ec.europa.eu/transport/modes/road/index_en.htm (accessed 15 March 2015).

waterways in the multimodal transport sector, though so far not by means of legislation except for a directive on technical issues.[52]

In the *rail sector*, in contrast, a single market is still the main focus for the EU, together with developing safety and infrastructure. A more competitive and efficient rail industry is seen as a prerequisite for achieving targets of emissions reduction and modal shift. Directive 2012/34/EU recasting the First Railway Package contains the basic provisions for market opening in the railway sector.[53] Further proposals are made in the Commission's 4th Railway Package.[54] Integrating rail in the multimodal transport chain is an important goal for the EU, as rail carriage is considered one of the more environmentally friendly modes of transport. It is also an important element in the Commission's goal of a sustainable transport chain.[55]

4.4 The contractual aspect

In its struggle for a sustainable transport industry, the Commission has so far been working on two different paths in terms of using contract law as a tool to promote the desired development. First of all, efforts have been made to create a *harmonised liability regime* for the growing multimodal industry, including a single European electronic transport document. The obstacles to this process are familiar from an international point of view, as EU progress on this point is hampered by the same legal and political problems as the international drive for a harmonised legal instrument. Most stakeholders agree that a harmonised system is needed, but the content of the system is hard to decide on.[56] In addition, legal problems arise from existing unimodal conventions, which might be difficult to harmonise with a new multimodal legal instrument.[57]

Furthermore, the Commission recognises that a modal shift to greener transport chains might lead to growth in a sub-group of multimodal transport organisers, or carriers, comprising the so-called green transport integrators, who are transport organisers committed to sustainable carriage. How the task of this group should affect the development of a future contractual framework for European carriage of goods has not yet been further developed by the Commission. Indeed, the Commission has been reluctant to include environmental obligations in the task of transport organisers, despite the fact that it is environmental

52 Directive 2013/49/EU amending Annex II to Directive 2006/87/EC of the European Parliament and of the Council laying down technical requirements for inland waterway vessels.

53 Directive 2012/34/EU establishing a single European railway area (recast).

54 Still in progress. The EU Parliament has completed its first reading. Available online at http://ec.europa.eu/transport/modes/rail/packages/2013_en.htm (accessed 10 March 2015).

55 Below in Chapter 5.

56 Below in Chapter 5 (at 5.1).

57 Below in Chapter 6 (at 6.1).

problems that started the whole process of regulating European multimodal contracts of carriage. The legal position of transport integrators and how environmental aspects can be included in the contractual legal regime will be discussed in Chapter 10.

So far the Commission has not succeeded in introducing any of its ideas on a harmonised legal framework for European multimodal contracts of carriage into European legislation, or even into proposals for legislation that could be discussed by the Council and the European Parliament. The project is still on the drawing board. This is, as mentioned above and as outlined below in Chapter 5, due to both political and legal obstacles. Another aspect is that the whole process has been administered by Directorate-General (DG) Move and its predecessor and *not* by DG Justice, which is the department working on harmonising European contract law on a general level.

Despite the progress of the single market, barriers between EU Member States still remain. Differences between national contract laws are recognised by the Commission as an important obstacle to cross-border trade.[58] DG Justice recognises that all economic transactions are based on contracts and on the perception that differences in contract rules need to be removed in order to strengthen European integration and the single market. Harmonising European contract law is, however, not an easy task. First, there are problems of variances between the different legal families in the European Union: the common law legal family, the civil law legal family and the Nordic legal family. These legal systems differ by tradition and it is not easy to agree on one contractual solution, and the similarities are probably bigger than the differences, although problems might arise even within individual legal families.

> One example is the Self-Employed Commercial Agents directive from 1986, which introduced mandatory rules on the agent's right to indemnity at termination.[59] At the time when the directive was agreed, a unanimous vote in the Council was required. The directive thus contained an optional solution to the rules on an agent's right to indemnity at termination of the contract. The Member States could choose between the so-called German and the so-called French indemnity system. The British, who were sceptical as to the whole idea of mandatory rules in business-to-business contracts, accepted the directive, but implemented a right for the parties to choose between the two systems. The result was at least three different solutions to the indemnity problem. Other difficult questions such as problems related to the agent's part in a contract between the principal and a third party (the classic agency problem), were totally left out of the directive. These

58 See the home page of the European Commission on transport. Available online at http://ec.europa.eu/justice/contract/index_en.htm (accessed 15 March 2015).

59 Council Directive 86/653/EEC of 18 December 1986 on the coordination of the laws of the Member States relating to self-employed commercial agents Official Journal L 382, 31/12/1986 P. 0017–0021.

problems were considered too difficult to agree on. As regards provisions on mandatory indemnity for the agent, two large continental Member States could not agree on a contractual solution departing from their own system. Furthermore, the common law countries of the United Kingdom had never even heard about mandatory rules protecting a self-employed person and therefore decided to keep as much party autonomy as possible. The result was that the parties were given a right to choose between the French and the German indemnity system. These examples are illustrative, not exhaustive. The mere fact that the EU has so far had little success in the area of harmonising contractual rules outside the area of consumer protection explains how difficult the process is.[60]

Huge efforts have been made to overcome the obstacles to a harmonised European contract law. With the Communication on European Contract Law of 2001,[61] the Commission started a process of public consultations on problems arising from differences between Member State contract laws. On the basis of the responses, the Commission issued an Action Plan in 2003,[62] proposing to improve the quality and coherence of European contract law by establishing a Common Frame of Reference (CFR) containing common principles, terminology and model rules. Between 2005 and 2009 the Commission financed a network of European contract law experts, who developed a Draft Common Frame of Reference (DCFR) based on extensive comparative law research. The DCFR was published in 2009.[63] However, all contracts related to transport were excluded from the DCFR.[64] Contracts of carriage were considered *lex specialis* and governed by international conventions.[65] In April 2010, the Commission set up an Expert Group on a CFR to assist the Commission in making further progress with development of a possible future European contract law instrument. The Commission asked the Expert Group to conduct a feasibility exercise on a draft instrument of European contract law of whatever legal form or nature. Furthermore, on 1 July 2010, the Commission published a 'Green Paper on policy options for progress towards a European contract law for consumers and businesses'.[66] In the Green Paper the Commission discusses different ways of

60 On the history of the Commercial Agency Directive, see Eftestøl-Wilhelmsson, E., *Fra etterprovision til avgangsvederlag*, 2005 (in Norwegian).

61 Communication on European Contract Law COM (2001) 398, 11.7.2001.

62 Communication on a More Coherent European Contract Law – an Action Plan, COM (2003) 68, 12 February 2003.

63 Von Bar, C., Clive, E. and Schulte Nölke, H. (eds), *Principles, Definitions and Model Rules of European Private Law. Draft Common Frame of Reference (DCFR)*, Sellier, 2009.

64 DCFR II.-5:201, IV.C-1:102 and IV.C.5:101.

65 Lorenzon, P., T*he European Contract Law Project and Maritime Law in The Emerging European Maritime Law, Proceedings from the Third European Colloquium on Maritime Law Research*, Ravenna, 17–18 September 2004, MarIus 2005, No 333, pp. 137–158 at p. 157.

66 COM (2010) 348.

harmonising the contract laws of Europe. One alternative is that the result of the Expert Group be used directly as an optional instrument, or it could be used as a toolbox available to European legislators when changing, or making new, legislation. If the toolbox were agreed between the different EU institutions it would be an even more important instrument. Another possibility is that the Commission attaches an instrument of European contract law to a Commission Recommendation addressed to the Member States. None of the above proposals are binding on the Member States, and the risk of incoherence would still be large.[67] The Commission is thus discussing whether a directive or a regulation setting up an optional instrument of European contract law would be a better alternative.[68] Additionally, the idea of a European civil code has been launched.[69] When the Green Paper consultation process closed in January 2011 the Commission had received 320 responses.

The responses were analysed by the Expert Group, which in the summer of 2011 published the results of its feasibility study: 'A European contract law for consumers and businesses' – a text of 189 Articles, which strives to constitute a complete set of contract law rules covering issues relevant in a contractual relationship in the internal market of the European Union.[70] The proposal consists of eight parts, of which the first three parts are general and apply to all contracts. The first part contains general provisions such as the principles of freedom of contract (Article 7) and the principle of good faith and fair dealing (Article 8). The second part is on making a binding contract and the third on assessing what is in the contract. Part four contains specific rules on the obligations and remedies of the parties to a sales contract, while part five deals with the same as regards obligations and remedies of the parties to a related services contract, which would be the relevant category for contracts of carriage. However, according to the proposed Article150 (2), '[t]his Part does not apply to transport services, training services, telecommunications support services, or financial services'. In other words, it seems as if the contract of carriage in the minds of the EU experts is also considered *lex specialis* and too different to be integrated in a European project on a harmonised contract law. Put differently, the traditional gap between general contract law and transport law remains in the minds of international experts, both in the international academic community and among decision-makers in the EU Commission. The European project for a harmonised liability regime for multimodal contracts of carriage seems to have been handled exclusively by DG Move and not at all by DG Justice.

It appears, however, that the rise of an EU instrument on general contract law is still very much in its initial phases. Instead, the Commission is focusing

67 Op. cit., at pp. 7–9.
68 Op. cit., at pp. 9–11.
69 Op. cit., at p. 11.
70 Available online at http://ec.europa.eu/justice/contract/files/feasibility_study_final.pdf (accessed 15 April 2014).

on establishing an optional instrument on European sales law. The work has progressed to such a degree that a proposal for a Regulation of the European Parliament and of the Council on a Common European Sales Law was pending in the EU legislative system.[71] However, the proposal has been withdrawn due to a new political situation in the Council. Although the proposed instrument was intended to apply to sales contracts and related services,[72] it still excluded contracts of carriage. According to the preamble, only *closely related* service contracts should be subject to the Regulation (at 19).[73] Furthermore, the proposal does not cover any related contracts by which the buyer acquires goods from, or is supplied with a service by, a third party (at 20).[74] Even though the withdrawn proposed sales law regulation excluded contracts of carriage, it remains an open question as to what this really means. The withdrawn regulation clearly had a wider approach than the international transport conventions, and the question as to what degree the general provisions of the Regulation nevertheless would apply to a contract of carriage also remains open.[75] This question has, so far, not been discussed by DG Move, which has been focusing on a harmonised liability regime for European multimodal transport.

71 Regulation of the European Parliament and of the Council on a Common European Sales Law, COM (2011) 635 final.

72 Op. cit., 'Article 1 Objective and subject matter

1 The purpose of this Regulation is to improve the conditions for the establishment and the functioning of the internal market by making available a uniform set of contract law rules as set out in Annex I ("the Common European Sales Law"). These rules can be used for cross-border transactions for the sale of goods, for the supply of digital content and for related services where the parties to a contract agree to do so.'

73 Op. cit., at 19: 'With a view to maximising the added value of the Common European Sales Law its material scope should also include certain services provided by the seller that are directly and closely related to specific goods or digital content supplied on the basis of the Common European Sales Law, and in practice often combined in the same or a linked contract at the same time, most notably repair, maintenance or installation of the goods or the digital content.'

74 Op. cit., at 20: 'The Common European Sales Law should not cover any related contracts by which the buyer acquires goods or is supplied with a service, from a third party. This would not be appropriate because the third party is not part of the agreement between the contracting parties to use the rules of the Common European Sales Law. A related contract with a third party should be governed by the respective national law which is applicable according pursuant to Regulations (EC) No 593/2008 and (EC) No 864/2007 or any other relevant conflict of law rule.'

75 More on the impact of general contract law and the goal of sustainable transport, see Chapter 8 (at 8.2).

5 The call for a European liability framework for multimodal contracts of carriage

5.1 The different stages of the EU discussion

The initial phase: a radical approach

So far, Directorate-General (DG) Move has led the discussion on a possible regional legal framework for multimodal contracts of carriage in isolation from the more general discussions on possible harmonisation of European Union (EU) contract law, which has been organised by DG Justice. The aim has never been to integrate the rules on contracts of carriage with other commercial contracts; on the contrary, the aim has always been limited to providing the transport industry with a harmonised legal framework on multimodal contracts of carriage. Based on the transport policy outlined in Chapter 4, the Commission appointed a group of legal experts ('the 1999 expert group'), to consider the possibilities of creating a regional liability regime for multimodal contracts of carriage.[1] The Director General for Transport at the time, Francois Lamoureux, stated in his preface to the group's publication, that the need for 'one transport – one document – one liability', identified 30 years, ago still applied. Different attempts to remedy the situation had failed and, according to Lamoureux, this was why the European Commission decided to make an inventory of the current liability arrangements and to identify possible approaches to resolve the current deadlock.

Certain key problems associated with lack of a coherent liability regime were addressed by the 1999 expert group. First, the group agreed that as multimodal transport is built up of unimodal stages, there are always unimodal conventions potentially applicable, so that allocation of responsibility is thus difficult. Moreover, if it is clear where the incident occurred, the parties may have agreed on different standard contracts that lead to different legal results, so that again lack of clarity is the result. Depending on where the incident happened, different

1 The group consisted of some of the most skilled scholars in international transport law. See: Asariotis, R., Bull, H.J., Clarke, M.A., Herbert, R., Kiantou-Pampouki, A., Morán-Bovio, D., Ramberg, J., deWitt, R. and Zunarelli, S., 'Intermodal Transportation and Carrier liability', European Communities, 1999. Available online at http://bookshop.europa.eu/en/intermodal-transportation-and-carrier-liability-pbC32599285/ (accessed 29 April 2015).

national or legal regimes might also be applicable. Another problem is connected with *identifying the carrier*, as in multimodal transport the counterpart of the consignor (sender) is often not the contractual carrier but an intermediary procuring the transport. The 1999 expert group thus concluded that uncertainty characterises the legal situation in current multimodal transport. This uncertainty could, according to the 1999 expert group, be grouped into three categories: uncertainty over the *location of loss or damage*, uncertainty concerning the *contract* and *identity of the carrier* and, finally, uncertainty regarding the *applicable legal regime* and *its effects*.[2]

Accordingly, a harmonised international legal tool was needed. An international convention would be the best, but was at the time considered unlikely.[3] Other options included different kinds of EU legal instruments, such as directives and regulations, or a regional convention. An inter-regional convention, for example between the EU and the United States (US) would be an attractive alternative, although considered not very realistic.[4] The problem is related to the fact that the differences as regards inland carriage are huge, particularly between the EU and the US. The so-called network liability system (see below) is favoured in European multimodal carriage of goods, whereas the uniform liability model seems to be more popular in the US.[5] The most difficult task would, therefore, be to create a legal regime acceptable to the industry. This would be difficult because of divergent interests in the industry and their home states. The industry has learned to cope with the inadequacies of the system and, according to the 1999 expert group, change will only appear attractive if it translates into tangible benefits.[6] As a solution, the 1999 expert group proposed a model rule, based on a default system, the application of which should be triggered unless the parties agreed otherwise. This was based on the idea that an optional regime is easier to accept, and an opt-out solution would give more coherence than the opt-in solution we have today. Regarding the material questions, both liability systems (uniform or network system) and the level of limitations were seen as central elements of a new liability regime. The 1999 expert group considered a *uniform liability* system more effective, provided that the level of liability would be in excess of established minimum levels.[7]

2 Op. cit., at pp. 16–17.
3 Op. cit., at p. 16.
4 Op. cit., at p. 26.
5 Ulfbeck, V., 'Multimodal Transport in the United States and Europe – Global or Regional Liability Rules?' *Tulane Maritime Law Journal*, 2009, Volume 34, pp. 37–90 at pp. 77–79. On recent development in the US as regards the law applicable to multimodal contracts of carriage, see Chapter 6 (at 6.2).
6 Asarioitis, R., Bull, H.J., Clarke, M.A., Herber, R., Kiantou-Pampouki, A., Morán-Bovio, D., Ramberg, J., deWitt, R. and Zunarelli, S., *Intermodal Transportation and Carrier Liability*, European Communities, 1999. Available online at http://bookshop.europa.eu/en/intermodal-transportation-and-carrier-liability-pbC32599285/ (accessed 29 April 2015).
7 Op. cit., at III 1.

The expert group was right in predicting that one of the most challenging tasks in the process of governing multimodal transport both on a regional EU level and on a global level would be to agree on a liability system that would satisfy all stakeholders. The problem is that there is no homogenous group of stakeholders; interests vary between governments as well as between organisations and private enterprises. As concluded in a 2003 United Nations Conference on Trade and Development (UNCTAD) report, and confirmed by a study performed on behalf of the European Commission in 2009,[8] the stakeholders clearly recognise that the existing legal framework is not satisfactory and that, in principle, an international instrument would be desirable. However, views on how this should be accomplished are divided. The UNCTAD secretary in the 2003 report suggests that future discussions should concentrate on two alternatives: either a *binding international liability regime* based on commercially accepted contractual solutions such as different standard contracts, or the development of a *non-mandatory regime that provides uniform and high levels of liability*.[9] Within the EU, a third alternative, in the shape of a *mandatory regime with optional liability limits*, has also been suggested.[10] As we shall see, in its initial phase the EU discussion concentrated on the non-mandatory uniform liability alternative, whereas the United Nations Commission for International Trade Law (UNCITRAL), through the Rotterdam Rules, reached agreement on a network solution in line with the present commercial situation. The latest news from the EU is that the Rotterdam Rules should also be regarded as an alternative.[11]

The first proposal: a uniform liability system and an opt-out regime

From the very beginning, the European Commission was aiming for a true multimodal legal regime. The first group of legal experts drafting a European legal regime on multimodal carriage (the 2005 EU draft), had a clear task: they were to prepare a set of uniform liability rules which *concentrate the transit risk on one party* and provide for *strict liability of the contracting carrier for all types of losses* (damage, loss, delay) irrespective of the modal stage where a loss occurs and of the cause of the loss.[12] The proposed basis of liability was accordingly 'strict' in the sense that the multimodal carrier, or transport integrator,

8 See below on the 2009 expert group.

9 Multimodal Transport: The Feasibility of an International Legal Instrument, UNCTAD/SDTE/TLB/2003/1 at 111.

10 See below.

11 See below in section 5.2.

12 This group of experts was smaller than the first group. As the first group consisted of nine outstanding legal scholars, the second was slimmed down to four. From the first group M.A. Clarke, R. Herbert and J. Ramberg continued the work. The new member of the expert team was F. Lorenzon. See Integrated Services in the Multimodal Chain (ISIC) Final Report Task B: Multimodal liability and documentation. Research report commissioned by the European Commission – DG TREN provided by an independent panel of legal experts, published by ECORYS Nederland BV, Rotterdam 2005 ('the 2005-EU Draft'), at p.17.

as described in the proposal,[13] should not be allowed to prove itself innocent of presumed fault. On the other hand, the carrier should be excused if the loss, damage or delay was caused by circumstances beyond its control. As far as limitation was concerned, liability was limited to 17 Special Drawing Rights (SDR) per kilogram of gross weight, which was the same as the highest monetary limit found in unimodal regimes established at the time of the proposal. This quite rough liability system was softened by the fact that the proposal did not aim for a new regional mandatory legal instrument. On the contrary, it was based on an *opt-out solution* where the parties could agree otherwise. The 2005 EU draft aimed to provide cargo interests with a simple and foreseeable method of indemnification irrespective of issues such as the transport operator's rights of recourse against subcontractors. This aspect was accordingly left out of the proposal.

The 2005 EU draft also contains provisions on *electronic transport documents*. According to the proposal, the draft was designed to have the smallest possible impact on international trade and banking practices. The particulars (on the content of the transport document) required by the proposal (Article 4) were hence a reflection of the current commercial standard. To avoid misunderstandings on the opt-out issue, the transport document should contain a statement that the contract is subject to the regime. This could, for instance, be done by a stamp or similar electronic registration.[14] Whether or not a statement in the document is sufficient to trigger a specific legal regime is open to discussion and depends on the possible existence of mandatory applicable colliding regimes. The proposal was not very extensive on the question of an electronic transport document and did not present any new ideas on the matter. The 1999 legal expert group recommended that the EU should wait for an international solution, such as the United Nations Convention on the use of Electronic Communications in International Contracts.[15]

Although the 2005 EU draft has been discussed extensively by the Commission and the stakeholders, this has so far not transformed into anything more than a proposal.[16] It was accordingly not mentioned in the mid-term review of the 2001 White Paper: Keep Europe moving – Sustainable mobility for our continent, published in 2006,[17] although the 2006 mid-term review focused on logistics to ensure sustainable and competitive mobility in Europe. The objective defined by the Commission remained the same: 'The trend towards integrated logistics companies needs to be matched by public policies enabling the optimal use and combination ("co-modality") of different modes of transport.'[18] The urgent need for a harmonised legal framework was, however, partially withdrawn.

13 Op. cit., at 5.2.
14 The 2005-EU draft at 3.2
15 The Convention was adopted on 23 November 2005, but is still not in force. Available online at http://www.uncitral.org/uncitral/uncitral_texts/electronic_commerce/2005Convention.html (accessed 15 March 2015).
16 More on the 2005-EU Draft below in Chapter 6 (at 6.3).
17 COM (2006) 314 final.
18 Op. cit., at 7.1.

The Commission stated in the mid-term review that the policy 'may include action to remove regulatory obstacles',[19] although it remains to be seen whether or not regulatory obstacles in the shape of unpredictable liability regimes need to be removed. Nevertheless, the Commission initiated an action plan to develop a framework strategy for sustainable freight.

Task reviewed after consultations with stakeholders

The Freight Logistics Action Plan was launched in 2007.[20] The plan presented several possible courses of action to promote multimodal transport, such as an 'internet for cargo', different solutions for sustainable quality and efficiency within the multimodal transport chain, harmonised vehicle dimensions and loading standards, and simplification of transport chains.[21] The last suggested course of action contained ideas on the simplification of administrative complaints and security and the development of a single transport document, as well as the question of liability.[22] Regarding liability, the Commission opened for deliberation on whether or not liability systems other than a uniform liability system could fulfil the demands spelled out 10 years earlier. As mentioned above, the intention of the Commission was initially that intermodal operators should be able to offer their customers a clear set of transparent liability conditions and procedures for any cargo that is damaged or lost during its journey. The rules should be uniform – not mode specific – and should not distinguish between national and international transport.

After large-scale discussions with the stakeholders, the Commission seems to have reduced its ambition. According to the Freight Logistics Action Plan, a uniform liability system is no longer the only option.[23] The Commission intends also to consider a network liability system as a solution to the European problem. This alternative would be based on the existing unimodal transport conventions.[24] According to the Action Plan, the major problem of undisclosed damages in a network system could be addressed by including a fallback clause.[25] It is likely that the shift in approach is related to the international situation where, shortly after the EU Action Plan was published, UNCITRAL reached agreement on the Rotterdam Rules. The future of those Rules was at the time (and still is) open and the convention is still not in force. However, the proposed alternatives were familiar to all. The Commission was at the time sceptical as to how the UN work would proceed as it decided to go on with its own project: 'failing rapid progress [at global level] the Commission will start exploring other options for Europe'.[26] It is, however, clear

19 Op. cit., at 7.1.
20 Freight Transport Logistics Action Plan. COM (2007) 607 final.
21 Op. cit., at 2.3.
22 Op. cit., at 2.3.3.
23 Op. cit., at 2.3.3.
24 More on the network system below in Chapter 6 (at 6.4).
25 Freight Transport Logistics Action Plan, COM (2007) 607 final, at 2.3.3.
26 L.C.

that the Commission was influenced by developments in UNCITRAL, as the idea of a uniform liability system was no longer the only possible European solution. However, the EU would explore whether or not a legal act with a standard fallback clause, in the case of no agreement between the parties, would automatically apply. Furthermore, legal gaps between the existing unimodal liability regimes could be addressed so that the parts of the logistic chain that currently fall outside mode-based liability regimes would be covered by the regime.[27] This is a solution that, to a large degree, corresponds with the network solution in the Rotterdam Rules.[28] The Freight Logistics Action Plan was followed up by a report in 2009 published by a third group of new (and not very well-known) legal experts ('the 2009 expert group') appointed by the Commission.

A second proposal: a uniform network system with optional liability limits

The report of the third group was published on the Commission's website in June 2009 ('the 2009 study').[29] This is a comprehensive study covering nearly 200 pages. In the same way as other studies, this study does not express the opinion of the Commission, but is to be considered as a piece of information that the Commission is assembling before taking a decision on whether or not to proceed with a legislative proposal.[30] After outlining the existing legal situation,[31] the 2009 expert group identifies the problem, as the other groups have done, to be a lack of coherent liability rules and a corresponding lack of uniform transport documents throughout the different freight transport modes in Europe.[32] The objective of the study is, accordingly, twofold: first, to assess to what extent the identified lack of uniformity as regards multimodal transport documents and liability is a barrier to seamless, streamlined, flexible and sustainable multimodal transport within the EU[33] and, second, to identify which legal regime would be best suited to promote a sustainable multimodal transport system.[34]

27 Op. cit., note 25.

28 More on the Rotterdam Rules as an alternative for the EU below in 5.2 and in Chapter 6 (at 6.3).

29 Study on the details and added value of establishing a (optional) single transport (electronic) document for all carriage of goods, irrespective of mode, as well as a standard liability clause (voluntary liability regime), with regard to their ability to facilitate multimodal freight transport and enhance the framework offered by multimodal waybills and/or multimodal manifests ('the 2009 study'). Available online at http://ec.europa.eu/transport/themes/strategies/studies/doc/2009_05_19_multimodal_transport_report.pdf (accessed at 28 April 2015).

30 The 2009 study was carried out for the Directorate-General for Energy and Transport in the European Commission and expresses the opinion of Gomez-Acebo & Pombo, Abogados SCP. See the Commission website. Available online at http://ec.europa.eu/transport/themes/strategies/studies/strategies_en.htm (accessed 28 April 2015).

31 Op. cit., (the 2009 study), pp. 31–94.

32 Op. cit., p. 94.

33 Op. cit., pp. 95–176.

34 Op. cit., pp. 177–197.

As for the first objective, the 2009 expert group conducted an empirical study among a group of 183 stakeholders representing 20 different categories, such as EU Member States, shipowners, terminal operators, transport workers, carriers and consignees.[35] Among the 58 stakeholders that answered the questions from the expert group, 34 were not satisfied with the legal situation today, 19 were satisfied and 5 did not respond to the question.[36] Furthermore, 32 of the respondents found that lack of certainty transfers into extra costs when transferring between transport modes, and that these costs are not reasonable, 10 found that this was not a problem and 16 stakeholders did not respond.[37] When asked about the use of electronic documents, 25 stakeholders reported that they used electronic documents, while 22 responded negatively and 11 stakeholders did not respond.[38]

The overall conclusion of the consultation was that *opinions diverged widely* on the way forward. The stakeholders agreed on the need for an electronic transport document, provided that the document could be printed.[39] However, when discussing the problem of diverging liability systems, the stakeholders did not agree on an optimal common solution. Almost all would like to see a liability system based on their own regime. Despite the fact that stakeholders in general were dissatisfied with the current situation, most of them would not like to see a change on a European level, but rather on a global level. A European regime is only regarded a first step towards a global solution (even by its supporters).[40] This is not surprising and is in line with the findings of UNCTAD published in 2003.[41]

In the 2009 proposal, five different policy options were presented for stakeholders: A – status quo/no action, B – opt-in network system, C – modified network system, D – modified uniform system whereby uniform, mandatory rules apply except as regards liability limits, which can be contractually opted out of, and E – a pure uniform system.

Based on the stakeholder survey, the 2009 expert group rejected options A and B as neither would bring anything new, and the ambition of the EU project is to improve the current situation. Option C, a modified network system, which is in line with the liability system in the Rotterdam Rules, was also counted out, the reason being that 'it does not provide any guidance in case of legal gaps or clashes related to the interpretation of the international unimodal conventions for the clauses to which the network regime applies'. The modified network system is thus not regarded as capable of providing legal certainty and predictability.[42] However, one could also argue that any harmonised liability system will be more predictable than the ungoverned situation of today. Option E – a uniform

35 A full list is presented op. cit., at p. 96.
36 Op. cit., p. 111.
37 Op. cit., p. 113.
38 Op. cit., p. 122.
39 Op. cit., p. 7.
40 Op. cit., at pp. 179–180.
41 Multimodal Transport: The feasibility of an International Legal Instrument, UNCTAD/SDTE/TLB/2003.
42 The 2009 study, at p. 185.

liability system, as proposed by both the 1999 and 2005 legal expert groups, was regarded as feasible by the 2009 study. However, the proposal was considered politically unviable and would 'certainly end in a similar way as the UN Multimodal Proposal of 1980'.[43] Considering the opinion of the stakeholders, the statement seems hard to argue with. However, if the Rotterdam Rules fail, this position might change.

After dismissing options A, B, C and E, the expert group suggested that the EU should consider option D, which is a ***modified uniform system*** whereby uniform, mandatory rules apply except as regards liability limits, which can be contractually opted out of. In other words, this would be a European mandatory uniform regime for all matters other than liability limits. The liability limits themselves should be based on an opt-out system, under which the parties are allowed to tie their contract to any of the existing unimodal liability limits. In the absence of express agreement to this, the rules of the 'longest mode' (in kilometres) would apply and in the case of disagreements that cannot be resolved, and the highest liability limit would then apply. When the study was published, this was 17 SDR/kg, but as the Montreal Convention has changed, the highest liability limit today is 19 SDR/kg.[44]

This proposal raises questions concerning the right of the contracting parties to agree on a specific liability regime. After all, the underlying unimodal legal regimes contain mandatory provisions on applicability. This will be discussed in Chapter 6.

5.2 Are the Rotterdam Rules an alternative for the EU?

As mentioned, the 2009 study concludes that an endorsement of the Rotterdam Rules at EU level is neither sufficient nor politically viable. Nevertheless, the question whether or not the Rotterdam Rules provide a solution to the lack of a multimodal liability regime applicable in the EU is under consideration by the Commission. Any explicit policy on this is, however, still not available. The uncertainty of the Commission regarding the potential of the Rotterdam Rules is visible in the recent White Paper from the Commission: Roadmap to a Single European Transport Area – Towards a competitive and resource efficient transport system.[45] The White Paper does not address the previous discussion on a regional liability regime for European multimodal transport. On the contrary, it merely mentions liability in the list of initiatives to be taken by the EU: 'Ensure that liability regimes promote rail, waterborne and intermodal transport.'[46] This might very well be due to the political situation in the European Council, which debated the status of the Rotterdam Rules at an informal meeting of Ministers

43 Op. cit., 42.
44 Op. cit., at p. 190.
45 Roadmap to a Single European Transport Area – Towards a competitive and resource efficient transport system, COM (2011) 144.
46 Op. cit., Annex 1: List of Initiatives, number 7, p. 19.

of Transport in 2010.[47] The ministers acknowledged that seamless, co-modal logistics, which is recognised as a goal for the common transport policy (CTP), requires co-modal arrangements for liability issues, as well as a single transport document. Despite this, the Ministers of Transport could not agree to recommend the Rotterdam Rules. Instead, the ministers restricted themselves to the conclusion that the Rotterdam Rules seem to have great potential in this context; '[h]owever, some further examination of how they could serve this purpose might still be necessary.'[48] The Commission has followed up this pronounced need for further examination. The Commission Staff working document accompanying the White Paper consequently states: 'Any comprehensive multimodal proposal of the Commission will have to take the global convention [the Rotterdam Rules] into account.'[49] How the rules should be taken into account is still an open question and the White Paper provides no solutions whatsoever. The Rotterdam Rules provide a network liability system as regards multimodal contracts of carriage (Article 26). It also contains rules to avoid collisions with existing unimodal conventions. How these provisions work, and whether they will fill the legal gap in international multimodal carriage in a satisfactory manner from an EU point of view will be discussed in Chapter 6 at 6.4. First, however, the main legal obstacles identified above will be examined.

47 Roadmap to a Single European Transport Area – Towards a competitive and resource efficient transport system, COM (2011)144 p. 19. Available online at http://register.consilium.europa.eu/doc/srv?l=EN&f=ST%2013971%202010%20INIT (accessed 15 March 2015).

48 Op. cit., at 5.

49 Commission Staff working Document Accompanying the White paper – Roadmap to a Single European Transport Area – Towards a competitive and resource efficient transport system, SEC (2011) 391 at 189.

6 The main legal obstacles to a European framework

6.1 The underlying unimodal conventions

The main legal obstacles to a European legal framework on multimodal contracts of carriage identified by the Commission and the different expert groups seem to mirror the obstacles identified on an international level. It is clear that the ungoverned situation leads to unpredictability. No international legal regime is directly applicable; hence, in some jurisdictions and situations, the unimodal legal frameworks apply and in others not. Exactly when the unimodal conventions apply is not clear and different jurisdictions have different practices. The problem has been analysed several times by academic scholars[1] and the Commission.[2] However, no legal regime acceptable to all stakeholders has so far been achievable.

Two main alternative solutions to the problem are available: the uniform solution and the network solution.[3] This was emphasised by the United Nations Conference on Trade and Development (UNCTAD), in its report *Multimodal Transport: The Feasibility of an International Legal Instrument* in 2003.[4] The UNCTAD report discusses the same problem as that addressed by the European

1 The leading book on the topic is Hoeks, M., *Multimodal Transport Law – The Law Applicable to the Multimodal Contract for the Carriage of Goods*, Kluwer Law International, 2010. In addition, several articles have been written on the topic. See e.g. Haak, K.F., 'The Harmonization of Intermodal Liability Arrangements', *European Transport Law*, 2005, Volume XL, Issue 1, pp. 13–51.

2 Above in Chapter 5.

3 In 1968, Swedish professor Kurt Grönfors launched five different solutions to the multimodal problem. However, a closer look at the proposed solutions shows that they all are varieties of either the network or the uniform liability system. As solutions 2 and 5, Grönfors discusses the possibility of the carrier being liable for the whole carriage according to one liability system, which is either the one corresponding to 'his own' liability rules (compare the Danish and US Supreme Courts in the cases discussed below) or to an 'external' liability system (as in the 2005 proposal which is based on a *sui generis* understanding of the multimodal contract of carriage). Solutions 1, 3 and 4 are all variations of the network system, where liability varies during the different legs of which the carriage consists. See Grönfors, K., *Successiva transporter*, P.A. Norsted & Söners Förlag, 2008, at pp. 239–275.

4 Multimodal Transport: The feasibility of an International Legal Instrument, UNCTAD/SDTE/TLB/2003.

Union (EU), although from an international point of view. The questions are, first, whether a demand exists for an international harmonised legal instrument on multimodal transportation and, second, if so, how this instrument should be drafted. To promote informed discussion on the topic, UNCTAD produced a questionnaire that was distributed to practically all interested parties, including transport service operators, freight forwarders, logistics service providers and terminal operators, liability insurers and cargo insurers, as well as shippers and transport service users, very much in the same way as the 2009 expert group did six years later but from a European position.[5] UNCTAD received responses from, inter alia, 60 governments from both developing and developed countries and 49 industry representatives.[6] On the question of the desirability of a new international instrument, the great majority (92%) of the respondents considered an international instrument governing liability arising from multimodal transportation desirable.[7]

The legal content of such an instrument was, however, less easy to agree on. Again on an international level, the key question concerned what kind of liability system the legal instrument should embody.[8] UNCTAD presented three options: the uniform liability system, the network system and the modified liability system, the last being basically a variation of the network system, or a combination of the network and the uniform liability systems. A uniform liability *system* was defined as a system that applies the same liability rules irrespective of the unimodal stage of transport during which loss, damage or delay (losses) occurs.[9] Under such a system, the result should be the same whether or not losses can be localised. This solution was proposed by the 2005 expert group assisting the Commission, and is discussed below in section 6.3. A network liability system was, on the other hand, defined as a system in which different liability rules will apply depending on the unimodal stage of transport during which losses occurred, but with a fallback clause if the location of the losses cannot be localised.[10] This is the solution in the Rotterdam Rules, which will be outlined below in section 6.4. The third system discussed by UNCTAD was described as a modified liability system. A modified liability system was described as a system where some rules apply irrespective of the unimodal stage of transport during which losses occur, whereas the application of other rules would depend on the unimodal stage of transport during which losses occur. This system more or less represents a compromise between the two liability systems mentioned above, and is in line with the proposal from the 2009 expert group (Chapter 5 (at 5.1)). Under a modified liability system, various arrangements are possible, making the system more uniform or more network-like. The potential advantage of this approach is, again according to

5 Above in Chapter 5 (at 5.1).
6 Op. cit., at p. 2.
7 Op. cit., at p. 27.
8 Op. cit., at p. 44.
9 Op. cit., at p. 45.
10 Op. cit., at p. 49.

UNCTAD, that it may provide a workable consensus, taking into account conflicting views and interests.[11]

The problem with a uniform liability system is, though, that in some areas of the transport industry, carrier liability would increase compared to the current situation. Two situations are particularly difficult. First, if uniform rules apply irrespective of the modal stage of transport during which losses occur, the carrier would no longer be able to take advantage of potentially less burdensome liability rules that might otherwise apply. Second, concern arises about the carrier's right to seek recourse against any responsible subcontracting actual or performing carrier. If a subcontracting unimodal carrier is subject to less burdensome liability rules, the multimodal carrier might not see its total loss reimbursed. A uniform liability system would, therefore, according to the UNCTAD report, meet resistance from the transportation industry.[12] The industry would thus, according to the UNCTAD report, rather support the idea of a network liability system. This is the alternative that differs least from the present international legal framework and also the system that provides the carrier with the possibility of relying on the less burdensome liability system. An international legal instrument based on a network system would provide various solutions to the questions relating to liability limits. The system would be flexible and allow for many different solutions and would also be in line with present contractual practice. On the other hand, such an instrument would lack the benefits of a uniform system, for example, the important aspect of predictability. As far as predictability is concerned, a uniform liability system would undoubtedly be better.

A uniform liability system should, however, be combined with a *sui generis* understanding of the multimodal contract of carriage in order to avoid collisions with the underlying unimodal liability conventions. The first problem to address is thus related to the *sui generis* discussion. Should – and could – multimodal contracts of carriage be considered contracts *sui generis* or not? What are the pro and cons? The issue will be addressed below. Currently there is no harmonised view on this matter in the different EU Member States. Instead, opinion diverges throughout Europe, as well as globally. As will be outlined, different national supreme courts have different opinions on the question, and thus different views on when the unimodal transport conventions are applicable to a multimodal carriage of cargo and when they are not. How to handle the present unimodal conventions is a legal problem, which has to be addressed whether the solution to the multimodal regulatory gap is a *sui generis* approach or the network system is selected. Moreover, under the latter system the contract of carriage needs to be identified in order to decide on the applicable unimodal liability system.

One solution, presented below, is to use the transport document as a connecting factor between the contract and the underlying legal regimes. If a uniform liability system is chosen the transport document needs to be combined with a declaration that the multimodal contract of carriage is *sui generis*. This would be

11 Op. cit., at p. 53.
12 Op. cit., at p. 47.

in line with the initial objective of the Commission on a uniform liability regime.[13] However, despite the EU initiative on a uniform liability regime, the common view in Europe seems to be to see the multimodal contract of carriage as a mixed contract to which a network of unimodal liability regimes apply. The problem of undisclosed damages, losses or circumstances is under this perspective solved by a fallback clause. Many scholars favour this solution.[14] The Rotterdam Rules are also based on a network solution. An outline of the network solution, as well as a discussion on whether the Rotterdam Rules provide a solution for the EU, are be presented below (in section 6.4). First, however, the question whether a multimodal contract of carriage should – or could – be regarded as *sui generis*, will be examined.

As already mentioned, a major problem in multimodal carriage of cargo, from a legal standpoint, is the lack of an internationally harmonised legal framework. Several attempts at tackling the problem have been initiated, but so far with no success. The industry has, however, managed to solve the problem (to a certain degree) by developing different standard contracts, which contain opt-in solutions and thus connect the multimodal contract to a specific set of legal rules. However, even these contracts often contain a step-back clause in case 'an applicable mandatory international convention or mandatory national law' applies.[15] This is due to the fact that the international unimodal transport conventions might apply to multimodal carriage, and, if this is the case, and the relevant provisions are mandatory, the standard contract must step back *ipso jure*. This is nothing exceptional; contracts always step back for mandatory law. The problem is, however, that it is not clear when the unimodal liability regimes are applicable in a multimodal context and when they are not. This differs in different jurisdictions and leads to unpredictability as regards the legal position of the parties to an international contract of multimodal carriage. The uncertain legal position of multimodal carriage is not only problematic from a practical point of view; the heterogenic interpretation of the unimodal regimes is also challenging regarding future international legislation on multimodal carriage. If the unimodal conventions are given a broad interpretation and thus a wide scope of application as regards multimodal contracts of carriage, then the room for adapting a new international legal instrument will be correspondingly narrow. We already see a difference in the approach to multimodal contracts of carriage in Europe.

Some states consider the multimodal contract of carriage as *sui generis*, that is a form of contract to which the unimodal regimes do not apply.[16] Others see the multimodal contract of carriage as a mixed contract and freely apply unimodal

13 See above in Chapter 5 (at 5.1).

14 See e.g. Hoeks, op. cit., note 1, pp. 483–490. See also Marten, B., 'A Multimodal Transport Reform and the European Union: A Minimalist Approach', *European Transport Law*, 2012, Volume XLVII, Issue 2, pp. 129–152 at p. 152.

15 See for example FIATA Multimodal Transport Bill of Lading 8.6. Available online at http://www.bifa.org/_attachments/resources/1079_s4.pdf (accessed 17 March 2015).

16 E.g. Germany, below in section 6.2.

legal regimes to the relevant part of the contract (if known),[17] or the multimodal contract might be considered as a form of unimodal contract of carriage, to which a unimodal legal framework is applicable to all modes performing the contract.[18] In our context the impact of describing the multimodal contract of carriage as a contract of its own kind would be that it is not a unimodal contract of carriage, and thus the unimodal legal regimes would not apply to this contract. The question is thus whether a multimodal contract of carriage is to be seen as something unique and not as a contract of carriage by road, or rail or sea or any of the other modes of transport, but simply as a contract combining these modes.

The alternative is to describe the contract functionally. That is to advocate that a multimodal transport contract is nothing more than the parts from which it is built. A multimodal contract carried out by air and road is accordingly, in addition to being a multimodal contract, also, for example, a contract of carriage by air and a contract of carriage by road. If the cargo is damaged or lost, or an event causing delay occurs during one of the two legs of the carriage, the relevant unimodal liability system will apply. Based on this approach, a network liability system should be implemented. If it is not possible to trace the source of losses, arrangements could be made for these so-called undisclosed cases, for example by implementing a fallback clause. As outlined in Chapter 2, this is the position in most jurisdictions where the multimodal problem is governed. Both the regional Andean and Mercosur agreements in South America, as well as the national German and Dutch models, apply a network liability system. This is also the underlying position of the standard contracts used today. Additionally, the Rotterdam Rules are built on a functional understanding of the multimodal contract of carriage and offer a network liability system. Under a functional approach the multimodal contract is considered as nothing more than the sum total of its components. But also under this viewpoint it is not clear what set of rules to apply and when.[19]

On the other hand, we also have the situation where a contract of carriage is considered unimodal, albeit performance is multimodal. What set of rules should apply in these situations? Should the contract be decisive, or should we use the rules applicable to the mode of transport where the losses actually occurred? If the cargo is damaged during a transport leg different from that agreed contractually, it is not always clear what set of rules to apply despite the fact that the losses are disclosed. Here we see different approaches in different legal systems. One approach is to argue that the contract of carriage applies throughout the entire transport regardless of where in the transport chain the losses occurred. This is the position in certain conventions with an extended application in multimodal situations. A typical example is Article 2 of the Convention on the Contract for the International Carriage of Goods by Road (CMR) regarding the called roll-on

17 E.g. England, below in section 6.2.
18 E.g. US and Denmark, below in section 6.2.
19 On the network solution below in section 6.3.

roll-off (ro-ro) transport.[20] As a main rule, CMR applies to ro-ro transport if the cargo is not unloaded and the losses could not be related to a specific event. Because of this, CMR is claimed to contain rules on multimodal transport.[21] However, in many situations we are outside the so-called multimodal scope of the unimodal conventions. A contract of carriage by air might, for example, be partly performed by another mode of transport, such as rail or road. Is this then a unimodal contract of carriage governed by a unimodal legal framework or is it a multimodal contract of carriage? And what legal regime is then applicable? These questions all boil down to the issue of how to interpret the scope provisions of the different unimodal conventions to which, as mentioned above, the answers vary greatly in different jurisdictions.

6.2 The role of the transport document

How the transport document can be decisive

Questions on the law applicable to multimodal carriage have been heard by several supreme courts in Europe as well as the Supreme Court of the United States. Both results and argumentation vary tremendously. In the following, the role of the transport document in determining the scope provisions of the unimodal conventions will be examined. The question asked is how important the transport document is in settling the scope of a unimodal transport convention. Can, or should, the transport document be described as a gateway to a particular legal framework?[22] And if the transport document is found important, can this give us a hint as to the problem? Could the problem be solved simply by connecting the liability system to the use of the document?

The following examples are gathered from court practice in three different legal systems in Europe, as well as from the US. Not all the cases deal with the transport conventions directly; some of the cases discuss the scope provisions of national legislation that implements international conventions. The arguments are still relevant for an understanding of the role of the transport document in finding the law applicable to multimodal contracts of carriage. The question to be discussed is the role of the bill of lading, as well as other transport documents, in this context. To what extent is the transport document relevant when solving the problem of applicable law in multimodal carriage of goods or, to be more precise, does the existence of a certain transport document used in a multimodal contract of carriage trigger a particular unimodal legal framework? This is again a question of interpreting the scope provisions of unimodal transport conventions.

20 Ro-ro transport is short for roll-on roll-off transport and applies typically to, e.g. ferries, where the lorries with their cargo are carried on board a vessel.

21 Herber, R., 'The European Legal Experience with Multimodalism', *Tulane Law Review*, 1989–1990, Volume 64, Issue 2 & 3, p. 611–629, at p. 614.

22 See Glass, D. and Nair, M., 'Towards Flexible Carriage Documents? Reducing the Need for Modally Distinct Documents in International Goods Transport', *The Journal of International Maritime Law*, 2009, Volume 15, pp. 1–28.

Most of the transport conventions have a contractual scope, which implies that they are applicable to a certain category of contracts used in international carriage. The CMR applies to 'every contract for the carriage of goods by road in vehicles for reward'[23] and the COTIF-CIM applies to 'every contract of carriage of goods by rail for reward'.[24] Furthermore, the multimodal scope of the COTIF-CIM is restricted to multimodal (rail) carriage 'subject of a single contract of carriage.'[25] This precondition is not directly expressed in the CMR, but follows from Article 2 read in context with Article 1. The contractual approach is also noticeable in 'wet' carriage. (CMNI convention)[26] has a contractual scope; it is applicable to 'all contracts of carriage whereby a carrier undertakes against payment of freight to carry goods by inland waterways'.[27] The Hamburg Rules (which are not used very much) are, according to Article 2, 'applicable to all contracts of carriage by sea'.[28] Most countries active in sea carriage are bound by the combination of a contractual and a documentary approach by the Hague-Visby Rules,[29] according to which the convention is applicable to every contract of carriage by sea,[30] as long as this is 'covered by a bill of lading or any similar document of title'.[31] The same system applies under the Hague Rules.[32] Carriage by air is seemingly in an exceptional position, as both the Warsaw Convention[33] and the

23 The Convention on the Contract for the International Carriage of Goods by Road (CMR) (Geneva, 19 May 1956), Art. 1(1).

24 Appendix B to the Convention concerning International Carriage by Rail (COTIF) of 9 June 1999 Uniform Rules Concerning the Contract of International Carriage of Goods by Rail (CIM) Applicable with effect from 1 July 2006. CIT Edition, the COTIF-CIM, Art. 1.

25 COTIF-CIM Art. 1.3 and 1.4.

26 Budapest Convention on the Contract for the Carriage of Goods by Inland Waterways (CMNI), Budapest, 25 September–3 October 2000 (the CMNI).

27 CMNI, Article 1, 'Definitions, In this Convention, 1. "Contract of carriage" means any contract, of any kind, whereby a carrier undertakes against payment of freight to carry goods by inland waterways and CMNI 2, This Convention is applicable to any contract of carriage.'

28 United Nations Convention on the Carriage of Goods by Sea (The Hamburg Rules) Hamburg, 30 March 1978, Art. 1. Despite the fact that the Hamburg Rules never became an international success, the Rules are, as far as possible without having to derogate from the ratified Hague-Visby Rules, implemented in the Scandinavian Maritime Codes, see above in Chapter 2 (at 2.2).

29 The Hague-Visby Rules – The Hague Rules as Amended by the Brussels Protocol 1968.

30 Hague-Visby Rules Art. II: 'Subject to the provisions of Article VI, under every contract of carriage of goods by sea the carrier, in relation to the loading, handling, stowage, carriage, custody, care and discharge of such goods, shall be subject to the responsibilities and liabilities and entitled to the rights and immunities hereinafter set forth.'

31 Hague-Visby Rules Art. I(b).

32 International Convention for the Unification of Certain Rules of Law relating to Bills of Lading (Hague Rules), and Protocol of Signature (Brussels, 25 August 1924), the Hague Rules Art. 1(b) '"Contract of carriage" applies only to contracts of carriage covered by a bill of lading or any similar document of title, in so far as such document relates to the carriage of goods by sea, including any bill of lading or any similar document as aforesaid issued under or pursuant to a charter party from the moment at which such bill of lading or similar document of title regulates the relations between a carrier and a holder of the same.'

33 Convention for the Unification of Certain Rules Relating to International Carriage by Air, Signed at Warsaw on 12 October 1929 (Warsaw Convention 1929).

Montreal Convention[34] apply to all international carriage of 'cargo performed by aircraft for reward'.[35] Therefore we may conclude that the 'air' conventions have a factual approach, although this does not prevent the transport document being used to identify the scope of the applicable law.

Beyond the unimodal scope, several of the conventions directly apply to situations normally characterised as multimodal. Article 2 of the CMR, for example, extends the scope of the conventions to so-called piggyback carriage, provided that the cargo is not transhipped.[36] According to Article 1.3 of the COTIF-CIM, the convention applies to supplementary carriage by road or inland waterways,[37] as well as to supplementary carriage by sea.[38] However, the extended scope of the COTIF-CIM is not applicable to multimodal carriage that includes international carriage by road. This was done in order to avoid possible conflicts with the CMR, which applies to international carriage by road.[39] The CMNI also has multimodal scope, although restricted to 'wet carriage'. According to Article 2.2, the CMNI Convention is applicable if the purpose of the contract is carriage of goods, without transhipment both on inland waterways and in waters to which maritime

34 Convention for the Unification of Certain Rules for International Carriage by Air – Montreal, 28 May 1999.

35 Montreal and Warsaw Conventions, both Art. 1.1.

36 CMR Article 2:

> 1 Where the vehicle containing the goods is carried over part of the journey by sea, rail, inland waterways or air, and, except where the provisions of article 14 are applicable, the goods are not unloaded from the vehicle, this Convention shall nevertheless apply to the whole of the carriage. Provided that to the extent it is proved that any loss, damage or delay in delivery of the goods which occurs during the carriage by the other means of transport was not caused by act or omission of the carrier by road, but by some event which could only occurred in the course of and by reason of the carriage by that other means of transport, the liability of the carrier by road shall be determined not by this convention but in the manner in which the liability of the carrier by the other means of transport would have been determined if a contract for the carriage the goods alone had been made by the sender with the carrier by the other means of transport in accordance with the conditions prescribed by law for the carriage of goods by that means of transport. If, however, there are no such prescribed conditions, the liability of the carrier by road shall be determined by this convention.
>
> 2 If the carrier by road is also himself the carrier by the other means of transport, his liability shall also be determined in accordance with the provisions paragraph 1 of this article, but as if, in his capacities as carrier by road and carrier by the other means of transport, he were two separate persons.

37 COTIF-CIM Art. 1(3): 'When international carriage being the subject of a single contract includes carriage by road or inland waterway in internal traffic of a Member State as a supplement to transfrontier carriage by rail, these Uniform Rules shall apply.'

38 COTIF-CIM Art. 1(4): 'When international carriage being the subject of a single contract of carriage includes carriage by sea or transfrontier carriage by inland waterway as a supplement to carriage by rail, these Uniform Rules shall apply if the carriage by sea or inland waterway is performed on services included in the list of services provided for in Article 24 § 1 of the Convention.'

39 CMR Art. 1.1.

regulations apply, unless a marine bill of lading has been issued in accordance with the marine law applicable or the distance to be travelled in waters to which maritime regulations apply is the greater.[40] The conventions governing contracts of carriage by air similarly extend their scope of application to certain multimodal situations. For example, the Montreal Convention applies to multimodal carriage performed within an airport as well as to multimodal carriage outside an airport for the purpose of loading, delivery or transhipment. The precondition, however, is that the carriage 'takes place in the performance of a contract for carriage by air'.[41] The same applies to a carrier which, without the consent of the consignor, substitutes carriage by another mode of transport for the whole or part of carriage that was initially intended by the agreement between the parties to be carriage by air.[42] It has been stated that the basic principle is 'that carriage outside the airport is not covered by the international air law conventions, but for exceptional circumstances and only in a supplementary manner'.[43]

In other words, all conventions, except the maritime, cover multimodal carriage to a certain extent. The multimodal scope is, however, limited. Both the CMR and the CMNI have as a precondition that the cargo is not transhipped. The Montreal Convention, however, only applies to intended multimodal carriage outside an airport if the purpose is transhipment, delivery or loading. As regards the conventions applicable to carriage by sea, they have no provisions on multimodal carriage whatsoever. These conventions merely apply to contracts of carriage by sea, and according to both the Hague Rules and the Hague-Visby Rules, only if a bill of lading (or a similar document) is issued as evidence of a contract of carriage by sea. Nevertheless, the limited scope provisions do not necessarily exclude other multimodal carriage from the scope of the conventions. The question is one of interpretation, which can be posed in relation to all general scope provisions.

40 CMNI Art. 2.2: 'This Convention is applicable if the purpose of the contract of carriage is the carriage of goods, without transhipment, both on inland waterways and in waters to which maritime regulations apply, under the conditions set out in paragraph 1, unless:

(a) a maritime bill of lading has been issued in accordance with the maritime law applicable, or
(b) the distance to be travelled in waters to which maritime regulations apply is the greater.'

41 Montreal Convention Art. 18.4: 'The period of the carriage by air does not extend to any carriage by land, by sea or by inland waterway performed outside an airport. If, however, such carriage takes place in the performance of a contract for carriage by air, for the purpose of loading, delivery or transhipment, any damage is presumed, subject to proof to the contrary, to have been the result of an event which took place during the carriage by air. If a carrier, without the consent of the consignor, substitutes carriage by another mode of transport for the whole or part of a carriage intended by the agreement between the parties to be carriage by air, such carriage by another mode of transport is deemed to be within the period of carriage by air.'

42 L.C.

43 Leloudas, G., 'Multimodal Transport under the Warsaw and Montreal Convention Regimes: A Velvet Revolution?' in Soyer, B. and Tettenborn, A. (eds), *Carriage of Goods By Sea, Land and Air – Unimodal and Multimodal Transport in the 21st Century*', Informa Law from Routledge, 2013, pp. 77–110 at pp. 90–91.

Three European cases

England – the Quantum *case 2002*

One of the most interesting cases on the law applicable to multimodal carriage of goods is a case heard by the English Court of Appeal, known as the *Quantum* case.[44] The case was about cargo damage during the road leg of a carriage performed by both air and road.

In September 1998, the air carrier Air France issued a waybill to the claimants, Quantum Corporation. The air waybill provided for carriage of hard disk drives from Singapore to Dublin by air. However, since the air waybill allowed trucking, parts of the air transport could, and were, substituted by road transport. Carriage from Singapore to Paris was accordingly performed by air and carriage from Paris to Dublin by road and roll-on-roll-off carriage. During the road leg the consignment was lost in a fake hijack in which the truck driver was involved. Air France admitted liability for the loss, but argued that carriage by air subject to the Warsaw Convention ended at Charles De Gaulle airport, and thereafter its liability was to be determined by reference to its own terms and conditions, which, according to Air France, were applicable to the extent that they were not inconsistent with the provisions of the Warsaw Convention. Furthermore, the Warsaw Convention liability limits should apply. At the time the liability limit was 17 Special Drawing Rights (SDR) per kilogram. This was more generous than the CMR limit of 8.33 SDR, but the conditions did not contain any provision, such as Article 29 of the CMR disentitling Air France from relying on the limit in the event of wilful misconduct. Air France argued that the contract of carriage was one of carriage by air and thus subject to the air law system. As the road part is not subject to air law, and there was no contract of carriage by air, there was a legal gap that should be filled by the standard conditions agreed between the parties.[45] Quantum, on the other side, argued that although the carriage was subject to only one contract of carriage, Air France had contracted not only for carriage of goods by air to Charles De Gaulle, but also for their carriage by truck to Dublin. Air France's conditions were contractual and thus subject to any applicable convention. According to the claimants, the relevant convention was the CMR. Under the CMR, Air France's liability would most likely be unlimited because of the wilful misconduct of the driver (CMR, Article 29).

The question for the court was, accordingly, if the CMR applied: 'The basic issue that we have to address is, . . . what constitutes a "contract for the carriage of goods by road in vehicles for reward" within the meaning of Art. 1(1).'[46] The Commercial Court had concluded that the correct approach was to characterise the contract as a whole, and that, unless the contract as a whole could be said to be for carriage by road internationally, any road carriage that it embraced fell outside the terms of the Convention. According to the Court of Appeal, the

44 *Quantum Corporation Inc. and Others v Plane Trucking Ltd* [2002] 2 Lloyds Rep. 25.
45 Op. cit., at p. 6.
46 Op. cit., at p. 10.

question could be divided into two parts. The first part was to what extent application of the convention (CMR) depended upon the carrier having obliged itself contractually to carry by road (and by no other means) and the second was to what extent a contract can be both for the carriage of goods by road, within Article 1, and for some other means of carriage, to which the CMR does not apply.[47]

Regarding the first question, the court listed four possibilities, each of which may actually lead to goods being carried by road internationally: (a) the carrier may have promised unconditionally to carry by road and on a trailer; (b) the carrier may have promised this, but reserved either a general or a limited option to elect some other means of carriage for all or part of the way; (c) the carrier may have left the means of transport open, either entirely or as between a number of possibilities, at least one of them being carriage by road; or (d) the carrier may have undertaken to carry by some other means, but reserved either a general or a limited option to carry by road.[48] The judge started by clarifying that it was really only alternative (d) (which the case was about) that was somewhat unclear as regards the applicability of the CMR and, '[i]f they are all within CMR, there seems to me much to be said for treating case (d) as also within CMR. Carriage by road contrary to the terms of a contract would raise different considerations.'[49] The conclusion was, in other words, that applying the CMR is not dependent on the carrier having obliged itself to perform the carriage by road only.

The judge continued by analysing the second question on whether the contract can be both for the carriage of goods by road and for carriage by some other means – so-called mixed or multimodal carriage – and still be governed by the CMR. Regarding the documentary approach, Air France had emphasised that the CMR, in contrast with, for example, the Warsaw Convention, focuses on 'the contract for the carriage of goods by road' and not on carriage as such and that the CMR therefore could not be applicable.[50] The Court of Appeal recognised that Article 4 of the CMR provides that 'the contract of carriage shall be confirmed by the making out of a consignment note' and Article 9 that 'the consignment note shall be prima facie evidence of the making of the contract of carriage, [and] the conditions of the contract'.[51] The transport document in use is, nevertheless, according to the Court, of no interest except in as far as it 'reflects the reality that the contract has now become'.[52] And as regards determining whether a contract exists for carriage of goods by road within Article 1, the Court of Appeal held that the actual operation of the contract under its terms was essential.[53] In this case the air waybill left the way open for carriage by road, and, according to the Court, as soon as this was taking place, there was a contract of carriage by road.

47 Op. cit., at p. 14.
48 Op. cit., at p. 15.
49 Op. cit., at p. 18.
50 Op. cit., at p. 19.
51 Op. cit., at p. 20.
52 Op. cit., at p. 21.
53 L.C.

Contrary to this, Air France argued that even if the contract should be established by the actual operation of the contract, it would have to be concluded that the place of taking over the goods specified in the contract was Singapore, which would result in the CMR Convention applying to air carriage from Singapore to Paris. According to the Commercial Court, this would be both 'absurd and contrary to the Warsaw Convention'.[54] In contrast, the Court of Appeal saw no problem stating that the road carrier received the cargo in Paris, despite the fact that no consignment note was handed over by the carrier. As regards the transport document, the Court pointed out that CMR, Article 4, clearly states that 'the absence, irregularity or loss of the consignment note shall not affect the existence or validity of the contract of carriage, which shall remain subject to the Convention'. In other words, lack of a transport document does not exclude the existence of a contract of carriage. Accordingly, the CMR applies to contracts of carriage with an option to carry by road when this option is actually performed.[55] The Court of Appeal was upholding the mixed contract perspective of a multimodal contract of carriage: 'Viewed overall, contracts can by their nature or terms have two separate aspects, and the present, despite the length of the air leg, was in my view just such a contract.'[56] The transport document involved was more or less a null argument for the judge, who determined the scope of the CMR by analysing the actual operation of the contract under its terms, and not by the document in use.

Despite a settled position in England and Wales,[57] the result of the *Quantum* decision is far from agreed either in legal doctrine or by other European courts.[58] It would probably not be an overstatement to say that today we can see a divided Europe as regards the law applicable to multimodal contracts of carriage. From Denmark we have a case, which also deals with a single contract of carriage performed by an air–road combination, in which the Danish Supreme Court reached a totally different conclusion than that of the Court of Appeal.

Denmark – Danish Supreme Court 2008

The *Salmon Roe* case from the Danish Supreme Court[59] illustrates how the problem of applicable law in multimodal contracts of carriage can be solved by

54 Op. cit., at p. 24.

55 Op. cit., at p. 56.

56 Op. cit. at p. 62.

57 *Datec Electronics Holdings Ltd & Others v United Parcels Services Ltd* [2007] UKHL 23 (16 Mary 2007).

58 The *Quantum* solution is approved by Professor Peter Wetterstien, who finds that the holding of the English Court of Appeal in the *Quantum* decision 'balances well the interests of the parties to the international contract of carriage, and therefore ought to be followed in other jurisdictions'. Wetterstein, P., 'The Application of the CMR Convention to Multimodal Transports – the Example of *Quantum Corp. v Plane Trucking*', *Tidskrift utgiven av Juridiska Föreningen i Finland* (JFT), 2014, Volume 6, pp. 442–458 at p. 458.

59 The *Salmon Roe* case (lakserognsaken) from the Danish Supreme Court (Dansk Høyesteret) is published in Ugeskrift for Rætsvesen UfR 2008.1638.

recognising the transport document as a document evidencing the legal nature of the contract of carriage. The contractual carrier (Mahe Freight) had taken on an obligation to carry salmon roe from Billund (Denmark) to Narita (Japan). The contract was evidenced by an air waybill issued by the agent of the Japanese carrier (Japanese Airlines) as air carriage from Billund to Narita. However, the carriage was, according to the contract, performed by road from Billund to Frankfurt (Germany), which was an option according to the contract. The contractual subcarrier (Haugsted) for the road leg issued a CMR consignment note for the carriage from Billund to Frankfurt. During the road leg the cargo was damaged and the question of applicable law arose.

The Danish Supreme Court (*Dansk Højesteret*) decided that the carriage was performed under a contract of carriage by air and that the Danish Air Carriage Act (implementing the Warsaw Convention)[60] was applicable to the contract of carriage. The fact that the contract contained an option to perform the carriage by another means of transport could not change this. However, the contract between the road carrier and the air carrier, for which a CMR consignment note was issued, was considered a contract of carriage by road. The contractual carrier was hence liable both according to the air law system and, based on its responsibility for its subcontractors, also according to the road law system. In the decision on which legal system to use, the Supreme Court decided that the consignee had the option to choose. The subcarrier was only liable according to the Danish CMR act.[61]

The transport document in the case was an air waybill, which included an option to choose other modes, including road transport. On the front was printed: 'Subject to the conditions of the contract on the reverse hereof, all the goods may be carried by any other means including road.'[62] This was the only document handed over to the shipper. The cargo owner claimed that this, therefore, was a contract of carriage by air. Although the air waybill contained an option to use other means of transport such as road, this did not imply acceptance of the contract turning into a contract of carriage by road and thus subject to different legal rules. If the contract could be characterised as a contract of carriage by road, the notification time limit would be one year. The notification time limit under the air law system was two years. This is more burdensome on the sender and could not have been accepted, although the contract accepted the substitute of air carriage by road.[63] The contractual carrier, on the other hand, argued that the applicable law was the CMR act. A key argument was that the issue of an air waybill does not imply a contract of carriage by air. Instead, the CMR-Convention is mandatory in both directions, and the parties cannot contract themselves out of its scope. Both the English *Quantum* case decision and legal literature were used to support this

60 The (previous) Danish Air Carriage Act (Lov om luftfart nr 408 af 11.09.1985).

61 The Danish CMR Act (CMR-loven nr 602 af 09.09.1986).

62 The *Salmon Roe* case, in UfR 2008.1638 at p. 1640.

63 Op. cit., at p. 1646.

position.[64] Nevertheless, the Supreme Court accepted the arguments presented by the cargo side and concluded that the Air Carriage Act was applicable. The reasoning is closely connected to the documents used: 'The transport is both in the booking note as well as in the air waybill specified as air transport from Billund in Denmark to Narita in Japan. The Supreme Court therefore agrees that the contract on this carriage as a whole must be considered to be a contract of carriage by air, and as such subject to the rules applicable to air carriage.'[65]

The Danish Supreme Court linked its arguments strictly to the contract as evidenced by the air waybill. The Court explained its opinion by reference to the fact that the booking note and the air waybill together specified the transport to take place from Denmark to Japan. The fact that the contract contained an option to substitute air carriage by other means of transport could not change the character of the contract. The reasoning was in two steps: first, the Court stated that the contract as a whole was to be considered a contract of carriage by air, and as a second step it declared that a contract of carriage by air is subject to the rules applicable to air carriage. The formal approach was also applied in relation to the actual carrier concerning the road leg of the carriage.

The fact that the contractual carrier might be held liable according to two sets of rules is criticised in Danish legal literature. The fact that the consignee should have an option to choose between different liability systems is considered unfair and in favour of the interests of the cargo owner at the expense of the carrier.[66] Another problem is that the Supreme Court could easily avoid commenting on the CMR act in relation to the contractual carrier, as the claim under this act was time barred. The statement was made as an *obiter dictum* and is thus not binding or at least does not have the same impact as statements directly relevant for the conclusion.

Nevertheless, for the time being we might conclude that, according to Danish case law, the transport document seems crucial when defining the scope of air law legislation. Furthermore, a contract of carriage performed by more than one mode of transport might very well be considered unimodal because the scope of a unimodal convention is settled in relation to the transport document in use. If an air waybill is issued for carriage between Denmark and Japan, the air law system applies even though the bill contains an option for the carrier to substitute air carriage with another mode of transport, such as road transport.

Because of the *obiter dictum* in the case, it is not clear if the mixed contract approach with the underlying network system is abolished or not under Danish law. If the cargo owner had benefited from the CMR act, it would have been entitled to apply this as well. The Danish Supreme Court seems accordingly to rest its decision on the one carriage – one document – one liability doctrine. The liability system follows the document in use, and if there are several documents, different

64 L.C.

65 The *Salmon Roe* case, at p. 1652 (author's translation).

66 See Roost, L.A., *Multimodale Transporter*, 2012, pp. 58–62 (in Danish). See also Ulfbeck, V., 'Options in Contracts of Carriage. The Air/Road Combination in Recent European Case Law', *Transportrecht*, 10/2010, pp. 370–376 at p. 375.

liabilities might be appropriate. As we shall see, this is not very far from the reasoning in the US Supreme Court, but far from the way the German Supreme Court sees the problem.

Germany – Bundesgerichtshof 2008

Neither England nor Denmark has any national legislation on international multimodal carriage of goods. A need to apply, in one way or another, the unimodal conventions to multimodal contracts of carriage therefore occurs. It is, however, different in Germany, where international multimodal contracts of carriage have been subject to national legislation since 1998, when the transport legislation was amended.[67] Today the Fourth Book of the Commercial Code governs multimodal contracts of carriage.[68] The code is to a large degree declaratory. However, certain provisions, which govern liability, are mandatory.

> Diverging rules on the basis of liability must be individually negotiated. General Conditions are accepted as regards the amount of liability, but only within a limit of 2 SDR and 40SDR/kg. The individually agreed liability limit must furthermore be shown in a particular kind of print so that the other party can easily recognize it.[69] The limitation is otherwise fixed at 8.33SDR (in line with the CMR).

In multimodal carriage the code applies a network system, which means that a party that can prove precisely during which mode of transport the cause of losses took place can invoke the rules of the liability system applicable to that mode of transport.[70] Before the amendment to the Commercial Code, there had been some divergence in court practice on how to deal with multimodal carriage of cargo. In 2008, however, the Court made a decision that clearly states that the unimodal conventions are not applicable to multimodal contracts, which the German Supreme Court considers *sui generis*.

In this case a Japanese manufacturer of copying machines entered into a contract of carriage with a Japanese freight forwarder (which acted as carrier) for carriage of 24 containers loaded with copying machines for transportation from Tokyo (Japan) to Mönchengladbach (Germany). According to the waybill issued, the Tokyo District Court should have exclusive jurisdiction in the case. The containers were carried by sea from Tokyo to Rotterdam. In the port of Rotterdam they were transferred to trailers to be carried by road from Rotterdam

67 Gesetz zur Regelung des Fracht-, Speditions- und Lagerrechts- Transportsrechtsreformgesetz-, Bundesgesetzblatt 1998 Teil I, 1558. For a general presentation in English see: Trappe, J., 'The Reform of German Transport Law', *Lloyd's Maritime and Commercial Law Quarterly*, 2001 volume 3, pp. 392–405.

68 The German Commercial Code (Handelsgezetzbuch) § 407 ff.

69 Op. cit., at p. 596.

70 Op. cit., at p. 601.

to Mönchengladbach. Before leaving the port area one of the containers was damaged because the trailer toppled over on a curve. The cargo owner claimed damages under the CMR Convention. The main question for the German Supreme Court (Bundesgerichtshof, BGH) was whether the Court had jurisdiction, which would have been the case if the CMR applied in this situation.

As the case was not about piggyback carriage as in Article 2, the court had to decide if the CMR applied to multimodal contracts of carriage with a road leg on the basis of Article 1(1) of the CMR. The response from the court was negative: 'weil die CMR grundsätzlich nicht auf multimodale Frachtvertrage anwendbar ist[71] [because the CMR in principle is not applicable to multimodal contracts of carriage]'.

The German Supreme Court started by stating that the contract was to be considered a multimodal contract of carriage because it would be performed by different modes of transport.[72] The Court neither discussed any of the different alternatives given by the English Court of Appeal, nor did it discuss the impact of the transport document issued. The analysis was limited to whether or not the CMR might be applicable to multimodal contracts of carriage. The Court admitted that the wording in CMR Article 1(1) does not prevent use of the CMR. However, an extended interpretation of the scope provision was considered not advisable, partly because of the wording in French that might lead to a more narrow interpretation, and partly because of CMR Article 2, which, according to the Court, solely deals with the multimodal issue. Additionally, the history of the CMR supported this way of reading the Convention.[73]

The final argument used to justify the narrow reading of CMR Article 1(1) is, however, the most important one. A narrow interpretation of the scope would be in line with the German legislator, which had taken the position that the national rules on international multimodal contracts of carriage would not be in conflict with the CMR.[74] Thereafter the Court spent some time on distinguishing the present case from previous German case law, as well as from the English *Quantum* case discussed above. The German court did not consider the use of transport documents at all, which indicates that the Court sees no connection between the document and the contract. The decision is at this point in line with the *Quantum* decision, although arriving at a different result. From a German point of view it might be concluded that the existence of a transport document has no impact on deciding the nature of the contract of carriage, which is the same position as taken by the English Court of Appeal, but contrary to the result in the Danish Supreme Court. The German Supreme Court clearly abolishes the mixed contract perspective, which because of national legislation on multimodal contracts of carriage was found to be an unnecessary construction.

71 BGH 17.07.2008 I ZE 181/05 at 16.
72 Op. cit., at p. 19.
73 Op. cit., at p. 23.
74 Op. cit., at p. 24.

This decision was followed by the Dutch Supreme Court (Hoge Raad) in a decision in June 2012 – the *Godafoss* case.[75]

Conclusion

These three decisions show two different attitudes towards the role of the transport document in assessing the nature of multimodal contracts of carriage under the scope provisions of two unimodal transport conventions: the CMR Convention and the Warsaw Convention. Both the German and the English courts ignored the transport document. The German court bypassed the issue in silence, whereas the English court explicitly stated that the transport document in use is of no interest as such, but only as far as it 'reflects the reality that the contract has now become'.[76] And as regards determining whether a contract exists for the carriage of goods by road under Article 1, 'the actual operation of the contract under its terms'[77] is decisive. We might say that these two cases (German and English) support the view that the contract of carriage and the transport document are not one and the same; the transport document only evidences the existence of a contract of carriage but has no further impact on evaluating what kind of a contract we are facing in relation to deciding on the applicable law. The Danish view is obviously more formal. The court pays a great deal of attention to the documents when deciding on the nature of the contract and the applicable law. The *obiter dictum* on making the CMR act applicable to a contract evidenced by a CMR consignment underlines this.

The three European cases were related to conventions with a contractual or factual approach. The CMR applies to contracts of carriage by road. The Warsaw Convention applies to air carriage and indicates a factual approach. Neither of the conventions requires a transport document to be issued as well. This is, however, different in the maritime conventions, in which the documentary approach is explicitly stated. Both the Hague Rules and the Hague-Visby Rules apply merely to 'contracts of carriage *covered by a bill of lading or any similar document of title*'.[78] In the German case, part of the carriage was performed by sea, but as the

75 HR (Hoge Raad) 1 June 2012, NJ 2012, 516 (Godafoss), with comment by K.F. Haak. See also Hoaks, M., 'Liability, Jurisdiction and Enforcement Issues in International Road Carriage: CMR-Carrier Liability in the Netherlands and Germany and the Influence of the EU', in Soyer, B. and Tettenborn, A. (eds), *Carriage of Goods by Sea, Land and Air. Unimodal and Multimodal Transportation in the 21st Century*, Informa Law from Routledge, 2013, pp. 45–64.

76 Quantum Corporation Inc. and others v. plane trucking Ltd. [2002] Lloyds rep. 25 at 21.

77 L.C.

78 Hague-Visby Rules Art. 1 (b): '"Contract of carriage" applies only to contracts of carriage covered by a bill of lading or any similar document of title, in so far as such document relates to the carriage of goods by sea, including any bill of lading or any similar document as aforesaid issued under or pursuant to a charter party from the moment at which such bill of lading or similar document of title regulates the relations between a carrier and a holder of the same.'

Court would only have had jurisdiction if the CMR applied, the sea carriage perspective was accordingly not raised. However, there are two US cases on the law applicable to multimodal contracts of carriage involving a sea and a rail leg where the transport documents involved were multimodal through bills of lading. As the US has implemented the Hague Rules, both cases are relevant to interpreting the scope provision of this convention in a multimodal context.

Two cases from the US

The law applicable to multimodal carriage in the US

The US has recently seen a development as regards the law applicable to multimodal carriage of cargo and the role of the bill of lading. This development was settled by two Supreme Court cases from 2004 and 2010. The cases abolish the previous mixed contract perspective, and follow the same path as the Danish Supreme Court in establishing a one carriage – one document – one liability doctrine from the perspective of predictability. However, the reasoning in the US Supreme Court is more comprehensive compared to that of its Danish counterpart. Whereas the Danish Supreme Court reached its conclusion with rather formal arguments linked to the transport document in use, the US Supreme Court showed a more substantive reasoning, although this was also based on the transport documents. Another difference between the Danish case and the cases from the US is that in the latter the relevant transport documents are multimodal through bills of lading as opposed to the unimodal air waybill and CMR consignment note in the Danish case. Moreover, the US cases do not concern an air–road combination, but a sea–rail combination.

Regarding the legal regime applicable to carriage by sea, the US has ratified the Hague Rules and implemented these into the Carriage of Goods by Sea Act (COGSA).[79] COGSA applies to contracts of carriage evidenced by a bill of lading,[80] but only when the cargo is on board the vessel. The parties are thus free to agree on the responsibility and liability of the carrier for the period prior to loading and after discharge.[81] In many contracts this is done through a paramount clause, which extends the COGSA to the inland part of a multimodal shipment.

79 US Code Title 46, Chapter 28, which according to §1315 might be cited as the 'Carriage of Goods by Sea Act' (COGSA).

80 Op. cit., § 1300: 'Every bill of lading or similar document of title which is evidence of a contract for the carriage of goods by sea to or from ports of the United States, in foreign trade, shall have effect subject to the provisions of this chapter.'

81 Op. cit., § 1307. 'Agreement as to liability prior to loading or after discharge.

Nothing contained in this chapter shall prevent a carrier or a shipper from entering into any agreement, stipulation, condition, reservation, or exemption as to the responsibility and liability of the carrier or the ship for the loss or damage to or in connection with the custody and care and handling of goods prior to the loading on and subsequent to the discharge from the ship on which the goods are carried by sea.'

In addition, a Himalaya clause permits the parties to extend the liability limitations and other terms to subcontractors. Both the latter options were exercised in the cases discussed below. The US is not a member of COTIF-CIM, which is mainly a European convention. Interstate rail transportation in the US is governed mandatorily by the Carmack Amendment.[82]

The Kirby case 2004

In *Norfolk Southern Ry. v James N. Kirby*,[83] the so-called *Kirby* case, cargo was transported from the port of Sydney, Australia, to the port of Savannah, Georgia, with Huntsville, Alabama, as the final destination. The transport was to be performed by different modes including a sea–rail combination. Two bills of lading were issued. The first was issued by a freight forwarder, and the second by the ocean carrier, Hamburg Süd. The latter was a through bill of lading, which invoked liability limitations provided by COGSA, as well as a Himalaya clause, which extended the carrier's limitations of liability to companies it hired. No separate bill was issued for the rail leg. Hamburg Süd carried the goods by ship to Savannah, Georgia, and subcontracted Norfolk Southern Railway to transport the goods inland to Alabama. The train derailed and the cargo was damaged. The Himalaya clause in the Hamburg Süd bill incorporated COGSA, which specified that liability was limited to $500 per package. The question in the case was whether the rail carrier was protected by the Himalaya clause and could limit its liability accordingly. This required that COGSA was applicable. COGSA applies only to maritime contracts, and the question which needed an answer was therefore whether a multimodal contract should be considered a maritime contract or not. This was again a question of whether or not the case would fall within admiralty jurisdiction, which was the first question to be addressed by the Supreme Court.

Prior to the *Kirby* case the position had been that multimodal contracts only fell under admiralty jurisdiction if (1) the dominant subject matter of the contract was maritime in nature and the land-based element was relatively minor or incidental to the transaction or (2) where the maritime segment and land-based segment were severable (composed of several separate contracts). Under the latter approach the court could exercise jurisdiction over the maritime dispute, but not over a dispute involving a land-based segment of a multimodal contract, as was

82 The Carmack Amendment is codified at 49 U.S.C. Section 14706 *et seq*. The courts have uniformly held that the Carmack Amendment pre-empts all state and common law claims and provides the sole and exclusive remedy to shippers for loss or damage in interstate transit. *Hughes Aircraft v North American Van Lines*, 970 F.2d 609, 613 (9th Cir. 1992). The pre-emptive effect of the Carmack Amendment also applies to claims of damage or loss relating to storage and other services rendered by interstate carriers. *Margetson v United Van Lines, Inc.*, 785 F. Supp. 917, 919 (D.M. 1991). Available online at http://corporate.findlaw.com/business-operations/the-carmack-amendment-a-uniform-system-of-liability-for.html (accessed 21 January 2014).

83 Pty Ltd., 543 U.S. 14 (2004).

the situation in the *Kirby* case.[84] The approach reflects the view of a multimodal contract being a mixed contract where different parts of the contract might be covered by different legal regimes.

This approach was turned upside down in the *Kirby* case. The court started its reasoning by stating its conclusion that '[t]his is a maritime case about a train wreck'.[85] It thereafter declared that it 'cannot look to whether a ship or vessel was involved in the dispute as . . . [it] would in a putative maritime tort case'.[86] Instead, the answer would depend upon 'the nature and character of the contract'.[87] The true criterion was whether the contracts involved had 'reference to maritime service or maritime transactions'.[88] The multimodal bills involved were considered maritime contracts because their primary objective was to accomplish transportation of goods by sea from Australia to the eastern coast of the United States. The fundamental interest giving rise to maritime jurisdiction was protection of maritime commerce, and according to the court the concept of maritime commerce has changed: 'While it may once have seemed natural to think that only contracts embodying commercial obligations between the "tackles" (i.e., from port to port) have maritime objectives, the shore is now an artificial place to draw a line.'[89] In other words, as maritime contracts nowadays are often door-to-door contracts, these contracts should be covered by the maritime legal regime.

It is interesting to observe that the Court did not distinguish between the contract and the transport documents involved as, for example, the English Court of Appeal did in the *Quantum* case. Instead, the through bills of lading are considered to constitute the contract. This is stated expressly on the first page of the judgment, where the controversy in the case is described as arising from 'two bills of lading (essentially, contracts).'[90] Later on, the Court was more precise and described the bills of lading as documents which formalise the contracts.[91] When the Court discussed whether or not the contracts were covered by COGSA, it was actually referring to the contracts as stated in the bills of lading. The fact that the transport document was important for the Court is also clear from how it justifies its judgement. One important justification is international harmonisation: 'Here, our touchstone is a concern for the uniform meaning of maritime contracts like the ICC and Hamburg Süd bills.'[92] And, furthermore, 'when a [maritime] contract . . . may well have been made anywhere in the world, it should be judged by

84 Force, R., 'The Aftermath of *Norfolk Southern Railway v James N. Kirby, Pty Ltd.*, Jurisdiction and Choice of Law Issues', *Tulane Law Review*, 2008–2009, Volume 83, pp. 1393–1433 at p. 1394.
85 *Norfolk Southern Ry v. Fames N. Kirby, Pty Ltd.* 543 U.S. 14(2004) p.1.
86 Op. cit., note, at p. 7.
87 L.C.
88 L.C.
89 Op. cit., at p. 8.
90 Op. cit., at p. 1.
91 Op. cit., at p. 2 and p. 4.
92 Op. cit., at p. 11.

one law wherever it was made'.[93] In this case, that law was US federal maritime law, the COGSA, which implements the Hague Rules.

The result has been criticised in some legal literature, with calls for a restricted interpretation of COGSA particularly in light of the application of the Carmack Amendment, which was not really a subject for discussion in the *Kirby* case.[94]

The Regal Beloit case 2010

The relationship between COGSA and the Carmack Amendment was the main issue in *Kawasaki Kisen Kaisha Ltd. v Regal Beloit Corp.*, a 2010 case.[95] Kawasaki Kisen Kaisha Ltd (Kawasaki) had, through its American agent, K-Line, agreed to carry Regal Beloit's (Regal) goods from China to the US, by any mode of transportation that K-Line chose. K-Line issued a through bill of lading to Regal covering the entire shipment, including both its ocean and inland parts. The cargo was damaged during the inland rail leg of the carriage. If the case was subject to COGSA, the forum-selection clause in the through bill would be valid and the case would be decided by Japanese law and resolved by the Japanese courts. If not, the case would be subject to the Carmack Amendment. Accordingly, a question of applicable law arose. According to the Supreme Court, the question was 'whether the terms of a through bill of lading issued abroad by an ocean carrier can apply to the domestic part of the import's journey by a rail carrier, despite prohibitions and limitations in another federal statute'.[96] The relevant statute was the Carmack Amendment, which governs the terms of bills of lading issued by domestic rail carriers.

The Supreme Court upheld the arguments from the Kirby case that the terms of a through bill of lading govern the whole of a shipment made partly by sea and partly by rail, despite provisions of state law to the contrary. Applying state law would hamper COGSA's purpose of achieving uniformity of general maritime law. In *Regal Beloit*, the court concluded that neither the text nor the history or purpose of the Carmack Amendment require a different result. Quite the reverse, the Carmack Amendment requires a bill of lading issued by a 'receiving carrier' in order to apply. A 'receiving carrier' is defined as 'the initial carrier, which "receives" the property for domestic rail transportation at the journey's point of origin'.[97] The result is justified by the idea of one carriage – one document – one

93 Op. cit., at p. 12.

94 See Sturley, M., 'Maritime Cases About Train Wrecks: Applying Maritime Law to the Inland Damage of Ocean Cargo', *Journal of Maritime Law & Commerce,* Volume 40, Issue 1, 2009, pp. 1–43 at p. 24: 'By its express terms, section 7 declares only that nothing in COGSA prevents the parties from agreeing to any risk allocation they like outside of the tackle-to-tackle period. It most deliberately did not address whether any other statute would regulate the parties before loading or after discharge. Section 7 plainly leaves open the possibility that other law, such as the Carmack Amendment, might prevent the parties from agreeing on a contrary risk allocation outside of the tackle-to-tackle period.'

95 *Kawasaki Kisen Kaisha Ltd. v Regal Beloit Corp.*, 561 U.S. (2010).

96 Op. cit., at p. 2.

97 Op. cit., at p. 10.

liability. 'If Carmack's bill of lading requirement did not refer to the initial carrier, but rather to any rail carrier that in the colloquial sense "received" the property from another carrier, then every carrier during the shipment would have to issue its own separate bill. This would be altogether contrary to Carmack's purpose of making the receiving and delivering carriers liable under a single, initial bill of lading for damage caused by any carrier within a single course of shipment.'[98]

The result, in other words, is that as no bill of lading was issued by the rail carrier at the journey's point of origin, the Carmack Amendment did not apply.

Conclusion

What the US Supreme Court does in the *Regal-Beloit* decision is to embrace the conclusion in *Kirby* that a multimodal through bill of lading is a maritime contract also as regards the inland parts of the journey. Uniformity of maritime contracts is essential for the Court in both decisions.[99] In the *Regal-Beloit* case, the impact of the Carmack Amendment, which is mandatorily applicable to inland rail carriage, was discussed. The Supreme Court found no conflict between the two sets of rules. The Carmack Amendment is only applicable if the receiving rail carrier issues a bill of lading. No such carrier existed in the case, as the ocean carrier received the cargo.

The law applicable to multimodal contracts of carriage in the US seems, according to the two cases discussed above, to be dependent on the nature and character of the contract in light of its primary objective and how this is evidenced in the bills of lading. This has to be decided at the point of origin of the carriage, which is where the cargo is delivered for carriage by the shipper. Contracts of carriage that include overseas maritime carriage and a US inland transport leg, will be subject to the maritime regimes if the carriage is inbound. What happens if carriage goes from the US with a receiving rail carrier issuing a bill of lading at the centre of origin of the journey is open. Thomas J. Schoenbaum, who was extensively cited by the Court, writes in a comment that after these cases the US might have two different liability regimes: one for imports and another for exports. Cargo going from the US and overseas would need two bills of lading: one issued by the inland carrier and one issued by the ocean carrier. The first bill would be governed by the Carmack Amendment and the second by COGSA.[100] Although this might lead to situations as described by Schoenbaum, the result promotes predictability. If you are the holder of a maritime bill of lading, the starting point is that you are protected by the maritime legal regime. And whether it is a unimodal

98 L.C.

99 The Court has been criticised for taking international uniformity for granted, see Force, R., 'The Regal-Beloit Decision: What, If Anything, Would Happen to the Legal Regime for Multimodal Transport in the United States If It Adopted the Rotterdam Rules', *Tulane Maritime Law Journal*, Volume 36, 2011–2012, pp. 685–706 at p. 697.

100 Schoenbaum, T., 'Important New U.S. Supreme Court Case on the Multimodal Carriage of Goods', *The Journal of International Maritime Law*, 2010, Volume 16, pp. 184–185.

or multimodal bill of lading makes no difference as long as the main purpose of the contract is maritime carriage in a broad sense.

Conclusions

The discussion above concerns the role of the bill of lading and other transport documents in defining the scope provisions of certain unimodal transport conventions and other relevant legislation covering unimodal contracts of carriage. The question posed was whether the existence of a certain transport document triggers a particular unimodal legal framework. International case law shows that the answer to this varies in different jurisdictions and perhaps with the character of the document.

According to the Danish Supreme Court, air law applies when both the booking note and the air waybill describe the carriage as carriage by air. The Danish Supreme Court takes a formal approach and uses the transport documents to identify the applicable law. The US Supreme Court takes the same approach in the above-discussed *Kirby* and *Regal-Beloit* cases. The Court does not distinguish between the contract and the transport documents involved. The transport document/contract defines and triggers the relevant applicable legal regime.

Both the Danish and the US Supreme Court cases diverge from the result in the case decided by the German Supreme Court. In the German case, multimodal contracts of carriage are treated as contracts *sui generis*. Because of national legislation on international multimodal transport of goods, there is no need to squeeze multimodal contracts into the unimodal legal framework; hence the impact of the transport document issued was not an issue for the German court. Likewise, the English Court of Appeal totally disregarded any impact of the transport document involved, although reaching a totally different result. This was the only court upholding the mixed contract perspective.

Both the consignee and the carrier would benefit from a predictable legal situation in international multimodal carriage. The cases discussed above reflect this. If the legal situation is predictable, as in Germany, no need arises for an extended interpretation of the scope provisions of the unimodal conventions. However, in a situation where there is no such legislation, the solutions provided by the US and the Danish supreme courts are understandable. The transport document issued by the receiving carrier will settle the legal regime covering all parts of the multimodal contract. Based on the argumentation from the two supreme courts, one could argue that the easiest way out for the EU in its struggle for a predictable liability regime for European multimodal transport would be to provide the industry with a transport document that connects with a certain liability regime simply by stating that a certain liability regime is connected to the use of a certain transport document. As outlined above, the 2005 proposal for a draft set of uniform liability rules for intermodal transport also suggested this.[101]

101 Above in Chapter 5 (at 5.1).

However, the main questions still remain: (1) What kind of liability regime should it be? A network system linking existing unimodal liability regimes together in a coherent system or a totally new uniform system for multimodal contracts only, as requested by the European Commission? And (2) how can the EU ascertain that the chosen document and connecting liability system do not collide with existing unimodal obligations?

6.3 The uniform liability system solution – a *sui generis* approach

The EU discussion

As mentioned, the European Commission was from the very beginning interested in a uniform liability system. The vision was 'a clear set of transparent liability conditions and procedures for any cargo that is damaged or lost in its journey . . . [with] . . . liability rules [that] should not be mode-specific and should not distinguish between national and international transport'.[102] The first legal expert group assisting the Commission accordingly suggested a uniform liability regime with strict liability and an opt-out possibility, the so-called 2005 EU draft.[103] Clearly, the idea was that a uniform liability system would benefit the multimodal transport industry and be the most efficient way to remove legal barriers. The group discussed possible clashes with the existing unimodal conventions. After analysing the scope provisions of the unimodal transport conventions, the expert group concluded that there is no big risk of such collisions: 'Generally speaking, such arguments will not be sustainable.'[104] Instead, the expert group argued that possible clashes could be avoided by defining the multimodal contract of carriage as *sui generis* and furthermore by connecting a mandatory liability regime for multimodal contracts of carriage to the use of a mandatory transport document. According to the proposed regime, a 'Transport Document' should contain 'a statement that the contract is subject to this Regime'.[105] The idea was that the parties would agree contractually that the regime should apply to their multimodal contract of carriage. This was in a way double security; first, multimodal contracts of carriage should be defined as something different from unimodal contracts of carriage to which we already have connecting international rules; second, a multimodal transport document should be issued for every multimodal contract of carriage and operate as a connecting factor between the multimodal contract of carriage and the underlying EU regime on multimodal contracts of carriage.

The 2005 expert group did not discuss the legal impact of a *sui generis* statement on multimodal contracts of carriage further. Instead, it seems as if the

102 COM (97) 243 final at 81, above in Chapter 5 (at 5.1).
103 Above in Chapter 5 (at 5.1).
104 The 2005 EU draft, p. 12.
105 Op. cit., Art. 3.

expert group presupposed that a *sui generis* definition of a multimodal contract of carriage would settle the problem and that no collisions would take place: 'Prima facie, such agreements [unimodal agreements] are different from contracts of transport subject to the Regime, which are intended to be sui generis: Article 1.1(a).'[106] Indeed, the *sui generis* solution could also be used without an EU regime. This would, however, leave the parties free to use the existing model rules or standard documents. This solution is fraught with risk, as the carrier would be in a position to contract out of any liability. It might thus be considered an 'evasion of the [mandatory] law and thus not upheld by national courts'.[107] The best solution would, therefore, be to combine a potential EU legal instrument on liability in multimodal contracts of carriage, such as a regulation or a directive, with an EU declaration on the *sui generis* nature of multimodal contracts of carriage.[108]

The *sui generis* solution proposed by the 2005 expert group is an easy way to deal with the underlying regimes; however, it needs some adjustment before it can be implemented. As outlined above, court praxis on the impact of the transport document in settling the nature of the contract varies. An agreement between the parties that a certain liability system applies will probably be an argument in identifying the legal nature of the contract agreed between the parties, but it will not be binding on the courts in relation to mandatory legislation. In the above-mentioned *Quantum* case, the English Court of Appeal pointed out that CMR Article 4 stated this clearly: 'the absence, irregularity or loss of the consignment note shall not affect the existence or validity of the contract of carriage, which shall remain subject to the Convention'. In other words, the lack of a CMR consignment note did not exclude the existence of a contract of carriage by road. And vice versa: the fact that an air waybill was issued did not convince the Court that air law should apply to the whole contract. The English Court found the transport document not relevant in establishing the applicable legal regime. However, we do have European examples of the opposite solution, for example from Denmark, where the Supreme Court emphasised the documents in use when choosing the relevant liability system in the *Salmon Roe* case discussed above.[109]

Bearing in mind that the impact of the transport document as a solution to the multimodal scope problem varies in various Member States, creating and issuing an obligatory European transport document linked to a harmonised European liability system for multimodal contracts of carriage might not be enough to convince the Member States that the EU regime does not collide with their obligations under the current unimodal transport conventions. This is particularly true

106 Op. cit., p. 13. See also Ramberg, J., 'The Future of International Unification of Transport Law', *Scandinavian Studies of Law*, 2001, Volume 41, pp. 453–458 at p. 458.

107 Haak, K. F. (2005) at p. 37.

108 In this direction Marten, op. cit., note 21, at p. 144.

109 Above in section 6.2.

if the Member State practises a wide interpretation of the unimodal transport convention's scope provisions, as in England, for example. In other words, tools are needed to make the Member States accept a narrow interpretation of the existing unimodal transport conventions.

This might sound like 'mission impossible' considering that the EU (at present) does not have external competence in the area of international unimodal contracts of carriage. However, there are ways around this problem, which have been used by the EU in other situations, and which could be used in the current situation. The solution is not complicated. The EU should use its competence to decide on an internal legal regime for international multimodal contracts of carriage. As there are at present no competing international multimodal conventions to collide with, no direct obstacles to internal legal regime arise. The problem is the grey zone, the area where the unimodal conventions apply in a multimodal context. To avoid collisions here, the EU regional multimodal regime should be equipped with two tools: The first should be a step-back clause, which gives the present unimodal conventions primacy, and second, the regime should contain a statement declaring the multimodal contract of carriage *sui generis*.

The step-back clause could be drafted in line with the provisions in the Rotterdam Rules, where Article 82 basically states that the Rotterdam Rules will step back from all situations where unimodal conventions directly apply in a multimodal situation.[110] The risk of collision would then be restricted to situations where the Member States insist on a wide interpretation of the existing unimodal legal regimes, as did the English Court of Appeal in its interpretation of CMR under English law. The risk of such collisions would, however, become minor if the EU fills the legal gap in multimodal transport by introducing a regional regime applicable to international multimodal contracts of carriage. Indeed, loyal implementation of such an EU regime would require a narrow interpretation of the multimodal scope of the unimodal transport conventions. Such an interpretation would allow the Member States to implement their EU obligations and exercise the principle of loyalty, without discarding their present obligations. Furthermore, the mere fact that unimodal scope provisions are presently subject to various interpretations in different jurisdictions within the EU shows that several legal solutions are possible. There should, in other words, be no formal or clear barriers for national legislators or courts to implement a new regime with the given instructions.

Indeed, the starting point is that the EU has no competence to interfere with the understanding of national legislation that stays within the competence of the Member States. This has been, and still is, the situation as regards business-to-business contracts for carriage of goods. However, it is common ground that the Member States have an obligation to align their national legislation with EU law. If the EU passes legislation on international multimodal contracts of carriage, it

110 More on this below in section 6.4.

would follow from the principle of loyalty[111] that the unimodal conventions are given a narrow interpretation, that is following the German Supreme Court's understanding of the scope of the CMR.[112] The relationship between EU law and national legislation has been addressed by the Court of Justice in several cases related to the CMR:

EU impact on existing unimodal conventions

The starting point is clear: interpretation of the unimodal conventions lies within the sovereignty of the Member States unless the conventions are made part of the *acquis communautaire* of the EU. EU legislation on contracts of carriage is so far restricted to carriage of passengers.[113] As none of the transport conventions on carrier's liability in relation to carriage of cargo are not part of the *acquis communautaire*, the point of departure is that the EU has no competence in relation to unimodal transport conventions, unless the conventions have been implemented in the EU law system.[114]

This has been stated in recent court practice from the Court of Justice related to possible conflicts between an EU regulation on recognition and enforcement

111 On the principle of loyalty as expressed in Art. 4(3) TEU, see above in Chapter 3 (at 3.1). In addition Art. 92 TFEU holds a *lex specialis* version of the principle of loyalty as regards discrimination of carriers: 'Until the provisions referred to in Article 91(1) have been laid down, no Member State may, unless the Council has unanimously adopted a measure granting a derogation, make the various provisions governing the subject on 1 January 1958 or, for acceding States, the date of their accession less favourable in their direct or indirect effect on carriers of other Member States as compared with carriers who are nationals of that State.' The duty of non-discrimination in the area of transport has been upheld by the CJEU in a very strict manner, see case C-195/90 *Commission v Germany (Heavy Goods Vehicles)* [1992] ECR I-3141, para. 36, were Germany was found in breach of the principle of loyalty by giving tax reduction to domestic carriers, although there was yet no direct EU law against this. However the CJEU found that Germany by this would make it more difficult for the Council to introduce the common transport policy and this was considered breach of Art. 92. It has been commented that this 'seems to *de facto* put Member States [as regards transport] in the same position as in areas of exclusive competence, such as the Common Commercial Policy': Klamert, M., *The Principle of Loyalty in EU Law*, Oxford University Press, 2014, at p. 17.

112 Above in section 6.2.

113 Some unimodal conventions on carriage of goods are part of EU Law. So far the *acquis communautaire* only includes the rules related to carriage of passengers. See e.g. in relation to air passengers: Council Regulation (EC) No 2027/97 of 9 October 1997 on air carrier liability in the event of accidents. OJ L 285, 17/10/1997. See also Regulation (EC) No 1371/2007 of the European Parliament and of the Council of 23 October 2007 on *rail passengers'* rights and obligations, OJ L 315, 3/12/2007. The same applies to carriage of passengers by sea: Regulation (EC) No 392/2009 of the European Parliament and of the Council of 23 April 2009 on the liability of carriers of passengers by sea in the event of accidents, OJ L 131, 28/5/2009. The EU also has community legislation on the rights of passengers in bus and coach transport: Regulation (EU) No 181/2011 of the European Parliament and of the Council of 16 February 2011 concerning the rights of passengers in bus and coach transport, OJ L 55, 28.2.2011.

114 On shared competence in the area of transport law, see above in Chapter 3 (at 3.1).

of judgments in civil and commercial matters, the so-called Brussels I Regulation[115] and the CMR, which also contains rules on jurisdiction in Article 31.[116] The point of departure is that the Brussels I Regulation steps back in case of conflict. The Regulation, according to Article 71(1), does not 'affect any conventions to which the Member States are parties and which in relation to particular matters, govern jurisdiction or the recognition or enforcement of judgments'.[117]

115 Council Regulation (EC) on recognition and enforcement on judgments in civil and commercial matters 44/2001 of 22 December 2001.

116 CMR Article 31:

1 In legal proceedings arising out of carriage under this Convention, the plaintiff may bring an action in any court or tribunal of a contracting country designated by agreement between the parties and, in addition, in the courts or tribunals of a country within whose territory:

(a) The defendant is ordinarily resident, or has his principal place of business, or the branch or agency through which the contract of carriage was made, or (b) The place where the goods were taken over by the carrier or the place designated for delivery is situated.

2 Where in respect of a claim referred to in paragraph 1 of this article an action is pending before a court or tribunal competent under that paragraph, or where in respect of such a claim a judgement has been entered by such a court or tribunal no new action shall be started between the same parties on the same grounds unless the judgement of the court or tribunal before which the first action was brought is not enforceable in the country in which the fresh proceedings are brought.

3 When a judgement entered by a court or tribunal of a contracting country in any such action as is referred to in paragraph 1 of this article has become enforceable in that country, it shall also become enforceable in each of the other contracting States, as soon as the formalities required in the country concerned have been complied with. These formalities shall not permit the merits of the case to be re-opened.

4 The provisions of paragraph 3 of this article shall apply to judgements after trial, judgements by default and settlements confirmed by an order of the court, but shall not apply to interim judgements or to awards of damages, in addition to costs against a plaintiff who wholly or partly fails in his action.

5 Security for costs shall not be required in proceedings arising out of carriage under this Convention from nationals of contracting countries resident or having their place of business in one of those countries.

117 Brussels I Article 71:

1 This Regulation shall not affect any conventions to which the Member States are parties and which in relation to particular matters, govern jurisdiction or the recognition or enforcement of judgments.

2 With a view to its uniform interpretation, paragraph 1 shall be applied in the following manner:

(a) this Regulation shall not prevent a court of a Member State, which is a party to a convention on a particular matter, from assuming jurisdiction in accordance with that convention, even where the defendant is domiciled in another Member State which is not a party to that convention. The court hearing the action shall, in any event, apply Article 26 of this Regulation;

(b) judgments given in a Member State by a court in the exercise of jurisdiction provided for in a convention on a particular matter shall be recognised and enforced in the other Member States in accordance with this Regulation.

The relationship between the two sets of rules was discussed by the Court of Justice of the European Union (the Court of Justice/CJEU) in *TNT Express Nederland BV v AXA Versicherung AG (TNT v AXA)*, a 2008 case.[118] The question in the case involved carriage of cargo by road from the Netherlands to Germany. The cargo was never delivered. The value of the cargo was high, but because of its low weight, the limited liability would be low. It would, accordingly, be in the interest of the cargo owner to argue that the limitation rules are not applicable due to wilful misconduct. At the time, German courts were known to be cargo-friendly whereas the Dutch courts were more carrier-friendly on this question.[119]

In order to be able to limit its liability under Dutch law, the carrier (TNT Express) made a claim for a negative declaratory judgment from the Dutch courts in 2002. The action was dismissed, but the case was appealed. The cargo underwriter, AXA Versicherung, did not accept this and went to court in Germany, claiming recovery for its loss. TNT was there ordered to pay damages, despite the *lis pendens* rule in CMR Article 31(2).[120] In the Dutch court system, the claim for a negative declaratory judgment was appealed to the Dutch Supreme Court, which turned to the Court of Justice to ask for advice. The questions at issue were:

a) Should the rules on jurisdiction, recognition and enforcement of CMR (Article 31(2), 31(3)) apply instead of the Regulation?
b) Does the CJEU have jurisdiction to interpret Article 31(3) (enforceability) of the CMR?

The Court of Justice gave the following answers:

First question:

Article 71 of Regulation 44/2001 must be interpreted as meaning that the rules governing jurisdiction, recognition and enforcement of a specialised convention, such as the *lis pendens* rules set out in Article 31(2) and the rules on

Where a convention on a particular matter to which both the Member State of origin and the Member State addressed are parties lays down conditions for the recognition or enforcement of judgments, those conditions shall apply. In any event, the provisions of this Regulation which concern the procedure for recognition and enforcement of judgments may be applied.

118 *TNT Express Nederland BV v ASA Versicherung* (Case C-533/08)

119 Aminoff, J., 'Article 71 of the Brussels I Regulation and the Application of Transport Law Conventions in the Light of Some Judgments of the European Court of Justice', *Tidskrift utgiven av Juridiska Föreningen i Finland (JFT)*, Volume 6/2014, pp. 420–441 at p. 428.

120 At the time, the German courts did not consider a liability claim and a claim on a negative declaratory judgment to be on the same ground, which was one prerequisite for the *lis pendens* rule in CMR Art. 31 (2): 'Where in respect of a claim referred to in paragraph 1 of this article an action is pending before a court or tribunal competent under that paragraph, or where in respect of such a claim a judgement has been entered by such a court or tribunal no new action shall be started between the same parties *on the same grounds* unless the judgement of the court or tribunal before which the first action was brought is not enforceable in the country in which the fresh proceedings are brought.' Aminoff, (2014) at p. 429.

enforceability in Article 31(3) of the CMR, apply provided that they are highly predictable and facilitate the sound administration of justice and enable the risk of concurrent proceedings to be minimised and that they ensure, under conditions at least as favourable as those provided for by the regulation, the free movement of judgements and mutual trust in the administration of justice in the European Union.

Second question: 'The ECJ [CJEU] does not have jurisdiction to interpret Article 31 of the CMR.'

As can be seen from the answer given to the second question, the starting point is that the Court of Justice has no jurisdiction to interpret conventions that are not part of EU law. However, this is only a starting point. When interpreting Brussels I Article 71, the Court did not discuss the Article; instead, the question was whether or not the CMR qualified to supersede the EU regulation. What the Court did, in other words, was to analyse whether or not the CMR qualified to supersede the Brussels 1 regulation, although there are no such preconditions in the regulation itself. Nevertheless, the Court stated that the competing convention (here the CMR) must ensure 'under conditions at least as favourable as those provided for by the regulation, the free movement of judgements and mutual trust in the administration of justice in the European Union'. The Court of Justice here shows that it distinguishes between a direct interpretation of the CMR (which it does not have competence to give) and clarification of the borderline of EU law, over which the Member States must not step.

This was further emphasised in a later judgment by the Court: *Nipponkoa v Inter Zuid*.[121] This case also involved carriage of goods between the Netherlands and Germany. Part of the cargo was stolen before discharge. Here, too, the value of the cargo was high and the limitation amount low. The carrier obtained a negative declaratory judgment by the courts in the Netherlands, and on that basis the recovery proceedings in Germany by the cargo underwriter were dismissed. Two questions were to be decided by the German Supreme Court, where the case finally ended. The first question the Court had to address was whether it had jurisdiction or not. This was a question of interpreting the *lis pendens* rules, Article 27 of the Brussels I Regulation[122] and Article 31(2) of the CMR. Furthermore, if the CMR was applicable, could the jurisdiction of the German court be based on an autonomous interpretation of Article 31(2) of the CMR regardless of the negative declaratory judgments from the Dutch court?

121 Case C-452/12, 19 December 2013.

122 Brussels I Art. 27:

1 Where proceedings involving the same cause of action and between the same parties are brought in the courts of different Member States, any court other than the court first seised shall of its own motion stay its proceedings until such time as the jurisdiction of the court first seised is established.

2 Where the jurisdiction of the court first seised is established, any court other than the court first seised shall decline jurisdiction in favour of that court.

The German Supreme Court stated two questions to the Court of Justice:

a) Does Article 71 preclude an international convention from being interpreted in such a way that it undermines the objective of the Regulation?
b) Does Article 71 preclude an interpretation of Article 31(2) of the CMR according to which an action for a negative declaratory judgement does not have the same cause of action as an action for indemnity brought about in respect of the same damage and against the same parties?

The Court of Justice ruled as follows:

First question: 'Article 71 of the Regulation must be interpreted as meaning that it precludes an international convention from being interpreted in a manner, which fails to ensure, under conditions at least as favourable as those provided for by the Regulation, that the underlying objectives and principles of the Regulation are observed.'

Second question: 'Article 71 of the Regulation must be interpreted as meaning that it precludes an interpretation of Article 31(2) of the CMR according to which an action for a negative declaratory judgment does not have the same cause of action as an action for the indemnity between the parties.'

In this case the CJEU is clear. Albeit that it does not have jurisdiction over the CMR (as stated in *TNT v AXA*), the Court still reached a decision on how the Convention should be interpreted: it cannot narrow the scope of a 'competing' EU instrument. And, of course, this is in a way an indirect interpretation of legal instruments outside the scope of the Court.[123]

In other words, there should be no restrictions on EU competence to declare that a multimodal contract of carriage is, according to EU law, to be considered *sui generis*, and thus subject to EU law. Any national legislation in a Member State derogating from this would accordingly be colliding with EU law. An EU declaration on the *sui generis* character of a multimodal contract of carriage, in combination with a regional multimodal liability regime, should in other words lead to a narrow interpretation of the existing unimodal transport conventions and in so doing avoid collisions with the new EU regime.

This solution is also presupposed by the Norwegian Maritime Law Commission, which suggests a narrow interpretation of the CMR under Norwegian law, provided that Norway implements the Rotterdam Rules. The Norwegian Maritime Law Commission did find it important to clarify the relationship to other transport conventions, and indeed the recommendation from the Commission was that the

123 Following the above-mentioned cases, one observer comments that the relationship between EU law and national instruments is not clear, and that mistakes can be done by national courts. A substantial body of case law from the CJEU would therefore be preferable. See Lamont-Black, S., 'Uniform Interpretation of EU Jurisdiction Rules in Jeopardy? Interaction of Specialised Conventions with the Brussels I Regime and the Mutation of *TNT v AXA*, *Tidskrift utgiven av Juridiska Föreningen i Finland* (*JFT*), Volume 6/2014, pp. 442–458 at p. 458.

transport conventions should be 'construed restrictively, in line with recent continental European Cases [for example, the German and Danish Supreme Court decisions] so that the issue of contradictions or overlapping scopes do not arise'.[124]

It seems unproblematic for the EU to move around the existing unimodal conventions by declaring that, under EU law, a multimodal contract of carriage is considered *sui generis* and hence is subject to EU law. Because of the broad scope of some unimodal conventions, this has to be supplemented by a specification of what constitutes a unimodal contract of carriage and what does not. Here a connection to the transport document in use could be a good way to start, simply by stating that under EU law a contract of carriage of goods under a European multimodal transport document is always considered multimodal and subject to the EU regime. In the case of conflict with any underlying unimodal legal regime, the solution would be to follow the point of view of the US Supreme Court in the two above-mentioned decisions,[125] although with the result that the applicable regime would be the EU regime.

How to opt out

A declaration stating that under the EU regime multimodal contracts of carriage are considered *sui generis* is one way of avoiding conflict with underlying mandatory legal regimes. The question still remains whether or not this EU regime would have to be mandatory, or if a declaratory regime would do the trick. The interest of the EU is, as stated several times already, to promote multimodal transport by providing the transport industry with a predictable legal regime. A mandatory and international regime has also been stated as the number one option of the EU Commission and would, of course, provide the greatest certainty through a high level of harmonisation. However, an international solution has so far been rather difficult to establish. To ease the level of political controversy, and at the same time increase the level of harmonisation compared to a situation where soft law (opt-in) solutions were chosen, the first expert group, which assisted the Commission and delivered the 2005 proposal, settled for a kind of middle way, a legal regime based on an opt-out solution. According to the proposed Article 2:

> The provisions of this Regime shall mandatorily apply to all contracts of transport . . .
>
> Unless the parties to the contract have agreed that it shall not be governed by the regime.

The parties should, in other words, be free to opt out and choose other solutions for their multimodal contract of carriage. However, if the parties have chosen the

124 Gjennomføringen av Rotterdamreglene i sjøloven. NOU (Norges offentlige utredninger) 2012:10. The implementation of the Rotterdam Rules in the Norwegian Maritime Code. Norwegian public report 2012:10. English summary, p. 14.

125 Above in section 6.2.

(proposed) EU regime, then they should not be able to pick and choose and leave out parts of it. The idea is that the parties will be bound by the regime in its entirety and any contractual provisions in conflict with the regime will be overridden.[126] With the exception of provisions on limitation of liability, it would not be possible to exclude only parts of the proposal from the contract, as this would prevent the proposal from being simple and transparent. On the other hand, it should not be possible to prohibit the parties from including parts of the regime in their contracts.[127]

The reasoning behind the opt-out alternative was more opportunistic than principled. The expert group were of the opinion that an opt-out solution would be easier for the stakeholders to accept than a mandatory legal regime: 'it would be more likely to achieve widespread application as it should avoid the strong opposition the adoption of mandatory measures would inevitably attract, while it would be triggered by mere inaction of the parties involved'.[128] Opting out could be done in several ways or 'in any form', as expressed in the comments to the proposal.[129] It would be sufficient for the agreement to emerge from a transport integrator's general conditions.[130] However, if the parties should want to use the EU transport document proposed in the regime, this document should, according to the proposal for Article 4.1(a) contain, 'a statement that the contract is subject to this regime'. If the parties want to use another transport document, the 'Transport Integrator may just stamp the front of a current multimodal bill with the statement that it "is subject to this Regime"'.[131] The latter sounds like an opt-in alternative, and the question arises as to what happens if the parties make no particular effort to opt in to an EU legal regime with an opt-out character. Probably the result would be the same. An opt-out regime means that the regime will apply unless the parties agree otherwise. If the parties explicitly agree, for example by a stamp, that the contract of carriage is *not* subject to the EU regime, that would clearly be an opt-out situation. The point of departure would be that if multimodal transport is performed under a multimodal contract of carriage, then the EU regime would apply unless the parties have opted out of the regime. If there is evidence of mutual agreement between the parties that they did not want to be governed by the EU legislation, then this must be accepted as we presume there is opt-out legislation on the EU level.

Now, how should the parties then opt out from the declaratory EU regime? Would it be enough that the parties use a multimodal transport document with a different legal regime for multimodal contracts of carriage, or is there a need for an explicit opting out, for example stamping, not subject to EU law? In my opinion there is no need for a specific declaration from the parties stating that the contract should not be subject to EU law. If the parties have chosen an EU

126 The 2005 EU draft at p. 12.
127 L.C.
128 L.C.
129 Op. cit., note, at p. 18.
130 L.C.
131 Op. cit., note, at p. 30 (at 8).

multimodal transport document stating that the EU regime applies to the contract of carriage, then of course the regime is applicable. The same must be the result if the parties use an EU multimodal transport document with no information on the applicable legal regime.

But, what is the situation if the parties use any of the other multimodal transport documents available, such as, for example, the FIATA (International Federation of Freight Forwarders Associations) multimodal transport bill of lading? Would this be enough to say that the parties have opted out of the scope of the EU regime, and the FIATA regime should govern the contract? In my opinion this would be a practical and predictable solution. In this case there is a legal regime governing the carriage, and the regime will be known by the parties to the contract of carriage, and also to different consignees that will be holders of the transport document and thus informed of the underlying legal regime. The legal situation of the parties will be predictable and there is no need for the EU regime to apply. A different approach would be to undermine the freedom of contract which is maintained under a declaratory system.

A practical and predictable way of solving the problem of applicable law would, in other words, simply be to use the transport document covering the transport as a guideline to identify the contract of carriage and the applicable law. If the parties have chosen a different transport document than the suggested European transport document, this would indicate that the parties have decided on another applicable legal regime. This would also solve any problems with a future maritime legal regime with a multimodal scope, such as the Rotterdam Rules. If the parties have chosen a multimodal bill of lading then the assumption is that the parties have opted out of the EU regime, and the Rotterdam Rules will apply.

So far the hypothesis has been that the parties have chosen a multimodal transport document and in so doing indicated that the carriage is multimodal. However, in many cases the problem is that the transport is carried out by more than one mode of transport, but the transport document is unimodal. Sometimes even more than one unimodal transport document might be issued. Could the transport document in these cases indicate anything on the choices of the parties? In the example of the English *Quantum* case, an air waybill was issued for the whole contract, but parts of the carriage were in fact by road. The English Court of Appeal nevertheless ruled that the CMR was applicable to the road part of the multimodal carriage. Under an EU regime, the multimodal contract of carriage would be considered *sui generis* and the solution of the English court (that the CMR applies to the road leg of the carriage) would not be possible. Instead, the solution would be that none of the unimodal legal regimes are applicable (unless we are within the extended scope provisions, such as the CMR Article 2), regardless of the transport documents issued. In such a situation it is not feasible to say that the parties have opted out from the EU regime, as no other multimodal transport regime is agreed. In these situations the presumption would be that the parties have not opted out of the multimodal legal regime, and the EU regime would govern the contract. Following the reasoning of the CJEU in the *Nipponkoa* case referred to above, an extended interpretation of the CMR, as performed by the English Court of Appeal in the *Quantum* case, would collide with EU law, and accordingly not be accepted.

One difference between the proposed EU regime and the Brussels I Regulation is, however, that the latter is mandatory law, while the proposed EU regime on multimodal contracts of carriage is proposed to be declaratory. Are the Member States not allowed to have mandatory law in conflict with declaratory EU law? Could the result be that use of any transport document other than multimodal transport documents would be interpreted as an opt-out of the EU regime?

This would not lead to a predictable legal situation, considering the various perspectives to the applicability of the unimodal legal regimes. A better solution would probably be to simply state that the EU regime applies unless the parties have clearly opted out. This can be done either by an explicit declaration in the transport document stating that the contract is not part of the EU regime, or by choosing a different multimodal transport document, which indicates that a different multimodal legal regime has been chosen. In all other cases the EU regime will apply.

The 2005 EU draft and its benefits

To base liability in multimodal contracts on the transport contract, rather on the means used to perform it, is in line with ideas presented by Professor Jan Ramberg, not only as a member of the 2005 expert group, but also as presented elsewhere, for example in his book *The Law of Transport Operators in International Trade*[132] where Ramberg advocates a drastic approach to international regulation of multimodal contracts of carriage: 'the better option seems to be to retain the conventions covering the different modes of transport in their present form, with some adaptations if necessary, and to develop an entirely new legal regime clearly based on the contract, rather than on the means used to perform it.'[133] According to Ramberg, this regime should follow the main principles of the 1980 Convention on Contracts for International Sale of Goods (CISG). After all, in most cases the contract of carriage is, together with the insurance contract and contract for payment, an ancillary contract to the international sales contract. Viewed in context, the contract of carriage covers only a small part of a larger economic pattern, and it is thus odd to have separate rules for this part of the whole logistical operation.

In addition to the proposed strict liability as the main rule for the liability of the multimodal transport operator, Ramberg suggests that the rules should cover all obligations arising from contracts, including labelling, packing, reloging, installation, adaptation, storage, transhipment and clearance of the goods for export or import, as well as collecting documents or money and all other services,[134] and apply from the time the transport operator receives the goods until they

132 Ramberg, J., *The Law of Transport Operators in International Trade*, 2005.
133 Op. cit., p. 184.
134 Op. cit., p. 186.

are delivered. Furthermore, Ramberg suggests 'full compatibility between the liability of the seller to the buyer and the liability of the service provider to either of them'.[135]

Ramberg's proposal responds well to the initial call from the Commission, where the instructions to the expert group assisting the Commission were to draft a set of uniform intermodal liability rules which 'concentrate the transit risk on one party and which provide for a strict and full liability of the contracting carrier for all types of losses (damage, loss, delay) irrespective of the modal stage where a loss occurs and of the cause of such a loss'.[136] As we shall see, however, Ramberg's ideas have been subject to compromises within the expert group in which Ramberg took part. The 2005 EU draft deviates from his private proposals, particularly as regards the liability rules, but also as regards what obligations a multimodal regime should cover. The latter questions will be discussed below in Part III, with particular focus on the environmental obligations. First, however, we shall take a closer look at the liability regime drafted by the expert group, including Professor Ramberg, in 2005.

Introduction

The 2005 EU draft might be characterised as uniform and efficient since it proposes strict liability as a main rule. This strict approach is, however, softened by the fact that the parties to the contract may agree to opt out of the regime. In contrast to the present international regimes that are either mandatory (conventions) or based on voluntary opt-in solutions (private rules), the 2005 EU draft aims to become the standard solution, but with a possibility for the parties to opt out. If the parties do not opt out of the regime, the carrier will, as mentioned, face strict liability for losses from the time it takes over the goods until the goods are delivered, except in the case of circumstances beyond the control of the transport integrator.[137] This is in line with the liability regime in the CISG, although not exactly the same.[138] Nevertheless, the solution is in line with the existing unimodal liability regimes covering carriage of goods by road or rail.[139] The 2005 EU draft in many aspects follows the same pattern as the present unimodal conventions. The transport integrator's right to limit its

135 L.C.

136 The 2005 EU draft, at p. 6.

137 The 2005 EU draft, Art. 8.

138 According to the CISG Art. 25, remedies of the buyer and seller depend upon the character of the breach of contract. If the breach is fundamental, then the other party is substantially deprived of what it expected to receive under the contract (strict liability). However, an objective test should show that the breach could not have been foreseen. CISG Art. 25: 'A breach of contract committed by one of the parties is fundamental if it results in such detriment to the other party as substantially to deprive him of what he is entitled to expect under the contract, unless the party in breach did not foresee and a reasonable person of the same kind in the same circumstances would not have foreseen such a result.'

139 See CMR Art. 17(2) and COTIF-CIM Art. 23(2).

liability is accordingly kept in the EU draft.[140] On this point the proposal leaves some freedom of contract to the parties, who may agree on a higher monetary limit on the transport integrator's liability than is provided by the 2005 EU draft itself. This is also in line with the main rule in general transport law. Only the CMR forbids such agreements.[141]

If the parties have not opted out of the regime, the 2005 EU draft would apply to international multimodal transports with a point of contact in the EU. The definition of a contract of transport in Article 1 paragraph 1 makes it clear that the proposed regime should not apply to domestic transport within EU Member States. The transport must be from 'a place in one country to a place in another country.'[142] Furthermore, the 2005 draft is not limited to international internal transport, but would apply to exports and imports to or from the EU. One point of contact with the EU would be sufficient. Either the place of loading or the place of delivery must be within the EU. This broad scope is in line with the transport policy of which the proposal forms part, but it is also probably partly the reason why the proposal has received such huge resistance from the parts of the transport industry that prefer a global solution.

The main rule on liability

Article 8 of the 2005 proposal holds the main provision on liability:

> 1 The Transport Integrator shall be liable for total or partial loss of the goods or damage to the goods occurring between the time he takes over the goods and the time of delivery, as well as for any delay in delivery.
> 2 Delay in delivery occurs when the goods have not been delivered within the time expressly agreed upon by the parties to the contract of transport or, in the absence of such agreement, within a reasonable time, having regard to the circumstances of the case.
> 3 If the goods have not been delivered within 90 consecutive days following the date of delivery determined according to paragraph 2, the claimant may treat the goods as lost.
> 4 The Transport Integrator shall not be liable for any total or partial loss of the goods, or damage to the goods, or delay in delivery of the goods to the extent that it was caused by circumstances beyond the control of the Transport Integrator.

140 See the 2005 EU draft, Art. 9.

141 CMR Art. 1(5): 'The Contracting Parties agree not to vary any of the provisions of this Convention by special agreements between two or more of them, except to make it inapplicable to their frontier traffic or to authorize the use in transport operations entirely confined to their territory of consignment notes representing a title to the goods.'

142 The 2005 proposal Art. 2 reads as follows: 'a) the place for the taking in charge of the goods by the Transport Integrator . . . is in a State member of the European Economic Community or b) the place for delivery of the goods . . . is in a State member of the European Economic Community.'

The first and fourth paragraphs cover the general provisions on liability, whereas the second and third paragraphs deal with delay. The first paragraph also contains a provision on the period of responsibility. According to the draft, the goods are considered taken over by the transport integrator when received into the transport integrator's custody and control. The time of delivery is when custody and control passes from the transport integrator to another person, the receiver or the consignee. This is not controversial as most modern transport conventions apply the custody principle.[143] In all present unimodal transport regimes governing land and air carriage, carrier liability attaches to the period from the time the carrier takes over the goods to the time of delivery, which is when the cargo is in the charge of the carrier.[144] It is only the 'old' maritime conventions, the Hague Rules and the Hague-Visby Rules, which apply a stricter scope of application, the so-called tackle-to-tackle principle.[145] However, in some regions, such as the Nordic area, the scope of the maritime liability regimes is expanded in line with the custody principle found in the more modern Hamburg Rules.[146] The pending Rotterdam Rules also apply the custody principle.[147]

Article 8, paragraphs 1 and 4 of the 2005 EU draft regulates the basis for liability, which according to the proposal is strict. This is apparent from the wording of the Article: 'The transport Integrator shall be liable.' The only exception from liability is provided for in Article 8, paragraph 4, which states the transport integrator will not be liable to the extent that the loss 'was caused by circumstances beyond the control of the Transport Integrator'. This is stricter than is proposed in other multimodal conventions. Liability under both the proposed Rotterdam Rules[148] and the failed MT convention is based on negligence with a reversed burden of proof,[149] which is a form of liability found in all maritime transport conventions.[150] The chosen strict liability is so far in line with the Commission's

143 On the terminology see e.g. Johansson, S.O., *An Outline of Transport Law*, 2nd edn, Bokbörsen, 2014, p. 78.

144 CMR Art. 17, COTIF-CIM Art. 23, the Montreal Convention Art. 18 (1) and (3) and the Hamburg Rules Art. 4.

145 HVR Art. I(e).

146 About the Nordic compromise, see above in Chapter 2 (at 2.2).

147 Rotterdam Rules Art. 12: 'Period of responsibility of the carrier: 1. The period of responsibility of the carrier for the goods under this Convention begins when the carrier or a performing party receives the goods for carriage and ends when the goods are delivered.'

148 See The Rotterdam Rules Art. 17, paras 1 and 2. According to Art. 17, para. 2: 'The carrier is relieved of all or part of its liability pursuant to paragraph 1 . . . if it proves that the cause or one of the causes of the loss, damage, or delay is not attributable to its fault of any person referred to in article 18, paragraph 1.' Art. 18 contains rules on the carrier's liability for other persons.

149 See the failed MT convention Art. 16, para. 1, according to which the multimodal transport operator is liable unless 'he, his servants, agents or any other person referred to in Article15 took all measures that could reasonably be required to avoid the occurrence and its consequences'. Art. 15 contains rules on the liability of the multimodal transport operator for his servants, agents and other persons.

150 HVR Art. IV(1), Hamburg Rules Art. 5.1, Rotterdam Rules Art. 17(2).

instructions to the expert group[151] and the Commission's attempt to create a European intermodal freight transport system, where the intention is to reduce the friction costs of changing from one mode of transport to another. Strict liability offers greater certainty to cargo interests and is therefore presented as the optimal solution in the European context.

Liability cannot, however, be unconditional. If failure in performance of the obligation in question is literally beyond the control of the transport integrator, it will face no liability. Furthermore, the transport integrator will not be liable if it can establish that the losses were 'caused or contributed to by fault on the part of consignor or consignee, to that extent the Transport Integrator will be exonerated'.[152] Although the transport integrator will be exonerated from liability due to the fault of the consignor or consignee, or actions or omissions beyond its control, liability will still be more burdensome than according to some of the existent unimodal liability regimes, for example under the maritime liability regimes where the basis of liability is culpa with a reversed burden of proof and the carrier has the benefit of generous exemptions.[153] On the other hand, as already mentioned, the proposed rule will be in line with the current liability system in carriage of goods by road and rail. Both the CMR and the COTIF-CIM apply strict liability. However, the carrier is relieved if the damage is caused by circumstances that the carrier could not avoid and the consequences of which it was unable to prevent.[154]

According to the second paragraph of the 2005 EU draft, the transport integrator will not only be liable for total or partial loss of the goods or damage to the goods, but also for 'any delay in delivery'.[155] If the time of delivery is not expressly agreed upon, the goods are delayed if they do not reach their destination within a 'reasonable time'. The goods are considered lost if they have not been delivered within 90 consecutive days following the agreed date of delivery.

Scope of liability

In terms of the scope of liability rule, the 2005 EU draft is also in line with the general idea of transport law and not in line with the rules in the CISG. Rules on limitation of liability are found in all present transport law regimes and the rules are all linked to an international agreed standard of SDRs, which is an international reserve asset, created by the International Monetary Fund (IMF) to supplement its member countries' official reserves. The value is based on a basket of four key international currencies, and SDRs can be exchanged for freely usable currencies.

Unfortunately, the level of limitation in the different unimodal liability regimes varies. One big obstacle to the harmonisation process has been – and is – this

151 The 2005 EU draft, p. 6.
152 The 2005 EU draft, p. 22.
153 The exemptions in the HVR listed in Art. IV(2).
154 See CMR Art. 17 (2) and COTIF-CIM Art. 23(2).
155 The 2005 EU draft, p. 22.

differentiation of liability limits. The challenge is how to create a harmonised liability system and still secure that the contractual multimodal carrier can be sure to have its loss covered in the recourse claim against the subcarrier responsible for the damage, loss or occasion causing delay. The proposed limitation rule (Article 9) reads as follows:

1 When the Transport Integrator is liable for loss resulting from loss of or damage to the goods according to article 8, his liability shall be limited to an amount not exceeding 17 units of account per kilogram of gross weight of the goods lost or damaged.
2 The liability of the Transport Integrator for loss resulting from delay in delivery according to the provisions of article 8 shall not exceed twice the amount of the charge payable under the contract of transport.
3 The aggregate liability of the Transport Integrator, under paragraphs 1 and 2 of this article, shall not exceed the limit of liability for total loss of the goods as determined by paragraph 1 of this article.
4 By declaration of value or otherwise, the Transport Integrator and the consignor may agree on limits of liability exceeding those provided for in the preceding paragraphs of this article.
5 The unit of account referred to in paragraph 1 is the Special Drawing Right as defined by the International Monetary Fund. The amounts referred to in paragraph 1 shall be converted into the national currency of a State according to the value of such currency on the date of the judgement or award or the date agreed upon by the parties. The value of a national currency, in terms of the Special Drawing Right, shall be calculated in accordance with the method of valuation applied by the International Monetary Fund, in effect on the date in question, for its operations and transactions.

The liability limit was set at 17 SDRs and was accordingly based on the highest monetary limit found in unimodal transport conventions at the time when the proposal was made, such as the COTIF-CIM and the Montreal conventions governing rail and air transport.[156] The expert group explains its choice in the introduction to the 2005 EU draft by a reference to the liability limit in rail and air carriage, which at the time were both 17 SDR. In doing so, the group seeks to avoid the limitation amount being deemed insufficient whenever an intermodal transport includes a leg by rail or air. As far as carriage involving a sea or road leg is concerned, the proposal would lead to an increase in limitation amounts. For road carriage, the limit would more than double from 8.33 SDR to 17 SDR and for sea carriage the limitation amount of 2 SDR per kilogram would increase greatly. Because of the alternative unit limitation system employed in sea transport, it is, however, the view of the 2005 expert group that the proposal will still sometimes provide the transport integrator with a lower limit than the combined

156 The 2005 EU draft, pp. 10–11.

unit/per kilo limitation under the Hague/Visby Rules.[157] As far as delay is concerned, a limit equal to twice the amount payable under the contract will apply.[158] However, combined liability for losses and delay will not exceed 17 SDR.[159]

It was important for the expert group to affirm that the new legal regime would not bring about a lower liability limit than the existing unimodal regimes. The cargo side should in other words not face a lower liability limit than it would have faced if a network system applied. Following this reasoning the liability limit should be at least 19 SDR per kilogram if the proposal is to be transformed into an EU regulation today. The problem arises in the recourse situation: when the transport integrator, which is responsible according to the multimodal contract, or its underwriter, claims recourse from its subcontractor that actually caused the damage. The transport integrator, which is the contractual carrier, will be liable to the consignee but with liability limited to a maximum 19 SDR. The problem in the recourse situation is whether the transport integrator can claim the whole amount from the subcarrier, or whether the liability of the latter will be limited according to the relevant unimodal transport law regime. The question is really a question of the legal basis for the recourse claim. Would the subcarrier be subject to a unimodal or multimodal transport regime? In order to keep things simple, the subcarrier should also be seen as a part of the multimodal transport arrangement and thus subject to the same regime. The separate contract between the subcarrier and the contractual carrier should make this clear for the subcarrier. The relevant contracts would, in other words, have to be adjusted to the new regime. It would also be effective to integrate a provision on this in the EU regime. A system for this could be found in the Hamburg Rules Article 10, which states that the subcarrier should be subject to the same rules as the actual carrier.[160] The provision is addressed to the shipper, who can choose which party to claim from. If the shipper was indemnified by the contractual carrier, the system

157 Op. cit., p. 11.
158 Op. cit., Art. 9, para. 2.
159 Op. cit., Art. 9, para. 3.
160 Hamburg Rules Article 10 – Liability of the carrier and actual carrier

1 Where the performance of the carriage or part thereof has been entrusted to an actual carrier, whether or not in pursuance of a liberty under the contract of carriage by sea to do so, the carrier nevertheless remains responsible for the entire carriage according to the provisions of this Convention. The carrier is responsible, in relation to the carriage performed by the actual carrier, for the acts and omissions of the actual carrier and of his servants and agents acting within the scope of their employment.
2 All the provisions of this Convention governing the responsibility of the carrier also apply to the responsibility of the actual carrier for the carriage performed by him. The provisions of paragraphs 2 and 3 of Article 7 and of paragraph 2 of Article 8 apply if an action is brought against a servant or agent of the actual carrier.
3 Any special agreement under which the carrier assumes obligations not imposed by this Convention or waives rights conferred by this Convention affects the actual carrier only if agreed to by him expressly and in writing. Whether or not the actual carrier has so agreed, the carrier nevertheless remains bound by the obligations or waivers resulting from such special agreement.

in the Hamburg Rules Article 10 would secure full compensation for the transport integrator, unless the parties have agreed otherwise.[161] The same freedom of contract should, in my opinion, apply under an EU regulation.

Neither of the groups of legal experts appointed by the Commission has questioned the need for a rule limiting liability. In the light of the legal context of the EU proposal, this would have been remarkable. Legal certainty is a key objective on the path towards an efficient European intermodal transport chain. A fixed cap on liability is therefore necessary in this context. However, if the ambition is to harmonise the liability scheme with the CISG, such a limitation is unfamiliar. The 2005 proposal is thus a compromise between the aims of harmonising future EU legislation on multimodal contracts of carriage with the existing law on international sales contracts on the one side and not deviating too much from existent international transport law on the other side.

In this context it is rather surprising that the 2005 EU draft contains no provisions on how to calculate the loss for which the transport integrator will be liable. If the transport integrator loses its right of limitation (which will be the case, according to Article 10, where the losses were caused *intentionally* by the transport integrator), the 2005 EU draft does not regulate how this loss should be calculated.

If transport integrators find that the 2005 EU draft does not satisfy their interests, there is always the possibility of opting out of the system. Otherwise, the proposal is based on a kind of take-it-or-leave-it principle. From this, however, there is one exception. The consignors are allowed to make a declaration of value and to obtain full compensation up to that value. In these cases the transport integrator will normally increase its charges by applying so-called *ad valorem* freight. The 2005 EU draft is here in line with the standard position on this question: there is no reason why the parties should not be entitled to agree on higher limits or, indeed, no limit at all and to do so in some other form than a declaration of value.[162] On the other hand, if the transport integrator by wrongful intent or recklessness has caused the losses, knowing that this would be the result of its actions or omissions, then the transport integrator will lose the right to benefit from the limitation of liability provided in Article 9. This follows from Article 10, Loss of right to limit responsibility:

> The Transport Integrator shall not be entitled to the benefit of the limitation of liability provided for in this Regime if it is proved that the loss, damage or delay in delivery resulted from a personal act or omission of the Transport Integrator

4 Where and to the extent that both the carrier and the actual carrier are liable, their liability is joint and several.

5 The aggregate of the amounts recoverable from the carrier, the actual carrier and their servants and agents shall not exceed the limits of liability provided for in this Convention.

6 Nothing in this Article shall prejudice any right of recourse as between the carrier and the actual carrier.

161 Hamburg Rules Art. 10(6).

162 The 2005 EU draft, p. 23.

done with the intent to cause such loss, damage or delay or recklessly and with knowledge that such loss, damage or delay would probably result.

Loss of the right to limit liability only applies if intent or recklessness resulted from 'a personal act' by the transport integrator. First, this means that the group of persons mentioned in Article 1, paragraph 2, 'the servants, agents or other persons engaged for the performance for the obligations under the contract of transport', is excluded.[163] Second, if the transport integrator is a corporation (which it normally will be), conduct will be categorised as personal if it is an act or omission of a human being concerning an executive matter which that person is authorised to decide without further reference to any other person in the managerial structure of the enterprise.[164] Finally, it should be mentioned that, to prevent cargo interests from seeking to put themselves in a better position than would be the case under the 2005 EU draft, the proposal limits the effect of a tort claim against the transport integrator in Article 11.[165] This rule also supports a harmonised system on recourse claims.

In my opinion the uniform liability system in the 2005 EU draft represents a good solution for the EU, provided that no international solution is found to the multimodal liability problem. However, as already stated, the uniform liability system is not a favoured solution among the stakeholders within the EU or among the majority of legal scholars. This fact has led to a discussion within the EU Commission on whether or not a network liability system would be predictable enough to ensure the desired modal shift. The discussion, as well as the discussion on whether or not the network solution of the Rotterdam Rules could be acceptable for the EU, is presented below.

6.4 The network liability system solution – a fallback clause

The EU discussion

According to the Freight Logistics Action Plan of 2007, a uniform liability system was no longer considered the only option.[166] Instead, the Commission intended also to consider a network liability system as a solution to the European problem. This alternative would be based on the existing unimodal transport conventions. The major problem of undisclosed damages in a network system would be addressed by including a fallback clause. It is likely that the shift in approach is related to the international situation, where the Rotterdam Rules are pending. The Rotterdam Rules are an extensive convention governing international

163 Op. cit., p. 16.
164 Op. cit., p. 24.
165 Art. 11: 'The defenses and limits of liability provided for in this Regime shall apply in any action against the Transport Integrator in respect of loss resulting from loss of or damage to the goods, as well as from delay in delivery, whether the action be founded in contract, in tort or otherwise.'
166 More on this above in Chapter 5 (at 5.1).

contracts of carriage, including multimodal contracts, provided that the carriage includes a sea leg. The liability system is a network system with a fallback clause and the Convention contains an option for electronic documents. Clearly, the EU Commission is considering whether this convention would solve the multimodal problem in the Union. The Convention is open for signature by the EU,[167] but so far the Union has not used this option.[168] It seems as if the Commission would like to keep the door open, as it has indicated that no further steps can be taken as regards an internal solution, without considering the Rotterdam Rules as an alternative.[169] The decision was taken despite negative advice on the Rotterdam Rules from the 2009 expert group, which dismissed the network alternative because it does not provide guidance for legal gaps or clashes related to interpretation of the international unimodal conventions for the clauses to which the network regime applies.[170]

As indicated above in relation to the uniform liability system, the problem with the unimodal conventions could be solved by a resolution from the EU stating that the existing unimodal conventions should be interpreted narrowly so that they do not collide with competing EU law. This would be in line with existing EU doctrine and enough to mend the legal gaps related to understanding the unimodal conventions. In addition, a future EU regime on multimodal contracts of carriage should contain specific step-back clauses in order to avoid clashes with the existing unimodal conventions that have an explicit extended scope and in some situations also apply to multimodal transport. The Rotterdam Rules Article 82 provides a solution. This will be outlined below, together with a presentation of the network model in the Rotterdam Rules (Article 26) and a discussion on whether or not the Rotterdam Rules could be an alternative for the EU.[171]

Does the network system of the Rotterdam Rules provide a solution for the EU?

The modified network liability system of the Rotterdam Rules

The basic objective of the Rotterdam Rules is to regulate international carriage of goods by sea and 'multimodal carriage when the carriage has a sea leg'. The state parties that adopt the Rotterdam Rules must make them applicable to contracts

167 According to the Rotterdam Rules Art. 93, a regional economic integration organisation (the EU) can also participate in the convention.

168 Currently the EU does not have competence to participate in the convention; this would require that the Union first make use of its internal competence and make the Rotterdam Rules applicable in the EU as a directive or a regulation. The EU would then have competence to access the Rotterdam Rules on the basis of TFEU Art. 216(1) or the principle of 'parallelism', see above in Chapter 3 (at 3.2).

169 White paper from 2011, see above in Chapter 5 (at 5.2).

170 The 2009 study, at p. 185; more above in Chapter 5 (at 5.1).

171 The following has also been discussed in Eftestøl-Wilhelmsson, E., 'The Rotterdam Rules in a European Multimodal context', *Journal of International Maritime Law*, 2010, Volume 16, pp. 274–288.

of carriage which 'shall provide for carriage by sea and may provide for carriage by other modes of transport in addition to the sea carriage' (Article 1(1)). Furthermore, this only concerns carriage that is international and linked to a contracting state (Article 5). Because of the maritime plus scope of the Convention, not only the port of delivery and discharge but also the place of receipt and delivery are accepted as linking factors. Both carriage end to end and the sea part of it must be international. The Rotterdam Rules go further than the current maritime conventions on carriage of goods[172] in that they present a harmonised instrument regulating almost the entire contractual relationship between the parties to a contract of carriage.[173] The Rotterdam Rules are in this respect more modern than the existing maritime conventions. This chapter relates, however, only to the liability system of the Rotterdam Rules applicable to multimodal contracts and the question of whether or not the Rotterdam Rules provide a sufficient alternative for the European Commission.

The modified network liability system applicable to multimodal contracts of carriage is based on an interaction between the different unimodal liability systems on carriage by road,[174] rail,[175] air[176] and inland waterways[177] and the liability system of the Rotterdam Rules.[178] Generally speaking, the carrier's liability will vary according to where in the multimodal chain the losses occurred. The main principle is that the mode-specific liability system will also apply under a multimodal contract of carriage. However, due to the fact that the period of responsibility of the carrier under the Rotterdam Rules is extended to include the place

172 International Convention for the Unification of Certain Rules of Law Relating to Bills of Lading, Brussels 1924 (the Hague Rules), Protocol to Amend the International Convention for the Unification of Certain Rules of Law Relating to Bills of Lading, Brussels 1968 (the Hague-Visby Rules) and United Nations Convention on the Carriage of Goods by Sea, Hamburg 1978 (the Hamburg Rules).

173 For more on the extended purpose of the Rotterdam Rules see Mankowski, P., 'The Rotterdam Rules – Scope of Application and Freedom of Contract', *European Journal of Commercial Contract Law*, 2010, Volume 2, Issue 1/2, pp. 9–21 at p. 12.

174 CMR The convention on the contract for the International carriage of goods by road (Geneva, 19 May 1956).

175 COTIF-CIM Appendix B to the Convention Conserving International Carriage by Rail (COTIF) at 9 June 1999 Uniform Rules concerning the contract of International Carriage of Goods by Rail (CIM). Applicable with effect from 7 July 2006.

176 Both the Warsaw Convention of 1929 with amendments and the Montreal Convention of 1999, which is meant to consolidate and replace the Warsaw Convention, are operating alongside each other. All EU Member States have, however, acceded to the Montreal Convention by Regulation (EC) No 889/2002 and Regulation (EC) No 2027/97 on air carrier liability in the event of accidents as amended by the Council (13 May 2002). Here reference will be made only to the Montreal Convention.

177 Budapest Convention on the Contract for the Carriage of Goods by Inland Waterways (CMNI) (Budapest, 22 June 2001).

178 On the liability system of the Rotterdam Rules, see e.g. Diamond, A., 'The Rotterdam Rules', *Lloyd's Maritime and Commercial Law Quarterly*, 2009, Part 4, pp. 445–536 at pp. 461–91. See also Yuzhou, S. and Hai Li, H., 'The New Structure of the Basis of Liability for the Carrier', paper presented at the Colloquium of the Rotterdam Rules 2009, 21 September 2009, De Doelen. Available online at www.rotterdamrules2009.com/cms/index.php?page=text-speakers-rotterdam-rules-2009 (accessed 9 April 2015).

of receipt to the place of delivery,[179] both the Rotterdam Rules and different unimodal liability regimes may be applicable simultaneously and lead to conflicts of conventions. Additionally, the unimodal conventions have an extended scope of application and are applicable to what might be seen as traditional maritime carriage.

In order to avoid conflicts with the unimodal conventions, the Rotterdam Rules liability system includes wide step-back clauses laid down in Articles 26 and 82. Article 26 regulates the situation where the liability regime of the Rotterdam Rules has extended its scope of application to multimodal carriage outside the vessel. Article 82, on the other hand, regulates situations where the unimodal regimes have extended their scope of application to what might be characterised as traditional maritime carriage, such as when the cargo is on board a ship or if the sea leg is supplementary to land transport. In the area of aviation, the legal regime has expanded to a great extent and the step-back clause in Article 82 is correspondingly wide.

Article 26: carriage preceding or subsequent to sea carriage

Article 26 is the key provision for understanding the limited network liability system of the Rotterdam Rules. The provision distinguishes between losses that occurred 'solely before . . . loading . . . or solely after . . . discharge from the ship' and other situations connected to the cargo being on board the vessel, or when the losses cannot be localised or are progressive. In the latter situations the liability system laid down in the Rotterdam Rules chapter 5 is applicable. In the first situation, the Rotterdam Rules step back for other international applicable legal regimes as specified in Article 26, provided the relevant international instrument contains mandatory liability provisions.

The difference between the liability system of the Rotterdam Rules and other liability systems starts from the event causing losses. According to paragraph 1 of Article 26, the Rotterdam Rules do not prevail over those provisions of another international instrument regulating this question if the event occurred 'during the carrier's period of responsibility but solely before . . . loading onto the ship or solely after . . . discharge from the ship'.

The word 'solely' suggests that the event should not be subject to any concurrent or contributory event after loading or before discharge and the burden of proof lies with the claimant, normally the shipper or receiver. If the losses started during the land leg of multimodal carriage governed by the Rotterdam Rules, but continued during the sea leg (or vice versa), then the Convention will prevail over, for example, the CMR. A typical case could be a refrigeration system starting to malfunction during the land leg of the transport and worsening during the sea voyage.

If the place where the losses occurred cannot be identified, it cannot be said that the event took place solely outside the vessel and the Rotterdam Rules will

179 Rotterdam Rules Art. 12.

apply as a default system. This is certainly a very important rule as a high percentage of container cargo damage is concealed.[180] A harmonised fallback solution for undisclosed events causing losses will definitely be one of the most important achievements of the Rotterdam Rules if they enter into force. The problem that exists when losses cannot be localised is at present partly solved, as regards liability limitation, through different optional general conditions, such as the FIATA FBL 1992 and MULTIDOC 95, both based on the UNCTAD/ICC Rules for Multimodal Transport Documents 1992.[181]

The Rotterdam Rules presuppose possible conflicts between the new convention and existing unimodal conventions. As mentioned above, this might be seen as acceptance of multimodal contracts as mixed contracts to which the unimodal legal regime of the particular mode where the losses are located will apply. The Rotterdam Rules, as a result, step back for conventions that 'would have applied to all or any of the carrier's activities if the shipper had made a separate and direct contract with the carrier in respect of the particular stage of carriage where the loss of, or damage to goods, or an event or circumstances causing delay in their delivery occurred'.[182]

Such hypothetical contracts are sufficient for the Rotterdam Rules to step back. It is not necessary to prove the unimodal legal regime applicable if there is no separate contract as they presuppose such applicability.[183] For example, if road carriage is part of a multimodal transport with a sea leg and the Rotterdam Rules apply, the system is that the CMR liability system will govern damages located to the road leg, provided that the preconditions of Article 26 are otherwise fulfilled. However, Article 26 does not solve all problems. If the losses that occurred at different stages of the transport are non-localised or progressive 'then two international instruments may both apply with potentially conflicting result'.[184] Neither Article 26 nor Article 82 regulates all the possible conflict situations that might occur. Furthermore, the Rotterdam Rules merely offer a so-called minimal network system.[185] The arrangement is called 'minimal' because it applies only to the carrier's liability, limitation of liability and time for suit.

Articles 26 and 82 of the Rotterdam Rules both deal with collisions of conventions and applicability, but with a different scope. Whereas Article 26 is placed in chapter 6 of the convention – Additional provisions relating to particular stages of the carriage – Article 82 is placed in chapter 17 – Matters not governed by this

180 Hancock, C., 'Multimodal Transport and the New UN Convention on the Carriage of Goods', *Journal of International Maritime Law*, 2008, Volume14, pp. 484–495 at p. 490

181 The text of the Rules can be found in ICC publication No 481.

182 Rotterdam Rules Art. 26(a).

183 See also Haak, K., 'Carriage Preceding or Subsequent to Sea Carriage under the Rotterdam Rules', *European Journal of Commercial Contract Law*, 2010, Volume 2, Issue 1/2, pp. 63–71 at pp. 64 and 70.

184 Diamond, op. cit., note 179, at p. 456.

185 Hoeks, M., 'Multimodal Carriage with a Pinch of Sea Salt: Door to Door Under the UNCITRAL Draft Instrument', *European Transport Law*, 2008, Volume 43, pp. 257–280 at p. 266.

convention. At first sight it is not easy to understand the relationship between the two provisions, which both seem to regulate the same situation. However, there are differences. Article 82 is constructed as a 'real' collision of convention provisions: it regulates whether or not the Rotterdam Rules as such are applicable. Article 26, on the other hand, presupposes that the Rotterdam Rules are applicable, but decides on what set of rules is to be used as regards carrier's liability, limitation of liability and time for suit when losses occur during the carrier's period of responsibility, but solely before the goods are loaded onto the ship or solely after their discharge from the ship. If the source of the losses is *solely* found before or after loading/discharge, the maritime liability system is not applicable. In other words, the Rotterdam Rules apply a (minimal) network liability system.

Article 82: step back

The subject of Article 82, on the other hand, is problems related to collision of conventions. In the matter of multimodal carriage, the challenge has been to sort out which convention is to be used when, since by definition more than one mode of transport is involved in multimodal carriage and thus several possible (unimodal) legal regimes. So far, sorting out under which means of transport losses occurred and then applying the appropriate legal regime for that mode of transport has normally solved the problem. This approach is based on an understanding of the multimodal contract as a mixed contract that is subject to an accumulation of regulations. With regard to the applicable law, the contract is regarded as the sum total of unimodal contracts.[186] The network solution, based on the mixed contract approach, works when the place where the place where the losses occured is located, but does not provide any solution when this is not the case. When losses are not located, something that might very well be the case, for example in container transport, the problem of legal uncertainty and unpredictability is particularly strong.

Article 82 deals with the relationship between the Rotterdam Rules and other international conventions regulating carriage by air, road, rail or inland waterways, as far as the mentioned conventions are *in force* at the time the Rotterdam Rules enters into force. At first glance, it seems as if Article 82 is a general conflict provision. According to Article 82, first paragraph, nothing in the Rotterdam Rules affects the application of any unimodal convention in force when the Rotterdam Rules enters into force regarding the liability of the carrier for loss of or damage to the goods. A general step-back rule as referred to above is, however, only applicable to conflicts with the international conventions on carriage of goods by air, such as the Montreal Convention (see the Rotterdam Rules Article 82(a)). In all other cases the step-back clause is restricted to certain situations mentioned in Article 82(b)–(d).

According to Article 82 (a), the Rotterdam Rules step back for any conflict with any convention governing the carriage of goods by air 'to the extent

186 This approach is chosen in the Netherlands regarding national multimodal transport: see above in Chapter 2 (at 2.4).

[it] . . . according to its provisions applies to any part of the contract of carriage'. The Montreal Convention is a unimodal convention with a wide scope of application. According to Article 1, the Montreal Convention applies to all international carriage of cargo by aircraft for reward. What this more precisely means is regulated in chapter III, Liability for the Carrier and Extent of Compensation for Damage. According to the Montreal Convention, Articles 18(1) and (19), the carrier is liable for damage to cargo and delay of cargo when the event which caused the damage or delay took place 'during the carriage by air'. According to Article 18(3), this means the period during which the cargo is 'in the charge of the carrier'. Regarding combined or multimodal carriage, Article 38(1) states that the convention '. . . shall . . . apply only to carriage by air'.

From the Montreal Convention Article 18(4) we can read that, inside the airport, carriage by air includes carriage by land, sea or inland waterways. A combination of carriage by sea and air inside an airport is perhaps not very practical. However, carriage *outside the airport* might also be included if 'such carriage takes place in the performance of a contract for carriage by air, for the purpose of loading, delivery or transhipment',[187] or when the carrier, without the consent of the consignor, substitutes air carriage by other modes of transport.

The Montreal Convention is, accordingly, applicable to other modes of transport either within the airport area or as part of, for example, a door-to-door agreement, or when the carrier, by itself, substitutes the means of transport. In other words, the Montreal Convention might be applicable in situations when air carriage includes a sea leg, a situation when the Rotterdam Rules might also apply. If we have such a situation, the Rotterdam Rules Article 82(a) state that it will not affect the application of 'any convention governing the carriage of goods by air'. This means that the liability system of the Montreal Convention might also be applicable when the goods are on board a vessel, if this is due, for example, to the fact that the air carrier, without the consent of the consignor, substitutes air carriage by other modes of transport, such as sea and road based modes. Article 82(a) was drafted 'in order to ensure that there is no conflict between the [draft] convention and the Montreal Convention',[188] and is by nature a general conflict provision. This is opposite to the other provisions in Article 82, which are all specific conflict provisions designed to cover some particular situations when other unimodal conventions may apply to carriage by sea performed by a vessel. In a conflict between the Rotterdam Rules and the Montreal Convention the result is quite predictable: the Montreal Convention will prevail.

Regarding road carriage, though, the situation is far from predictable. The conflict between the Rotterdam Rules and CMR is regulated by Article 82(b), which is limited to the situation where the goods 'remain loaded on a road

187 Montreal Convention Art. 18(4).

188 Berlingieri, F., 'Multimodal Aspects of the Rotterdam Rules', paper presented at the Colloquium of the Rotterdam Rules 2009, 21 September 2009, De Doelen. Available online at http://www.rotterdamrules2009.com/cms/uploads/Def.%20tekst%20F.%20 Berlingieri%2013%20OKT29.pdf, p. 15 (accessed 9 April 2015).

cargo vehicle carried on board a ship'.[189] The same wording is used in CMR Article 2, which states that the convention is applicable to lost, damaged or delayed goods 'carried over part of the journey by sea . . . [when] . . . the goods are not unloaded from the vehicle',[190] in other words the same piggyback situation as mentioned in the Rotterdam Rules. In this situation the Rotterdam Rules Article 82 states that the CMR will prevail as far as it is applicable. This is not unclear.

Problems arise when trying to figure out the liability system of the CMR convention, Article 2(2).[191] The CMR also operates with a network liability system in a multimodal context. According to CMR, Article 2(2), second sentence, the crucial question in deciding on which liability system to use is the source of the losses: If caused by 'some event which could only occurred in the course of and by reason of the carriage by that other means of transport [than the road based transport]', then the liability system of the relevant convention for this means of transport is applicable. This means that, in certain situations involving piggyback transport, chapter 5 of the Rotterdam Rules will apply, despite the fact that the CMR would prevail. During sea carriage, a typical situation would be that the road vehicle and its cargo has fallen overboard and is lost (roll-on–fall-off). In that situation the CMR is normally not applicable, and the Rotterdam Rules would apply. If on the other hand the cargo remains unloaded and damage is due to problems with the containers (e.g. temperature), the CMR will be applicable despite the fact that the damage took place at sea and according to Article 82(b) the CMR prevails over the Rotterdam Rules. The provisions on conflict of conventions in the Rotterdam Rules are complicated in relation to the CMR, and might for that reason be characterised as unpredictable.

If the Rotterdam Rules apply to the contract of carriage, the network solution in the Rotterdam Rules, Article 26, still leads to the result that the CMR will be applicable to events causing losses when the event has *solely* taken place outside the vessel and during the road leg of the transport. If losses are connected to the sea leg or are non-localised, then the Rotterdam Rules apply (the fallback clause). However, in the situation of piggyback transport the Rotterdam Rules will step back if the CMR is applicable. The question when CMR liability is applicable in these situations is, however, not easy because of the difficult preconditions laid

189 The sea carriage in such a situation might be performed by a roll-on–roll-off (ro-ro) vessel designed to carry wheeled cargo that is driven on and off the ship on its own wheels or by lo-lo (lift on-lift off) vessels which use a crane to load and unload cargo to and from the vessel. CMR will typically only apply to the ro-ro situation.

190 This is, however, not valid if the means of transport has changed according to the instructions of the sender as regulated in CMR Art. 14.

191 CMR Art. 2 is one of the most complicated provisions in transport law. A good overview of the different possible conflict situations that might arise is given by Ralph de Witt, *Multimodal Transport*, LLP Professional Publishing, 1995, at pp. 102–107.

down in CMR, Article 2. From an EU perspective, this solution is far from optimal, but familiar to the industry, as CMR Article 2 is not a new provision.

Again, regarding conflict of conventions regulating carriage by rail, we face problems. According to Article 82(c), the Rotterdam Rules step back for the convention regulating international carriage by rail, the COTIF-CIM,[192] as far as it applies to the carriage of goods by sea as a supplement to the carriage by rail. This is the same expression used in the CIM, Article 4, as a precondition for applying the CIM on a sea leg of a multimodal contract including a rail and a sea leg. Deciding on what is supplementary might be a challenge and in some situations lead to unpredictability regarding the applicable legal regime. One way to distinguish the supplementary criteria is by distance. A sea leg can be a supplement to rail carriage when the distance the goods are transported by sea is short and only ancillary to the rail transport, such as in rail transport between Paris and London. In contrast, if the sea distance is clearly the longer one, it is difficult to consider it supplementary to rail carriage. Overseas carriage from New York to Paris, where only the last part is performed by train from a European port, cannot be characterised as supplementary. If the sea part is the more important part of the carriage, the CIM is, according to Article 1(4), not applicable. Another way to distinguish the sea part as supplementary is to consider the carrier's position. Is it mainly performing rail carriage, or are we dealing with a maritime carrier? The position of the carrier might influence the evaluation. However, even though the sea leg (of multimodal carriage by rail and sea) is found supplementary to the rail leg, this is not sufficient for the CIM also to apply on the maritime leg. If rail carriage is the main object of the contract of carriage, then CIM applies to the sea leg only 'if the sea carriage . . . is performed on services included in the list of services provided for in Article 24 § 1 of the Convention'. According to COTIF, Article 24, there are two lists, the CIV Uniform rules concerning the International Carriage of Passengers by Rail (CIV). Appendix A to COTIF, and the CIM list.[193] The lists can be found on the homepage of OTIF (Intergovernmental Organisation for International Carriage by Rail).[194] To complicate the matter even further, if the CIM is applicable, it is not clear what liability system should be used. The CIM applies a kind of network system. Even though the CMI main rule, according to Article 23, is strict liability with some exemptions, a different fault-based liability

192 Convention concerning the Contract for International Carriage by Rail (COTIF) of May 1980. Appendix B: Uniform Rules concerning the Contract for International Carriage of Goods by Rail (CIM).

193 Art. 24: Lists of lines or services § 1 The maritime and inland waterway services referred to in Article 1 of the CIV Uniform Rules and of the CIM Uniform Rules, on which carriage is performed in addition to carriage by rail subject to a single contract of carriage, shall be included in two lists:

a) the CIV list of maritime and inland waterway services,
b) the CIM list of maritime and inland waterway services.

194 Available online at http://www.otif.org/en/publications/cim-lists-of-lines-or-services/cim-list-of-maritime-and-inland-waterway-services.html?type=98 (accessed 14 April 2015).

system is available for the sea carrier in respect of sea–rail traffic.[195] It is, however, necessary that the Member States of the CIM *opt in* to this possibility.[196]

As the last conflict of collision rule, the Rotterdam Rules, Article 82(d) contains a provision on potential conflict with any convention applicable to inland waterways, which applies to carriage of goods *without transhipment* both by inland waterways and sea. The relevant convention here is the CMNI, in force from 1 April 2005. Members of the Convention are mainly from the EU.[197] According to Article 2(2), the CMNI Convention applies if the purpose of the contract is carriage of goods, without transhipment both by inland waterways and in waters to which maritime regulations apply, unless a marine bill of lading has been issued in accordance with the marine law applicable or the distance to be travelled in waters to which maritime regulations apply is the greater.[198] In other words, if the goods are carried without transhipment and a marine bill of lading has been issued, the CMNI Convention is not applicable.

The next-best solution

The question raised above was whether or not the modified network liability system of the Rotterdam Rules provides a sufficient alternative to the European Commission's plan for increased use of multimodal transport by providing transport users with a predictable liability system needed to reduce transaction costs by changing mode of transport.

Based on a study of the modified network system, and recognising all the questions regarding the content of Article 26 and the complicated network of scope of application in the unimodal conventions, which has to be measured against the collision rules in Article 87, it is easy to criticise the Rotterdam Rules for their multimodal attempts.[199] The answer to the above question must therefore be

195 CIM Art. 38.

196 By requesting a suitable note to be included in the list of services to which the CIM apply, s. 38(2) provides liability based on negligence with a reversed burden of proof for the sea carrier from the time the goods are loaded on board the ship to the time they are unloaded from the ship, section 5.38(2). Such a note is requested for lines between Sweden and Denmark as well as Sweden and Finland for example. Available online at http://www.otif.org/fileadmin/user_upload/otif_verlinkte_files/07_veroeff/07_liste_CIM/CIM_Sude_3.8.2006_1.1.2008.pdf (accessed 15 May 2015).

197 The Convention was agreed at a diplomatic conference organised jointly by the Central Commission for the Navigation of the Rhine, the DANUBE Commission and the United Nations Economic Commission for Europe. CMNI is therefore characterised as a pan-European legal instrument in the field of inland water transport. It is signed by 12 European nations, including Germany, France and the Netherlands, and Russia, altogether 13 nations. Available online at http://www.unece.org/trans/main/sc3/sc3_cmni_legalinst.html (accessed 28 April 2015).

198 CMNI Art. 2.2(a) and (b).

199 See for example Tetley, W., 'A Summary of General Criticisms of the UNCITRAL Convention (The Rotterdam Rules)' (20 December 2008). Available online at http://www.mcgill.ca/files/maritimelaw/Summary_of_Criticism_of_UNCITRAL__No_1.pdf (accessed 13 April 2015).

'no'. The system is not easy and predictable. Instead, many legal obstacles need to be overcome and the network-based interaction with the unimodal conventions is not without loopholes.

However, the modified network liability system laid down in the Rotterdam Rules is based on the network liability system in operation at present: if losses can be localised to a specific mode of transport, the liability system of that mode will apply. The problem of un-localised losses is at present not governed by any international binding legal regime, but by different general conditions, such as the FIATA FBL 1992 and MULTIDOC 95.[200] These general conditions only harmonise the limitation rules. In other words, the existing European multimodal liability system is a network liability system with an opt-in solution for un-localised losses. By providing a fallback solution, as achieved by Article 26, the Rotterdam Rules have improved the legal clarity of the network system.[201]

One criticism of the Rotterdam Rules has been that they do not 'provide any guidance in case of legal gaps or clashes related to the interpretation of the international unimodal conventions for the clauses to which the network regime applies'.[202] According to this criticism, the modified network system of the Rotterdam Rules is not regarded as capable of providing legal certainty and predictability. This was the reason why the 2009 expert group dismissed the Rotterdam Rules as an alternative for the EU and is also the reason why multimodal scholars do not favour the convention. According to, for example, Marian Hoeks, the limited network system of Article 26 in the rules is 'tremendously complicated' and 'unlikely to work without at least a few glitches'. The foremost of these being that the rules do 'not take views on the applicability of carriage conventions such as the CMR to international road stages of multimodal contracts'[203] (see the court praxis reviewed above in section 6.2.) However, nothing prevents the EU from making a resolution or other statement on the *sui generis* character of multimodal contracts of carriage and in doing so demanding a narrow interpretation of the unimodal transport conventions. This is the position of the Norwegian Maritime Law Commission when considering whether or not Norway should implement the Rotterdam Rules.

The modified network liability system of the Rotterdam Rules represents a step forward in the international regulation of multimodal carrier liability. Keeping in mind the history of international harmonisation of multimodal transport, this is no small achievement. If the Rotterdam Rules enter into force, the Convention will become the first international mandatory regime on multimodal transport. Among the ratifying states, non-regulated liability gaps will not exist.

200 Both based on the UNCTAD/ICC Rules for Multimodal Transport Documents 1992 (n 52).

201 Hoeks, op. cit., note 1, at pp. 348–349 points out, however, that this also has negative consequences as the low liability limit of the Rotterdam Rules will not stimulate carriers to reveal where loss or damage occurred.

202 The 2009 study, p. 185.

203 Hoeks, op. cit., note 1, at p. 477.

A downside is, however, that the Rotterdam Rules do not include multimodal transport without a sea leg, nor do they regulate all legal issues in multimodal transport. Nevertheless, as Haak points out, they represent the 'next-best solution for international multimodal cases' simply because they will increase the level of uniformity in international multimodal transport.[204] This is also stated by Schoenbaum.[205] Additionally, Hoeks is of the opinion that if the Rotterdam Rules enter into force, 'the best we can do is to hope that [they are] accepted globally instead of sporadically. Only then will the new regime add to the much sought – after uniformity of carriage law.'[206] Nikaki and Soyer are of the same view, admitting that the objective of the rules as stated in the Preamble, has 'been realized to an extent'. Thus, although the Rules are in other words not totally unacceptable, nevertheless the worst scenario would be that the Rotterdam Rules are ratified by enough states to enter into force, but still not ratified by the major shipping nations such as the US, Canada, China, Spain and the UK.[207]

The question of whether or not the Rotterdam Rules in such a situation will satisfy the EU remains to be answered. As mentioned, one of the main obstacles in the process towards a European multimodal transport chain has been the friction costs resulting from the uncertain legal position of the multimodal carrier, especially in relation to the question of carrier liability. This issue has been under discussion internationally for decades. It is no secret that the main problem has been the industry's response to proposed new legal instruments. Even though there is apparently a demand for a clear and predictable legal solution, no one wants their own liability to be increased beyond the existing system. The early EU proposals advocated a strict uniform liability system, which would probably best fulfil this demand. However, recent studies show that it is almost impossible to reach consensus on such a proposal.[208] The European Commission also recognised this as it opened discussions on a modified network system in the 2007 Freight Transport Logistic Action Plan.[209] If the Rotterdam Rules enter into force and are accepted on a global level, this will be a strong argument for the EU to link its regional solution to the global convention and settle for a modified network system. At present both the EU and the Member States are examining this option.[210]

204 Haak, K., 'Carriage Preceding or Subsequent to Sea Carriage under the Rotterdam Rules', *European Journal of Commercial Contract Law*, Volume 2, Issue 1/2, at pp. 63–71 at p. 71.

205 Schoenbaum, T., 'An Evaluation of the Rotterdam Rules', *The Hamburg Lectures on Maritime Affairs, 2011–2013*, Volume 28, pp. 21–43 at p. 43.

206 Hoeks, op. cit., note 1, at p. 478.

207 Nikaki, T. and Soyer, B., 'New International Regime for Carriage of Goods by Sea: Contemporary, Certain, Inclusive AND Efficient, or Just Another One for the Shelves?' *Berkeley J. Int'l L.*, 2012, Volume 30, Issue 2, pp. 303–348 at p. 46.

208 See above in Chapter 5 (at 5.1) on the 2009 study.

209 See above in section 6.4.

210 Above in Chapter 5 (at 5.2).

Summary

The idea of a uniform liability regime for multimodal contracts of carriage where liability is based on the contract and not on performance would certainly solve many legal problems in the transport industry and provide predictability as called for by the Commission. If the EU used its competence to issue an EU regulation according to which the multimodal contract is defined as *sui generis*, the problem of conflict of conventions would also be solved due to the shared competence between the EU and the Member States in the area of transport. If the EU uses its competence, the competence of the Member States will be similarly reduced. The principle of loyalty implies that the Member States must interpret other international conventions narrowly so that they will not collide with EU legislation. This is possible as regards the transport conventions, as demonstrated by the German Supreme Court. Additionally, the recourse problem would also be solved by a *sui generis* approach as the unimodal conventions would not apply to a contract between transport integrator and subcarrier, which would be made subject to the EU regime on the same conditions as the transport integrator.

However, because of the risk of a higher liability limit and removal of the right to apply certain specific exemptions from liability, such as exemptions for navigational errors and fire which appear in the main maritime conventions, it is not likely that consensus on the proposed regime will be reached by the stakeholders in the EU. As mentioned, the Commission is thus also examining the role of the Rotterdam Rules, which of course could also be used by the EU. One should, however, raise the question of how effective a harmonised liability regime is, as regards the goal of increased multimodal carriage of goods and sustainability. This question will be discussed below.

7 Does a harmonised legal regime really enhance multimodal carriage?

7.1 Introduction

As has been outlined in the above chapters, reducing the negative impacts of transport and creating a sustainable European transport industry are important goals for the European Union (EU) and a core part of the common transport policy (CTP). The aim is to drastically reduce CO_2 emissions while at the same time keeping an efficient transport industry. A modal shift towards more multimodal carriage of goods, accompanied by more effective use of each mode, will, according to the EU Commission, contribute to the desired development. In order to reach this goal, all barriers hindering the desired development should be identified and removed. The unpredictable legal situation of the parties involved in a multimodal contract of carriage has been identified as one such barrier that needs to be removed and replaced, for example with a regional liability regime. In economic terms, the unpredictable legal situation is defined as a transaction cost preventing the parties from choosing the multimodal alternative. In order to increase the use of multimodal transport, the identified transaction cost must be reduced. As outlined above,[1] this is, in combination with the slow progress on an international solution to the multimodal problem, the reason why the EU started to examine whether or not a regional legal regime for multimodal contracts of carriage was possible – and feasible.

Stakeholders and scholars do not question the unpredictable liability situation in multimodal transport as problematic and expensive. On the contrary, it is treated as a fact that both the Commission and legal experts agree on. The first legal expert group (the 1999 expert group) assisting the Commission concluded that the unpredictable situation could lead to unnecessary costs, such as costs related to claims handling and litigation.[2] The multimodal problem has been subject of international discussion for decades. All stakeholders seem to agree that the legal situation is unclear, but before the EU Commission entered into discussions, nobody claimed that the unpredictable legal situation was a barrier to increased use of multimodal carriage.[3]

1 Above in Chapters 3, 4 and 5, and on friction costs, see particularly Chapter 4 (at 4.2).
2 The 1999 expert group, at p. 20.
3 On the previous discussion, see Chapter 2 (at 2.3).

The economic impact study

As no study had been carried out regarding loss of money as a result of the inadequacies of the fragmented liability framework, the Commission ordered a study on The Economic Impact of Carrier Liability on Intermodal Freight Transport, in order to disclose the legal friction costs. The study was published in 2001 ('the 2001 study').[4] The scope of the study was twofold: partly to analyse the loss and damage characteristics of shippers and their use of insurance to mitigate risk, and partly to analyse the current freight transport liability arrangements for all actors taking the perspective of the supply chain.[5] In line with Commission assumptions,[6] the 2001 study defined the friction costs related to an unpredictable liability system as costs stemming from loss, damage, delay and consequential losses (actual losses), plus those arising from the administration of the regime that supplies insurance and deals with claims (administrative costs).[7] In the study, the friction costs of all stakeholders – shippers, carriers and insurers – were calculated. The 2001 study revealed that friction costs in multimodal transports are generally low and that they vary for different types of journey depending particularly on consignment (cargo) value, journey length and level of risk.[8] In order to illustrate the share of friction costs in total transport costs/freight charges, the study refers to three markets: national, intra-Europe (including non-EU Eastern European countries) and extra-Europe (transfer between Europe and North America).[9] By using the share of friction costs in the three markets and weighing them by their share of multimodal consignments, the level of intermodal transport friction costs in the EU was calculated to approximately 450–550 million euro yearly.[10]

The 2001 study started by stating that the key driver of the economics of carrier liability is the actual loss and damages incurred. If there were to be a transport system without these, no need would arise for any liability system and associated administrative costs.[11] In order to understand the economics of carrier liability, a study was needed of the shippers' experience of the level of loss and damages and insurance costs, in relation to the value of transported cargo as well as the applicable liability regime. A survey to collect this information was therefore carried out. The survey showed that one-quarter of the shipments had a value above 17 Special Drawing Rights (SDR)/kg (the highest level of liability at the time, found in rail and air transport), but that 67 per cent of the shipments

4 IM Technologies (England) and Studiengesellschaft für den kombinierten Verkehr e.V (Germany), 'The Economic Impact of Carrier Liability on Intermodal Freight Transport', London, 22 January 2001.

5 Op. cit., at 1.2.

6 Above in Chapter 4 (at 4.2).

7 The 2001 study, at 4.1.

8 Op. cit., at 5.1.

9 L.C.

10 Op. cit., at 5.2.

11 Op. cit., at 3.1.

had a value under 8.33 SDR/kg (the liability level in road transport) and 39 per cent of these had a value of not more than 2 SDR/kg (relevant in sea transport).

Loss and damage varied according to means of loading unit/mode used. Containerised freight suffers from a lower rate of loss and damage than non-containerised freight. Much of the intra-EU freight was moved in non-secured loading units, such as swap bodies with canvas side-covers. The rate of loss was accordingly not only related to distance, but it appeared that the risk of damage and loss is highest at transfer points.[12] As these are more numerous in multimodal transport, losses are higher in multimodal than in unimodal transport.[13] In national EU transport, the level of friction costs was the highest, at an average of 6.3 per cent of freight charges. Intra-Europe (including Eastern European countries) transport had a friction cost level of 3.9 per cent, while extra-European transport (in this study, a transfer between Europe and North America) had the lowest friction cost level of 2.4 per cent.[14] The total level of intermodal transport friction costs in the EU was calculated to approximately 450–550 million euro per year.[15]

Introducing a strict and full liability regime would not, according to the 2001 study, change the situation very much. The rate of loss or damage was already considered very small. Eliminating the three types of uncertainty related to location of damage or loss, identification of carrier/contract and the question of applicable liability regime (as identified by the 1999 legal expert group) would only reduce friction costs by 20 per cent. Most of this would accrue in the first instance to forwarders and insurers, the two parties mainly concerned with the pursuit of claims. The savings, as far as multimodal transport is concerned, would thus amount to no more than 50 million euro a year.[16] The researchers who performed the study concluded accordingly that '[s]trict and full liability on balance might therefore lead to some reduction in the administrative friction costs, though the potential for reduction may not be as large as some proponents suggest.'[17] Introducing a voluntary, uniform liability system would accordingly probably not reduce legal friction costs to a large degree. As an alternative, the 2001 study mentions that greater harmonisation of conditions among the international conventions, thereby resulting in common legal positions across the EU, would be another means of reducing friction costs.[18] In other words, according to the economists, the level of friction costs associated with an uncertain legal situation in multimodal transport is low, while both a uniform as well as a network-based liability system will probably reduce friction costs sufficiently. Choosing an adequate legal framework for the European multimodal transport project therefore seems more of a political than an economic problem.

12 Op. cit., at 4.2.
13 Op. cit., at 5.3.2.
14 Op. cit., at 5.1.
15 Op. cit., at 5.2.
16 Op. cit., at 5.4.2.
17 L.C.
18 L.C.

The Helsinki study

The results of the 2001 study were verified by a study at the University of Helsinki and Aalto University School of Business in the joint InterTran research project running from 2010 to 2014.[19] A short presentation of the results was published in 2014.[20] A sample of Finnish service providers, carriers, involved in rail-based multimodal transport were asked, inter alia, (1) whether there is a need for a harmonised legal instrument for better support of the multimodal transport industry, and (2) whether liability issues are a problem in the current legal framework. The results were clear. According to the Finnish service providers involved in multimodal carriage involving a rail leg, liability issues are not a problem. Damage occurs seldomly and liability issues are *not* considered a limiting issue as regards use of multimodal transport alternatives.[21] The interviewees did not see any need for a new instrument. In general, the current legal instruments were considered good enough. Instead, as cargo insurance is used by customers (the shippers), the interviewees did not see liability and damages as a huge economic risk. Problems would normally arise in relation to other service providers (subcarriers), although these issues were normally solved by negotiation.[22] However, a few of the interviewees commented that a harmonised liability regime would be beneficial.[23]

7.2 Conclusion

It is undoubtedly true that an international or regional liability regime for multimodal carriage would be beneficial in many ways. It might even have some impact on the choice of transport modes, although the effect is probably small. As a tool in the struggle for more sustainable carriage of goods in the EU, a harmonised liability regime might be one of the tools in a larger toolbox. However, it is not likely to be a very effective tool. The friction costs related to change of transport mode are low and have only a minor impact on the choices made by transport integrators and their customers. The total outcome of the liability project seems to be marginal and not at all in line with the rather extensive policy goal on reduction of CO_2 emissions from transport, which according to the Commission should be 80–95 per cent below 1990 levels by 2050.[24] If nothing is done, by

19 The research project is presented in the preface.

20 Bask, A. and Eftestøl-Wilhelmsson, E., 'Is a Harmonised Liability System a Necessary Prerequisite for European Multimodal Transport? The Finnish Logistic Service Providers' Point of View', in Mäenpää, O. et al., *Oikeuden Historiaasta Tulevaisuuden Eurooppaan*, Suomalainen Lakimiesyhdistys ja kirjoittajat, 2014, pp. 41–50. A full version of the study will be published later in 2015, both in a scientific article in *MarIus* as well as in the InterTran research project final report.

21 Op. cit., note 20, at p. 49.

22 Op. cit., note 21.

23 Op. cit., note 21.

24 Roadmap to a Single European Transport Area – Towards a competitive and resource efficient transport system, COM (2011) 144 at 1.6.

2050 CO_2 emissions from transport will remain one-third higher than their 1990 level and congestion costs will increase by about 50 per cent.[25] It seems clear that a harmonised liability regime is not an effective tool to promote sustainable, multimodal transport in the EU. Leaving the issue to the transport industry is not an alternative either – so far this has merely produced negative results. European transport is constantly growing and road carriage is expanding its already high share.[26] Current development is, in other words, inconsistent with the aim of the transport policy. If the Commission is serious about its environmental commitment, more effective tools should be considered.

To provide the industry with a smooth liability system, as suggested by the Commission, contract law should be used as a tool to enhance sustainable carriage. Although the proposed solutions seem to be non-effective as tools to influence the behaviour of the parties in a transport arrangement, the idea is innovative and should be developed. The question is whether and how contract law could be used in a better way to achieve the goal of a shift in European transport flows towards more environmentally friendly alternatives, such as multimodal carriage.

A relatively easy and not too burdensome alternative or supplement to a harmonised liability regime would be to create a regional legal regime that imposes an obligation on the multimodal transport integrator to choose the most environmentally friendly transport alternative for a certain assignment, or to impose a duty on the transport integrator to inform shippers of the environmental impact of different transport alternatives, so that the shippers can choose between different transport alternatives on an informed basis. This duty requires functional methods of measuring the environmental footprints of different transport alternatives. The Commission is currently working on a method to register the carbon footprint of transport in the EU.[27] Once this method is functioning, it should be integrated with the transport integrator's and the carrier's duty to make use of it.

Other ways to promote multimodal carriage are hence the main issue in Part III: Contract Law as a Tool to Promote Sustainable Carriage of Goods, which discusses whether contract law could provide more in the struggle for sustainable transport patterns than merely being an instrument to smooth the use of multimodal carriage. Part III starts with a discussion on whether or not general environmental obligations under the EU treaties (the Treaty of the European Union (TEU), Article 3, and the Treaty on the Functioning of the European Union (TFEU), Article 11) have any tangible impact on how transport policy should be implemented in EU legislation and continues with a discussion on

25 Op. cit., at 1.13.

26 Road transport contributes about one-fifth of the EU's total emissions of carbon dioxide (CO_2), the main greenhouse gas. CO_2 emissions from road transport increased by nearly 23% between 1990 and 2010, and without the economic downturn growth might have been even greater. Transport is the only major sector in the EU where greenhouse gas emissions are still rising. See online at http://ec.europa.eu/clima/policies/transport/vehicles/index_en.htm (accessed 14 April 2014).

27 Available online at http://ec.europa.eu/transport/themes/sustainable/consultations/2014-06-13-harmonised-carbon-footprinting-measures_en.htm (accessed 14 April 2015).

whether or not general principles of EU contract law entails environmental obligations on the transport integrator. Thereafter, the question of how the contractual duties of a transport integrator could be utilised to enhance environmental carriage is examined. Private environmental procurement is launched as an idea, meaning that the environmental footprint of a consignment should be made part of the offer from the carrier and this information should also be accessible to the public. A prerequisite, however, is that the EU develops a method for registering the carbon footprint of transport within the Union.

Part III

Contract law as a tool to promote sustainable carriage of goods

8 Integration of sustainability in EU contract law

8.1 The integration principle in Article 11 TFEU

As already stated above, sustainable transport of goods has become a core goal of the common transport policy (CTP). Following the 2001 White Paper – The future development of the common transport policy – A global approach to the construction of a Community framework for sustainable mobility[1] – European Union (EU) transport policy has had a clear focus on sustainable carriage of goods.[2] In other words, transport policy is in line with the general duty of the EU to integrate sustainable development and environmental protection into its policies and activities, as stated in Article 11 of the Treaty on the Functioning of the European Union (TFEU) (ex Article 6 of the Treaty of the European Community (TEC)): 'Environmental protection requirements must be integrated into the definition and implementation of the Union policies and activities, in particular with a view to promoting sustainable development.' Accordingly, it is clear that the EU has an obligation to integrate sustainable development and environmental protection into its policies, as the Union has done as regards the CTP.

The question to be asked in the following is, however, whether Article 11 of the TFEU, which embraces the so-called integration principle, contains something more than a general guideline and thus can be used to direct EU institutions as to how environmental protection should be integrated not only into the policies of the Union, but also into its 'activities'. Professor Beate Sjåfjell, who has examined the question,[3] states in a recent publication that '[t]his [the integration principle] entails that each institution [including the Union legislator: The Council, the Commission and the Parliament], when carrying out its task according the Treaties, has an independent obligation to ensure that the environmental integration duty is carried out.'[4] According to Sjåfjell, this shows that

1 COM (92) 494 final.

2 Above in Chapter 4.

3 For a general analysis see: Sjåfjell, B., *Towards a Sustainable European Company Law. A Normative Analysis of the Objectives of EU Law, with the Takeover Directive as a Test Case*, Kluwer Law International, 2009, Part III.

4 Sjåfjell, B. 'The legal significance of Article 11 TFEU for EU institutions and Member States', in Sjåfjell, B. and Wiesbrock, A. (eds), *The Greening of European Business under EU Law. Taking Article 11 TFEU Seriously*, Routledge 2015, pp. 51–71 at pp. 61–62.

'EU law [has] the potential of taking the lead globally' and turning the trend of what she describes as a 'short-term mania into a reflective, long-term sustainable development'.[5] In other words, Sjåfjell is of the opinion that the EU institutions have an obligation to integrate environmental protection into their decisions and in so doing ensure that sufficient action is taken to promote sustainable development. The question is, however, what this exactly means on a more tangible level.

Article 11 of the TFEU must be read in context with Article 3 of the Treaty of the European Union (TEU), which states the EU's obligation to 'work for the sustainable development of Europe based on balanced economic growth and price stability, a highly competitive social market economy, aiming at full employment and social progress, and a high level of protection and improvement of the quality of the environment'. In other words, the environmental obligation must be understood in context. The Court of Justice of the European Union (CJEU) has reached the conclusion that sustainability need not be realised by each individual measure. It is enough that a high level of protection is aimed at, and that the environment is improved.[6] This probably means that the relevant institutions have a certain amount of discretion in deciding on the level of environmental protection in relation to a certain issue. Or – to put it in the words of Professor Ludvig Krämer in an article on the integration principle – 'everybody agrees that there should be integration. And that's it.'[7]

Trying to use a harmonised liability regime as a tool to promote sustainable carriage of goods is perhaps an example of this – a tool, for which there is a call from the legal profession and parts of the industry, but which really has no impact on sustainability and environmental issues. The conclusion is hence that the integration principle in the TFEU welcomes and expects sustainability to be included in EU policies and activities. How this should be done is, however, left to the institutions, and in particular to the Commission, which is the institution mainly involved in the legislative initiative.[8] Efforts from the Commission towards a harmonised European liability regime are thus in line with the integration principle in Article 11 of the TFEU, although research reveals that a harmonised liability regime will have very little – if any – impact on transport patterns.[9] On a tangible

5 Op. cit., at p. 72.

6 Court of Justice, C/341/95 Betatti, ECR 1998, p. I-4355. In this case, the CJEU explicitly stated that: 'whilst it is undisputed that Article 130r(2) of the Treaty requires Community policy in environmental matters to aim for a high level of protection, such a level of protection, to be compatible with that provision, does not necessarily have to be the highest that is technically possible', at 47.

7 Krämer, L., 'Give a Voice to the Environment by Challenging the Practice of Integrating Environmental Requirements into Other EU Policies', at p 16. Available online at http://www.clientearth.org/aarhus-centre-documents/lk-integrating-requirements.pdf (accessed 15 April 2015).

8 Nowadays, to a large degree shared with the EU Parliament. On the ordinary legislative procedure see Art. 294 of the TFEU.

9 Above in Chapter 7.

level, the objective of European sustainable transport seems to be more of a political aim than a legal obligation for the European institutions.

However, as the goal of sustainable transport is set and clearly defined as a core target of the CTP, the Commission should search for other ways to accomplish its goal of more multimodal contracts of carriage within the EU. The trick is to find solutions that are within the competences of the EU, acceptable on a political level, but not too complicated to accomplish within the present international legal framework. As considerable work and resources have been exploited in the liability project, it would be wise to start from here and consider whether or not the liability regime could be used in a more direct manner to accomplish a modal shift or more efficient use of the transport chain. This has so far not been examined by the Commission.

8.2 The integration principle in general contract law

Most of the activities of the EU as regards contract law have focused on making the inner market more effective, and not on promoting sustainability. The main efforts have been on removing barriers that, so far, have been found in national public law restrictions. For the transport sector *security* has also been an important area.[10]

In the area of commercial contract law, however, not much has happened, and particularly not in the area of transport law. Despite huge efforts from both the Commission and a large group of European academics, we still do not have a common European contract law, far less a European civil code. A common framework on European contract law currently exists only on the drawing board and in textbooks produced by various research groups, which to a large extent is financed by the European Commission.[11] However, none of these efforts include transport law or contracts of carriage. According to the study group on a European civil code, '[t]ransport, which is already heavily regulated by international treaties, may be regarded as too politically sensitive at this stage to include in the European Contract Code project.'[12] All the proposed legal instruments accordingly exclude transport from their scope.

A proposal for a regulation on a common European sales law has been pending in the EU legislative system.[13] The proposal is currently withdrawn. However, although this legal instrument should apply not only to sales contracts, but also to related services,[14] the instrument still excludes contracts of carriage.

10 Greaves, R., *EC Transport Law*, Longman, 2000 p. 15.

11 Above in Chapter 4 (at 4.4)

12 Position paper by the Study Group on a European Civil Code, Team on Services. Cited from Lorenzon, F., 'The European Contract Law Project and Maritime Law', *The Emerging European Maritime Law*, MarIus 330, 2004, pp. 137–158 at p. 157.

13 Regulation of the European Parliament and of the Council on a Common European Sales Law, COM (2011) 635 final.

14 Op. cit., Article 1 Objective and subject matter

1 The purpose of this Regulation is to improve the conditions for the establishment and the functioning of the internal market by making available a uniform set of contract law rules

According to the preamble, only 'closely related service contracts' should be subject to the regulation.[15] Furthermore, the proposal clearly states that it does not cover related contracts by which the buyer acquires goods from, or is supplied with a service by, a third party.[16] Any EU statutory contract law relevant to the contract of carriage of goods is, apparently, hard to find.

The same is true when examining the slowly developing general principles of EU civil law. According to Norbert Reich, seven principles of EU civil law can be identified: the principle of 'framed' autonomy, the principle of protection of the weaker party, the principle of non-discrimination, the principle of balancing, the principle of proportionality and, finally, an emerging principle of good faith and of a prohibition of abuse of rights, but the last two are with a question mark.[17] None of these principles relate to external matters such as sustainability, which seems to be an 'alien' in the *inter partes* relationship that the contract covers. There are apparently no general principles of EU law or EU contract law that impose duties on the parties to a contract of carriage to take environmental issues into consideration. Furthermore, there are no explanations as to why this is so. The explanation is probably found in old traditions and settled views on what contract law entails.

Nevertheless, a modern harmonised liability regime that aims to enhance sustainable carriage of goods should cover rules on the environmental duties of transport integrators, the logistical service providers that procure and perform multimodal contracts of carriage, such as carriers and freight forwarders. Environmental issues should, in my opinion, be integrated into the contractual framework, and not only be presupposed by the mere existence of a harmonised liability regime, as the policy of the Commission has been so far. As will be outlined below, only small changes to the present proposals are needed.

as set out in Annex I ('the Common European Sales Law'). These rules can be used for cross-border transactions for the sale of goods, for the supply of digital content and for related services where the parties to a contract agree to do so.

15 Op. cit., note, at 19: 'With a view to maximizing the added value of the Common European Sales Law its material scope should also include certain services provided by the seller that are directly and closely related to specific goods or digital content supplied on the basis of the Common European Sales Law, and in practice often combined in the same or a linked contract at the same time, most notably repair, maintenance or installation of the goods or the digital content.'

16 Op. cit., note, at 20: 'The Common European Sales Law should not cover any related contracts by which the buyer acquires goods or is supplied with a service, from a third party. This would not be appropriate because the third party is not part of the agreement between the contracting parties to use the rules of the Common European Sales Law. A related contract with a third party should be governed by the respective national law which is applicable according pursuant to Regulations (EC) No 593/2008 and (EC) No 864/2007 or any other relevant conflict of law rule.'

17 See Reich, N., *General Principles of EU Civil Law*, Intersentia, 2014.

In the following chapters the question of how the idea of sustainable carriage of goods can be integrated into a harmonised liability regime for European multimodal contracts of carriage will be addressed. The examination will start with the role of the transport integrator in the 2005 proposal, which is the only proposal so far containing a coherent system of uniform liability for EU multimodal contracts of carriage.

9 The role of the freight integrator

9.1 Introduction

To procure and perform transport

The above review of current contractual principles and proposed liability rules shows that no rules on sustainable carriage have been integrated into the contractual framework of a future European liability system for multimodal contracts of carriage, either in any of the proposed liability regimes[1] or in the existing general principles of European Union (EU law). It seems that the integration principle in Article 11 of the Treaty of the Functioning of the European Union (TFEU) has no tangible impact on individual proposals such as the 2005 EU draft. Furthermore, the 2005 EU draft does not itself contain provisions that directly enhance sustainable carriage. This is rather depressing, as one could imagine that sustainability and environmental protection would be part of the proposal, as these issues were the main drivers behind the whole project for a European multimodal liability regime.

However, the proposal contains *one* interesting feature that opens up the possibility of adding rules that might be used to enhance sustainable transport patterns within Europe. The possibility is attached to the scope provision: that is, the proposed liability regime is not restricted only to carriers that *perform* contracts of carriage, it will also apply to freight integrators that might have taken on an obligation to *procure* such carriage. As mentioned in the chapter one,[2] and as will be discussed below, freight integrators are defined as carriers or freight forwarders that focus on green logistics. The latter group is normally distinguished from carriers by not having taken on an obligation to perform a contract of carriage, but only to organise it.[3] This means that all actors involved in *planning* transport will be covered by the 2005 EU draft. Such an expansion of a liability regime opens up new possibilities as regards the policy goal of sustainable transport within the EU. With very small changes to the existing 2005 EU draft, an obligation on the transport

1 As outlined in Chapter 5 (at 5.1).
2 Above in Chapter 1 (at 1.2).
3 See below at pp. 133–134.

integrator to consider environmental issues and sustainability when planning transport could be integrated into the proposed regional regime. A regional EU regime on multimodal contracts of carriage should contain an obligation on the freight integrator to find out about, and offer, the most sustainable mode(s) of transport for a specific consignment. This would be in line with the CTP (common transport policy), on which the proposal rests, and, as no existing legal regime contains an environmental obligation as regards the planning process, such an obligation will not contradict any existing unimodal legal regime, nor will it contradict the proposed Rotterdam Rules, if the Rules enter into force in Europe.

The proposed transport integrator

The 2005 EU draft does not use the term freight integrator. Instead, the term 'transport integrator' was chosen to reflect the overall project of 'Integrated Services in the Intermodal Chain', of which the 2005 EU draft forms part,[4] and to distinguish the 2005 EU draft from other transport regimes, and the transport integrator from other operators in the field. The task of the transport integrator is, therefore, according to the 2005 EU draft, not only to *carry* goods (i.e. to perform transport), but also to *procure* carriage. According to the 2005 EU draft, the transport integrator is a legal entity that 'concludes a contract of transport whereby . . . [it] undertakes to perform or procure the transport of goods from a place in one country to a place in another country, whether or not through a third country, involving at least two different modes of transport, and to deliver the goods to the consignee'.[5]

This wide scope is in line with the solution chosen in the failed 1980 MT (United Nations Convention on International Multimodal Transport of Goods) convention. This convention used the term multimodal transport operator (MTO)[6] (basically the same as multimodal transport integrator) to describe the legal entity that would assume responsibility for a multimodal transport contract. According to the MT convention, an MTO takes responsibility not only for performing multimodal carriage of cargo, but also for procuring performance of such transport.[7] This is more than is expected from a unimodal carrier where only one mode of transport is involved, but a necessity in a situation where more than one mode of transport is to be used. It is therefore disappointing that the authors of the Rotterdam Rules, which aim to be a 'wet' multimodal convention, have not taken this into account. Instead, all activities related to procuring carriage are excluded from the wording of the scope provision. The Rotterdam Rules apply merely to a carrier that undertakes 'to carry goods from one place to another'.[8] The solution is in line with all existing unimodal transport conventions in which

4 The 2005 EU draft p. 16.
5 Op. cit., Art. 1(f).
6 Op. cit., Art. 1.2.
7 Op. cit., Art. 1.3.
8 Rotterdam Rules, Art. 1.1.

the definition of a contract of carriage and a carrier is based on performing transport, not on procuring it. The choice is, however, understandable, as a further widening of the scope of the rules would probably lead to even stronger political resistance than the rules in their present form. As will be outlined below, the obligation to carry in any case includes an obligation to procure carriage. It is the inclusion of freight integrators that *only* undertake to procure carriage that is new. However, widening the term (from 'carry' to 'procure') might also open the way for a wider interpretation of what the duty to procure a multimodal contract of carriage entails.

In the context of the CTP, where sustainable carriage of goods is a key issue, it is particularly interesting to address the question how the duty to procure multimodal carriage of cargo could entail environmental obligations. This question has not been discussed previously, but is highly relevant today. In a convention designed to govern multimodal transport, one could imagine that the performing party would have an obligation to take environmental issues into consideration when planning the logistic transport chain. Protection of the environment is, however, not mentioned as an obligation of the performing party either in the failing MT convention or in the 2005 EU draft of a regional liability regime for European multimodal transport. In the latter case, this is particularly disappointing as environmental protection has been the most important factor behind the entire project for a European legal regime on multimodal transport. In fact, none of the legal regimes mentioned contains provisions that describe the obligations of the performing party in any detail.[9] The question is therefore whether we can conclude anything on the contractual obligations of transport integrators from how their task is described.

Includes carriers and freight forwarders

By including the task of procuring carriage of goods, the 2005 EU draft aims to widen the scope of the liability regime, compared to the present unimodal regimes, and also includes those who merely procure such carriage of cargo. Procuring carriage differs from the obligation to perform it, as the former relates to organising carriage, and is not restricted to merely carrying.

To procure something has been defined as to 'initiate a proceeding, to cause a thing to be done, to instigate, to contrive, bring about, effect or cause'. Synonyms for procure are, for example, 'get', 'obtain', 'acquire'.[10] Professor Jan Ramberg, who was one of the authors behind the 2005 EU draft, uses the term 'procure' to describe the fact that the task is 'not limited to perform the transport in a physical sense, but also to procure performance by using another party or

9 On the duties of the carrier to exercise care for the cargo, see Nikaki, T., 'The Carrier's Duties Under the Rotterdam Rules: Better the Devil You Know?' *Tulane Maritime Law Journal*, 2010, Volume 35, Issue 1, pp. 1–44.

10 *Black's Law Dictionary*, 6th edn, West, 1990.

parties as sub-contractors'.[11] The term transport integrator furthermore includes, unless the context otherwise requires, any reference (in the 2005 EU draft) to the 'servants or agents, and any other person engaged for the performance of the obligations under the contract of transport'.[12] It is a wide definition also in terms of other tasks related to the contract of carriage. Arranging for multimodal carriage clearly lies within the scope of the definition. The idea behind the extended scope has been to include persons involved in the intermodal chain other than merely traditional carriers, such as those persons who *plan and organise* carriage, an operation typically taken care of by freight forwarders. Freight forwarders are excluded from the existing unimodal transport liability regimes, as well as from the pending Rotterdam Rules.

The definitions of a transport integrator and a traditional freight forwarder are not far apart. A freight forwarder is an independent professional who organises and coordinates carriage from departure to destination. Their work includes negotiating contracts of transport that are concluded in their own name, but on behalf of their customer. They have complete freedom to choose the means of transport, but normally do not perform the carriage themselves, although they may do so.[13] The task of a freight forwarder is, in other words, in many respects identical to the task of a transport integrator, and in many jurisdictions freight forwarders are considered to be carriers if they charge a fixed price for their services.[14] In other words, the borderline between a freight forwarder and a traditional carrier is not clear and indeed varies between different jurisdictions. To include freight forwarders in the EU regime would be a great step forward and make the system more coherent and easier for practitioners to apply. As Kiantou-Pampouki remarks, the international situation is confused regarding both the activities of freight forwarders, as well as their legal status.[15] It would, therefore, be a step forward if freight forwarders were included in the EU regime on multimodal contracts of cargo, as the different approaches to categorisation of freight forwarders in different Member States would be irrelevant. If not opted out from, the EU regime would apply to anybody who falls within the scope of the EU regime. If freight forwarders wish to exclude themselves from the proposed liability system, they may opt out under the rules in Article 2, Scope of Application, and fall back on their standard agreements or other applicable law.[16]

11 Ramberg, J., *The Law of Transport Operators in International Trade*, *Norstedts* juridik, 2005, p. 19.
12 The 2005 EU draft, Art. 1(2).
13 See Kiantou-Pampouki, A., 'Multimodal Transport Carrier Liability and Issues Related to Bills of Lading', in Kiantou-Pampouki, A (ed.), *Multimodal Transport. Carrier Liability and Issues Related to Bills of Lading*, XVth International Congress of Comparative Law, Bristol, 26 July–1 August 1998, Brussels, 2000, pp. 3–66 at pp. 11–24.
14 The 2005 EU draft, p. 18.
15 Op. cit., note 13.
16 The 2005 EU draft, p. 18.

9.2 The present legal framework

The unimodal conventions

The freight forwarder and the multimodal carrier play a key role in organising freight. These two groups of actors are of essential importance in the effort on greening transport through extended use of multimodal transport, and their role is, accordingly, most interesting. A question to be asked is whether these groups already have an obligation to take environmental protection into account when planning transport, for example by providing the shipper with a green transport alternative. As the EU at present does not have a regional legal regime on multimodal transport, and no international binding regime is in operation either, European international carriage of goods is to a large degree regulated by the international conventions governing the different modes of transport in use. As outlined in Chapter 6 (at 6.2), these conventions are to a large degree also utilised to settle disputes in multimodal contracts of carriage. In contrast, contracts with freight forwarders are, except when the freight forwarder is considered to be a carrier, for all practical purposes governed by standard contracts, such as the FIATA (International Federation of Frieght Forwarder Associations) Model Rules for Freight Forwarding Services 2007. The question to be asked in the following is whether any of the unimodal legal regimes contain a mandatory duty of the carrier or multimodal service provider to take environmental issues into consideration when planning a transport arrangement.[17]

In most unimodal transport conventions a carrier is defined as a person who enters into a contract of carriage with a shipper or consignee. A contract of carriage, however is defined as a contract that contains an obligation to '*carry goods from one place to another*'.[18] The definition of a contract of carriage contains no elements of the nature and quality of the task. Environmental issues are not mentioned. A contract of carriage is simply a contract for transport from A to B, performed with a certain mode of transport. Possible norms on how this transport should be performed, and under what conditions, must be found in the provisions specifying the contractual obligations of the carrier.

Regarding maritime carriage, the duties of the carrier are regulated in the Hague Rules and the Hague-Visby Rules, Article III rules 1 and 2, which contain an obligation to handle cargo with care and exercise due diligence regarding the seaworthiness of the vessel. The carrier must accordingly 'properly and carefully load, handle, stow, carry, keep, care for and discharge the goods carried', as well as exercising due diligence to make the ship seaworthy. The Hamburg Rules govern the question indirectly through the liability provision in Article 5.1, but

17 The question has also been discussed in Eftestøl-Wilhelmsson, E., 'European Sustainable Freight: The Role of Contract Law', in Wetterstein, P. and Rak, H. (eds), *Environmental Liabilities in Ports and Coastal Areas – Focus on Public Authorities and Other Actors*, Institute of Maritime and Commercial Law Åbo Akademi University, 2011, pp. 229–245.

18 See for example, Rotterdam Rules, Art. 1.1.

also under this regime the main rule is that the cargo should be transported with due care. The loyalty and responsibility of the carrier must be evaluated in light of the expectations of its contractual counterpart, the shipper. When the carrier receives the cargo into custody, it is responsible for any damage, loss (or delay) to the cargo, and thus has a duty to handle the cargo with care. This is an obligation derived from the contractual relationship between the parties. External issues, such as environmental issues, are not included in the due diligence duty of the carrier. They are simply not part of the contract.

Additionally, in the other conventions regulating unimodal transport of goods, the environmental obligations of the carrier are practically invisible. Neither the COTIF-CIM nor the CMR contains any obligation on the carrier to take environmental issues into consideration. In international rail carriage, the rail carrier has an obligation to transport the cargo to a certain place and to deliver it to the right receiver.[19] The obligations of a road carrier are not outlined in the CMR at all, though its duty to carry goods with due dispatch is implied by the liability rules.[20] And regarding inland waterways, under the relatively new CMNI (2000) on carriage by inland waterways, the obligation of the carrier is also limited to carrying goods to the place of delivery within a set time and delivering them to the consignee.[21]

This rather traditional approach to contract law is maintained in the Rotterdam Rules. The main rule is that the carrier should carry the goods to the destination and deliver them to the consignee.[22] If not agreed otherwise,[23] the obligation includes to 'properly and carefully receive, load, handle, stow, carry, keep, care for, unload and deliver the goods'.[24] All requirements are intended to protect the cargo and the interest of the carrier's contractual counterpart, the shipper. The obligations of the carrier are, in other words, designed in line with the present conventions on unimodal transport at sea.

Because of the multimodal element in the Rotterdam Rules, the obligations of the carrier are extended somewhat. Instead of using the phrase 'load and discharge', as in the Hague Rules and Hague-Visby Rules, the Rotterdam Rules contain an obligation to receive and deliver the cargo. This is linked to the extended scope of responsibility of the Rotterdam carrier, which, because of the multimodal aspect of the convention, has responsibility for the goods from receiving to delivery, which can both take place on land, before loading and discharge.[25] The tackle-to-tackle period is extended to a door-to-door period. However, no

19 CIM, Art. 6(1): 'By the contract of carriage, the carrier shall undertake to carry the goods for reward to the place of destination and to deliver them to the consignee.'

20 CMR, Art. 17.

21 CMNI, Art. 3.1.

22 Rotterdam Rules, Art. 11.

23 Rotterdam Rules, Art. 13.2.

24 Rotterdam Rules, Art. 13.1.

25 Rotterdam Rules, Art. 12.

obligation to protect the environment, for example by organising a sustainable transport chain, is mentioned.

Nevertheless, an important innovation regarding environmental protection in the Rotterdam Rules can be found in the liability rule in Article 17. According to Article 17(1), the carrier is liable for loss of or damage to the goods, as well as for delay in delivery during their period of responsibility unless they prove themselves or any person they are responsible for blameless.[26] In any case, the carrier is relieved of liability if one of the events mentioned in Article 17(3)(a)–(o), is fulfilled. According to Article 17(3)(n), the carrier is not liable for damaged, lost or delayed cargo caused by: 'Reasonable measures to avoid or attempt to avoid damage to the environment.' The carrier will thus be encouraged, for example, to participate in salvage operations, not only when there is a risk to human life or property, but also when there is a risk of damage to the environment. This might also encourage the carrier to choose alternative routes for the voyage of its vessel when an environmental risk arises along the original route.[27]

Accordingly, the Rotterdam Rules do not impose any duty on the carrier to take environmental issues into account when making commercial decisions, such as organising the most environmentally friendly transport chain, this has been questioned by reseachers.[28] However, compared to previous international unimodal conventions, environmental issues have a place in the convention. In general, however, the current international legal framework on contracts of carriage does not contain any environmental duties. As mentioned, the transport legal framework does not apply to the freight forwarder if the freight forwarder has not taken on the obligation to perform carriage. If they have only undertaken an obligation to procure carriage, no mandatory legal regime is applicable. Any environmental duties must derive from standard agreements or contracts.

The FIATA Model Rules

The freight forwarder is an independent professional who organises and coordinates carriage from departure to destination. The work includes negotiating contracts of transport that are concluded in the name of the freight forwarder, but on behalf of their customer. As a starting point, the freight forwarder has complete freedom to choose the mode of transport, but normally does not perform the carriage in person, though may do so.[29]

26 Rotterdam Rules, Art. 17(2) and Art. 18.

27 See Munari, F. and La Mattina, A., 'The Rotterdam Rules and Their Implications for Environmental Protection', *Journal of International Maritime Law*, 2010, Volume 16, Issue 5, pp. 370–379.

28 Røsæg, E., 'The Rotterdam Rules as a Model for Multimodal Transport Law', *European Journal of Commercial Contract Law*, 2010, Volume 1/2, pp. 94–97 at p. 96.

29 See Kiantou-Pampouki, op. cit., note 13, at p. 11.

The services of a freight forwarder are regulated by standard conditions that the parties might opt into. The main standard form is the FIATA Model Rules for Freight Forwarding Services 2007.[30] If agreed, the FIATA Model Rules supersede any additional terms of the contract, except in so far as they increase the responsibility or obligations of the freight forwarder.[31] According to this, a freight forwarder is a person who enters into a contract of freight forwarding services, which is defined as:

> services of any kind relating to the carriage, consolidation, storage, handling, packing or distribution of the Goods, as well as ancillary and advisory services in connection therewith, including but not limited to customs and fiscal matters, declaring the Goods for official purposes, procuring insurance of the Goods and collecting or procuring payment or documents relating to the goods.[32]

As far as the choice of method and route of transportation, this is regulated in Article 5:

> The Freight Forwarder shall carry out his services according to the Customer's instructions as agreed. If the instructions are inaccurate or incomplete or not according to contract, the Freight Forwarder may at the risk and expense of the Customer act as he deems fit. Unless otherwise agreed, the Freight Forwarder may without notice to the Customer arrange to carry the Goods on or under deck and choose or substitute means, route and procedure in the handling, stowage, storage and transportation of the Goods.

The FIATA Model Rules give the freight forwarder a great deal of freedom in how to arrange transport. Although environmental protection is not mentioned as an obligation of the freight forwarder, the Model Rules enable the freight forwarder's counterpart, the customer, to increase the responsibility and obligations of the freight forwarder, for example in terms of choosing an environmentally friendly route of transport. Nevertheless, this is not a main issue in the Model Rules. Like the international transport conventions, the FIATA Model Rules are designed to ensure that the freight forwarder uses due diligence in relation to their customer and the cargo, but not in relation to the environment. External, societal or environmental interests were not an issue when issuing the FIATA Model Rules. The legal obligations of performing due diligence are related to protecting the cargo, not the environment.

30 Available online at http://www.weiss-rohlig.com/sites/default/files/model_rules_07.pdf (accessed 28 April 2015).
31 FIATA Model Rules 2007, Art. 1.2.
32 FIATA Model Rules 2007, Art. 2.1.

9.3 Green solutions in the market

The policy of service providers

Despite the fact that neither legal regimes nor standard documents in use take environmental issues into account, the clear indication is that a green transport market is emerging. Accordingly, environmental issues are visible on a policy level. FIATA is marketing freight forwarders as a green branch of industry with a responsibility for the environment. Under the strapline 'Promoting Sustainable Distribution to the Global Market', FIATA is highlighting how environmental issues are of importance to the freight-forwarding industry:

> **Promoting the environment**
>
> Congestion, pollution, safety. These are among the watchwords in today's society. Everyone is aware of them and it is clear that concern for the environment is the responsibility of everyone. The transport industry arguably has a greater responsibility than many, because [of] it[s] . . . ever visible effects on . . . [everyone's] daily life. Forwarders invest heavily in environmentally friendly transport modes and support policies for cleaner vehicle emissions.[33]

The trend is also visible in the marketing of many large logistic service providers. They all offer environmental protection and sustainable carriage of goods. The world's largest logistic service provider, DHL, claims to offer green logistics solutions by assisting their customers in supply chain optimisation and strategic decision-making.[34] It is, however, unclear if this is something DHL does by itself, or if the service must be required from their shippers.

Another large service provider, Kuehne + Nagel, has established an environmental policy that commits them to offering environmentally sound, sustainable and innovative supply chain solutions. This means that reducing negative impact on the environment and promoting sustainability features are integral parts in the formulation of their strategy and decision-making at every level.[35] According to its published environmental policy, Kuehne + Nagel has committed itself to 'reduc[ing] its natural resource consumption by focusing on opportunities to minimise, reuse, and recycle goods used in its operations, and to use recycled products and those from sustainable sources where possible. Provid[ing] environmentally sensitive product alternatives (transportation and warehousing) that

33 Available online at http://fiata.com/uploads/media/architect_of_transport_11.pdf (accessed 28 April 2015).

34 Available online at http://www.kn-portal.com/about_us/corporate_social_responsibility/environment/ (accessed 20 April 2015).

35 Available online at http://www.kn-portal.com/contract_logistics/environment (accessed 20 April 2015).

allow customers to meet their sustainability commitments.'[36] Certainly, this is a demanding approach to environmental protection and a statement that seems to include green choices as regards transport means and routes.

The trend is followed by DB Schenker, another big player in logistics, and that operates with several pages under the sustainability link available on the Internet.[37] DB Schenker is presented as an environmental pioneer and, accordingly, the company offers products that set the standard for efficient use of available resources. DB Schenker supports the DB Group to reduce specific CO_2 emissions by 20 per cent between 2006 and 2020. To reach this goal, it has launched a variety of initiatives and is continuing to expand its range of green products. Acting with the environment in mind is an important issue at DB Schenker. The attitude is supported through initiatives from its business units. Examples of this include continuing to improve the capacity utilisation of their modes of transportation, modernising their equipment and facilities across the board, using a low-emission fleet and training their drivers in energy-saving driving techniques. Furthermore, DB Schenker offers eco solutions for every mode of transportation, allowing customers to reduce, compensate for or avoid CO_2 emissions altogether along the entire supply chain.[38]

In other words, the industry is preparing for the demand for sustainable carriage of goods. Yet we do not see the desired reduction in the negative effects of transport. Instead, as exposed by the Commission, the trend is the opposite.[39]

The freight integrator study

The key question for the Commission has constantly been how European transport could be organised in a more environmentally friendly way. As long ago as the 1997 Communication, 'Intermodality and Intermodal Freight Transport in the European Union',[40] the Commission recognised the importance of freight integrators and declared that it would conduct a survey of the various types of actors in the transport market. The purpose of the study would be to identify the obstacles and opportunities that each type of actor faces in order to fulfil intermodal transport functions and meet logistics requirements.[41] This was followed up in the 2001 White Paper 'European Transport Policy for 2010: time to decide',[42] in which the Commission decided to encourage what was defined as

36 Available online at http://www.kn-portal.com/fileadmin/user_upload/documents/about_us/CSR/documents/Environmental_Policy.pdf (accessed 20 April 2015).

37 Available online at http://www.dbschenker.com/ho-en/sustainability/ (accessed 20 April 2015).

38 L.C.

39 Above in Chapter 4.

40 Intermodality and Intermodal Freight Transport in the European Union a Systems approach to freight transport, Strategies and Actions to Enhance Efficiency, Services and Sustainability COM (97) 243 Final.

41 Op. cit., at 58.

42 European transport policy for 2010: time to decide, COM (2001) 370.

a new profession, that is freight integrators. These freight integrators should be able to 'combine the specific strengths of each mode at European and world level to offer their clients and, consequently, society at large the best service in terms of efficiency, price and environmental impact in the broadest sense (economic, ecological energy etc.)'.[43]

The green element should, in other words, be integrated into the services of the freight integrator. Efficiency and price should no longer be the only factors to consider – environmental issues should also be included. In order to encourage the development of these green freight integrators, the Commission ordered a study on freight integrators active in the EU. The 'Study on Freight Integrators' was performed on behalf of the European Commission and published in 2003.[44] It starts by defining freight integrators as 'transport service providers who arrange full load, door-to-door transportation by selecting and combining without prejudice the most sustainable and efficient mode(s) of transportation'.[45]

Within the EU the freight integrator study identifies between 200 and 500 companies that it estimates to qualify as freight integrators, actively supporting the idea of environmental sustainability.[46] However the study discloses a 'hidden' potential for multimodal transport within existing unimodal transport. The potential consists of transport that would be efficient from an economic point of view but which is still performed unimodally because transport providers do not have the relevant information and knowledge.[47] Other barriers to more sustainable integrated carriage of goods are also identified in the study. These are: infrastructure and technical problems, lack of incentives, mentality/attitude and issues related to liability and documentation.[48]

Lack of infrastructure and technical problems lie outside the scope of this book and will not be commented on further. As regards liability and documentation issues, the freight integrator study does not really add anything to previous studies. On the contrary, the interviews in the freight integrator study support the results of the Economic Impact Study and the Helsinki Study, which both conclude that the impact of friction costs related to unpredictable liability systems in intermodal transport is minor.[49] Nevertheless, the conclusion in the freight integrator study is that due to concern in the industry about legal issues, it would be prudent to address hidden/contingent problems and analyse them in relation

43 Op. cit., p. 47.

44 Commission of the European Communities, Study on Freight Integrators. Final Report, Berlin, 16 April 2003. The study was carried out by a consortium of five partners under the co-ordination of Zentrum für Logistik und Unternehmensplanung (ZLU). The others were International Scheldt Faculty (ISF), European Intermodal Association (EIA), Kravag-Logistic and European Logistics Association (ELA).

45 Op. cit., at 1.

46 In the study, 10 indicators were used to qualify a freight integrator, freight integrator study at 5.2.

47 Op. cit., at 7.

48 Op. cit., at 6.3.

49 Op. cit., at 7.1.

to liability for intermodal freight integration.[50]As research shows that the impact of liability issues is minor with reference to choice of transport routes, it is more interesting to address the other obstacles that green freight integrators face: lack of incentives, mentality/attitude problems and lack of information/knowledge. All these relate to internal issues within freight integrators.

A freight integrator is by definition an entity that is supposed to choose the most efficient and environmentally friendly mode of transport from among all available modes. However, according to the freight integrator study, mentality and attitude qualify as major obstacles in the area: 'Although environmental issues are definitely on people's minds, they do not in any way influence their behaviour.'[51] The desired modal shift can, according to the study, 'only happen if no additional costs or longer transport costs would result'.[52] Furthermore, there are no incentives to change this attitude: 'Companies today not engaging in the field of intermodal transportation often see no reason why they should do so.'[53] This might be due to the lack of information and knowledge mentioned as an obstacle to multimodal carriage. Transport organisers are simply not aware of other modes and their possibilities.[54] However, many service providers today hold contracts containing special arrangements with specific operators, which make them less neutral in decision-making or in choosing the most environmentally friendly route. An example of this is the IATA (International Air Transport Association) agent system.[55] However, the freight integrator study also suggests ideas on how problems can be overcome: 'If governments want more balance between the different modes of transport to become more environmental[ly] and social[ly] friendly (sustainability), they have to create the atmosphere, the legislation and control it. . . . In our opinion, there are two possibilities: Firstly, the use of intermodal transport should be obligatory where possible, defined by . . . governments or [the] EU, for all forwarders.'[56]

The study recommends that freight forwarders implementing multimodal transport be granted state help in various forms. For the purpose of this book, the suggestion cited above is the most interesting: 'intermodal transport should be obligatory where possible'. One possibility, which has not been discussed in the EU or in relation to the Rotterdam Rules, is to integrate an obligation to take environmental issues into consideration when planning transport in the contractual framework governing multimodal contracts of carriage. Despite good intentions, the EU Commission has not taken any initiative to encourage the expert

50 On the Economic Impact Study, see above in Chapter 7 (at 7.2). The Helsinki Study is presented in Chapter 7 (at 7.3). It is interesting to note that the freight integrator study does not refer to the Economic Impact Study although it was published on the home pages of the Commission before the freight integrator study was published.

51 Freight Integrator Study (2003), Op. cit. note 44, at 6.3.7.

52 L.C.

53 Op. cit., at 6.3.8.

54 Op. cit., at 6.3.7.

55 Op. cit., at 4.

56 Op. cit., at 6.3.8.

groups to include environmental obligations in the different proposals on legal regimes for multimodal transport. The instruction given by the Commission has been to draft a harmonised liability regime, which by its predictability will remove legal transaction costs linked to the change of transport systems. However, the connection between predictable rules and the change to environmentally friendly transport systems has been questioned by economists. It is, therefore, reasonable to question the role of contract law in this context as the whole potential of this instrument is not being utilised by the Commission.

Indeed, good examples of how contract law can support sustainable carriage of goods do exist. One innovative suggestion has been presented by the Norwegian Maritime Law Commission in its proposal to the Norwegian Parliament on whether or not Norway should ratify the Rotterdam Rules. In this proposal, the Norwegian Maritime Law Commission, under the leadership of Professor Erik Røsæg from the Scandinavian Institute of Maritime Law at the University of Oslo, manages to convert the principles of sustainability into practical rules. The Norwegian example is an excellent example of how the integration principle in Article 11 of the Treaty on the Functioning of the European Union (TFEU) could be implemented in national or EU legislation.

9.4 The proposal from the Norwegian Maritime Law Commission

The Norwegian Law Commission on implementation of the Rotterdam Rules in the Norwegian Maritime Code[57] recognises that the authors of the Rotterdam Rules had no ambition to use the convention as a tool to promote sustainable transport. The purpose was restricted to harmonising the rules on multimodal transport and, in doing so, as far as possible to avoid the jigsaw puzzle that at the moment characterises the legal situation in international multimodal transport. Nevertheless, the Norwegian Law Commission approves the idea of using contract law as a tool to promote sustainable transport and has accordingly supplemented the Convention in two important areas: transport planning and slow steaming.

As regards planning, the Norwegian Law Commission suggests that the carrier should have an obligation to consider the environmental impact of carriage and to choose the most environmentally friendly transport alternative. This obligation will encourage the use of ship and rail, which are considered more environmentally friendly than, for example, road transport. The duty is not part of the general obligations of the carrier but constructed as a rule of interpretation. Moreover, the Rotterdam Rules also have a rule of interpretation. Article 2 states that in interpreting the convention, regard is to be had to its international character and to the need to promote uniformity in its application and the observance of good faith in international trade. This has been adopted by the Norwegian

57 Norge Offentlige Utredninger (NOU) 2012: 10 Gjennomføring av Rotterdamreglene i Sjøloven,

Law Commission in the first sentence of its proposal § 261, which is almost identical to the wording of Article 2 of the convention and has the following wording: 'In the interpretation of this chapter, regard is to be had to its international character and to the need to promote uniformity in its application and the observance of good faith in international trade.' The second sentence, however, has no equivalent in the Rotterdam Rules, or in any other transport regime. I translate it as: 'It should be assumed that the transport must be planned and implemented with due regard to the environment.'

In its comments on the provision, the Norwegian Law Commission states that the carrier has an obligation to choose the most environmentally friendly transport alternative, unless otherwise agreed. The provision is on interpretation and is, therefore, not sanctioned by penalties. Accordingly, it will probably be difficult to claim any economic loss under the contract for environmental damages. However, taking environmental issues into consideration will not be held against the carrier under this provision, even if the sender were to claim so.

The environment is also protected under Norwegian proposal § 278, second sentence, which contains a rule on slow steaming. Slow steaming refers to deliberately reducing a vessel's cruising speed in order to cut fuel costs. When a ship's speed is reduced, its engine power is also reduced.[58] This results in less fuel consumption and, in effect, the CO_2 emissions released in line with the vessel's fuel consumption are reduced. Slow steaming is, accordingly, not only a means of protecting the environment, but also of saving energy costs for the carrier. According to the Norwegian proposal, the carriage should also be performed with due dispatch regarding speed. However, if reducing speed reduces CO_2 emissions, the carrier should have a right to do so.

The proposal by the Norwegian Law Commission regarding the carrier's duty to plan and carry out transport with a view to reducing greenhouse gas emissions is, hence, of great interest, not only because it represents a totally new approach to environmental protection from a private law point of view, but also because of the legislative technique used. The duty is not implemented in the proposed draft legislation as a contractual duty of the carrier, but as a rule of interpretation. This is a regulatory tool that could be utilised much more than is done today,[59] for example as regards understanding the contractual obligations of freight organisers, carriers and freight forwarders, whether they are called freight integrators, transport integrators or something else.

58 Cariou, P., Is Slow Steaming a Sustainable Means for Reducing Liner Shipping CO_2 Emissions? paper presented at Euromed Management Mare Forum, 14 September 2010, Marseilles. Available online at http://www.mareforum.com/EUROMED_PRESENTATIONS_2010/CARIOU_paper.pdf, pp. 1–15 (accessed).

59 See the discussion above (Chapter 6) as to how to avoid collisions between existing unimodal liability conventions and possible new international and/or regional regimes on multimodal contracts of carriage.

10 Conclusion

10.1 Freedom of contract is not enough

As outlined in previous chapters, the Commission has made the policy decision that the desired modal shift should be reached by reducing the transaction costs of a modal shift, not by imposing obligations on the parties to a contract of carriage. In the communication 'Intermodality and Intermodal Freight Transport in the European Union',[1] the Commission describes the role of the Commission and the Member States so as to define the framework in which the market can operate. The idea of the Commission is that increased use of multimodal carriage should be voluntary and not forced upon the parties: 'It [the Commission] will increase its support to the development of competitive intermodal transport solutions through positive actions such as the financing of research and demonstration projects.'[2] The Commission sees its own role as a catalyst in an area where the market does not easily solve problems on its own, and where Commission action can bring clear benefits.[3] As economic research points out, this approach will probably not lead to the desired modal shift.[4] A more pro-active approach from the Commission is therefore needed.

Unfortunately, the aim of sustainability has, as described in previous chapters, had no impact on the content of the different proposed liability regimes. From the point of view of the European Union (EU), the task has been to provide the industry with an efficient and predictable liability regime. Accordingly, green values are today only apparent in the legal policy behind (possible) new legislation on the carriage of goods within the EU and not in the content of those rules.

Bringing the discussion one step forward, one could ask, as indicated by those interviewed in the freight integrator study, whether sustainable transport should be mandatory. This could, for example, be achieved by imposing an obligation

1 'Intermodality and Intermodal Freight Transport in the European Union a Systems approach to freight transport, Strategies and Actions to Enhance Efficiency, Services and Sustainability' COM (97) 243 Final.

2 Op. cit., at 111.

3 Op. cit., at 110.

4 Above in Chapter 7.

on providers of transport services to offer the most environmentally friendly transport alternative as an option for shippers. An obligation on logistic service providers – freight integrators – always to offer a sustainable transport alternative would force the group to be informed on sustainable transport alternatives, thus overcoming one of the obstacles to multimodal carriage that was mentioned in the freight integrator study.

Such an obligation could have different legal foundations.[5] One way to organise this could be, as noted, to impose on freight integrators operating in Europe a duty to be informed, and to inform, about sustainable carriage alternatives. This could form part of freight integrators' obligations; indeed, in line with the current duty of due care, it could even be integrated in the duty of due care. In other words, the freight integrator could be directed, by an instruction on how to interpret the duty of care, to take environmental issues into consideration when organising carriage of cargo within the EU,[6] or at least to find out about and inform shippers of the most environmental friendly transport alternative.

Freight integrators therefore need methods to consider the environmental impact of the chosen mode of transport. How to measure the environmental impact of different transport alternatives is not a straightforward task. Despite many initiatives at both European and global level on identifying the carbon footprints of transport services, there is no universally accepted definition of the concept of carbon footprint. Instead, the methods and tools for measuring (and comparing) the carbon footprints of the transport industry in Europe show numerous divergences and inconsistencies.[7] Currently, there is no uniform tool to measure the carbon footprints of different transport alternatives.[8]

In order to contribute to the harmonisation of carbon footprint measurement for transport services in Europe, the Commission is considering the development of harmonised carbon footprinting measures for both freight and passenger transport services. According to a background document,[9] the overall policy objective of the Commission initiative is to increase the CO_2 emission efficiency of both passenger and freight transport. The objective can be achieved if companies report CO_2 emissions, on the one hand, and whether reported carbon footprints are comparable and reliable, on the other hand.[10] The idea is that both

5 For a broad approach, see: Sjåfjell, B., *Towards a Sustainable European Company Law: A Normative Analysis of the Objectives of EU Law, with the Takeover Directive as a Test Case*, Kluwer, 2009.

6 As proposed by the Norwegian Maritime Law Committee, see above in Chapter 9 (at 9.4).

7 Available online at http://ec.europa.eu/transport/themes/sustainable/consultations/2014–06–13-harmonised-carbon-footprinting-measures_en.htm (accessed 21 April 2015).

8 L.C.

9 'Consultation on the Introduction of a standardised carbon footprint methodology. Background document'. Available online at http://ec.europa.eu/transport/themes/sustainable/consultations/doc/2014–06–13-harmonised-carbon-footprinting-measures/background.pdf, p. 3. (accessed 21 April 2015).

10 L.C.

transport users and providers, when informed about the CO_2 emission performance of a service, will be able to change their behaviour; that is, the transport users – the shippers – will choose the most environmental friendly alternative, and the transport providers – the carriers – will be encouraged to reduce the carbon intensity of their services. The person who has to obtain this information is, first and foremost, the freight integrator, who will inform customers about the CO_2 performance of different alternative modes of transportation and their impact on the environment.

The most interesting legal question, however, is whether it should be mandatory to measure the carbon footprints of a specific voyage, or whether this should be a voluntary option for the industry. In light of developments in the business-as-usual era, with increased transport and an increased share of road transport, it is not likely that the industry will be able to cope with the environmental challenges that transport is facing. One could thus advocate that it should be mandatory to measure the environmental footprint of a specific voyage, but that it should still be optional for the shipper to decide whether it will make use of the more environmentally friendly transport option or not. Most important is that shippers are able to make an informed decision as to the mode of transport. One solution is, in other words, that freight integrators would have a mandatory duty to find out about and inform shippers of the environmental footprints of different transport alternatives for a specific consignment. Once a system for this is up and running, the choice of the parties could be integrated in the transport documents, so that it is clear to everybody whether the cargo has been carried 'green' or not.[11]

Albeit that environmental protection seems to be on everybody's lips, this does not seem to affect their behaviour.[12] Different ways of integrating good intentions should, therefore, be developed. There are several ways in which contract law could be used as a tool to promote sustainable carriage of goods. One way is to use interpretation as a tool to promote sustainability. This is utilised by the Norwegian Maritime Committee in its proposal on the Rotterdam Rules for a rule on interpretation, stating that: 'It should be assumed that the transport must be planned and implemented with due regard for the environment' (author's translation).[13] This will influence, for example, the obligations of the carrier as regards packing, carrying, choice of subcontractors, and so on. The expectation is that the carrier will carry the cargo in the most environmentally friendly way. That is, the system will encourage the carrier to find out about and offer the most environmentally friendly mode of carriage, so that choosing environmentally friendly alternatives should be the first choice. Other solutions must be expressly agreed between the parties.

11 This information should then be integrated in the calculations performed in relation to deciding whether the cargo is green or not. Information that seems to be missing in the calculations relates to green public procurement, where the life cycle of a product is used as a basis for procurement.

12 See the freight forwarder study referred to in Chapter 9 (at 9.22).

13 Above in Chapter 9 (at 9.4).

Another possibility is to use what has been described as the 'full contractual tool',[14] that is, to establish sustainable contractual standards to be incorporated into international law of contract obligations, such as, for example, the fundamental norms of *lex mercatoria*. This could, for example, be done through the doctrines of good faith, legitimate expectations, constructive knowledge, and others. A full contractual tool approach would fill the gap where now a legal vacuum exists. This is an interesting approach, but something that will most likely not become a reality in the near future.

A third, and more pragmatic approach is, as proposed in Chapter 9, to impose on freight integrators a duty to find out about and to inform about the most environmentally friendly mode of carrying a specific consignment. This is neither about interpretation nor about utilising the potential of the full contractual tool, but could instead be described as a decision support tool.[15] Here the idea is to provide companies with standards to be incorporated in their contractual framework as a support tool in the decision-making process. To make it very simple, transport documents could contain a box marked 'sustainability' where the parties mark whether the transport should be performed in the most environmentally friendly way or not. One could also combine this with the idea from the Norwegian Maritime Law Commission and make a rule that, if the parties have not agreed otherwise, the presumption will be that the freight integrator will choose the most environmentally friendly mode of carrying the consignment. Indeed, the idea requires that the EU Commission should come up with a system for measuring the environmental footprints of different forms of carriage. However, as several systems are up and running, this should not be too challenging. Once the survey on the development of harmonised carbon footprinting measures for transport services in Europe is completed,[16] the Commission should integrate the solution in a European transport document, which again should be promoted in the Union. Additionally, the EU could cooperate with the Baltic and International Maritime Council (BIMCO) and other organisations under which transport documents are agreed.

10.2 Need for a shift in the role of contract law

The proposals listed above with the aim of boosting the European project on sustainable carriage of goods are not, from a legal point of view, very radical. Instead, they should be considered a small step forward in bringing external, societal issues, such as environmental issues, into contractual legal regimes governing

14 See Queinnec, Y., 'Sustainable Contracts Concept's Outlines and Exploration Tracks', January 2010. Available online at http://www.reports-and-materials.org/sites/default/files/reports-and-materials/Sherpa-on-sustainable-contracts-Jan-2010.pdf (accessed 21 April 2015).

15 Op. cit., at. p. 3.

16 Available online at http://ec.europa.eu/transport/themes/sustainable/consultations/2014–06–13-harmonised-carbon-footprinting-measures_en.htm (accessed 26 January 2015).

multimodal transport today. External issues have always lain far outside the scope of contract law. The aim of the Hague Rules and Hague-Visby Rules was to balance the interests between carriers (read: ship owners) and cargo owners regarding liability claims. The more recent Hamburg Rules aimed at repairing what was criticised as an imbalanced international solution in international carriage of goods.[17] The CMR, COTIF-CIM and CMNI were also designed to balance the interests between the parties under a contract of carriage. The interests involved have been represented by the contracting parties and their organisations, including insurance interests. If states, or other bodies of governance, have been involved, the perspective in the negotiations has always been the main interest of the national (or regional) transport industry. External, societal interests have not been an issue.

Generally, the use of green arguments in modern transport law is very modest. Environmental issues are not part of the mandatory international regimes governing carriage of goods, neither are such interests viewable in the present discussion on a harmonised European contract law. One might argue that this is the only possibility as contract law was not designed to do anything other than serve the parties in resolving disputes among themselves. Other rules, such as those under tort law, protect the environment. Private law rules are intended to be used by marked actors, each promoting their own self-interest in individually determined relationships with one another. Private law is self-implementing by nature. No public authority supervises application of the rules. On the contrary, implementation of the rules is left to the parties themselves or, to be more exact, to the party whose rights have been infringed – in our context, the cargo owner. Furthermore, the cargo owner is not forced to make use of the contract law material it is provided with. It can decide if it wishes to make a claim, or if it wishes to accept an offer from the carrier. In other words, the use of civil law rules as means of controlling the behaviour of parties to contracts presupposes that one or other party sees it as being in their interest to refer to those rules.

This leads to a situation where environmentally related contract law arguments in practical terms will normally only be considered where one party has suffered from the other's environmentally harmful acts or products. A typical example of this is transport of dangerous goods, where the parties are protected by mandatory contractual rules. Another example could be where the carrier has not performed due diligence in preparing the vessel, or other means of transport, before the voyage. If the cargo is delayed, lost or damaged, the cargo owner might claim damages from the carrier. If the damage is simultaneously dangerous to the environment, normally public regulations deal with this particular issue.

Because of the intense focus on environmental issues in current European transport policy, it is, hopefully, only a matter of time before the problems outlined above are overcome. Traditional contract law is today at a crossroads. Sustainability is a key word guiding all official decision-making, and it will eventually

17 On the historical development in maritime carriage, see: Falkanger, T., Bull, H.J. and Brautaset, L., *Scandinavian Maritime Law*, Universitetsforlaget, 2004, pp. 260–265.

find its way into the realm of contract law. We already see some signs of this in the latest transport convention, the Rotterdam Rules, although attempts to use the convention to protect the environment are extremely modest.[18] With a growing green transport industry, the element of sustainable transport contracts will increase, and probably affect the contractual regimes governing these contracts. The European effort towards a legal regime on multimodal transport that emphasises sustainability can be seen as an example of a new development where the role of contract law is changing. External interests such as protecting the environment are emerging and influence possible new private law regulation. The EU could, however, speed up this process by integrating in its regional legal regime for multimodal contracts of carriage a duty for freight integrators to take environmental issues into account when planning carriage and to share information on the environmental impact of different transport alternatives with shippers. Operators in the transport industry need to know the exact environmental impact of different transport alternatives in order to make an informed decision on which transport alternative to choose. Information is the key to all behavioural change.

18 Above in Chapter 3 (at 3.2).

Bibliography

Aguirre, C., 'The Rotterdam Rules from the Perspective of a Country that Is a Consumer of Shipping Services,' *Uniform Law Review*, 2009, Volume 14, pp. 869–884.

Alcántara, J.M. , 'The New Regime and Multimodal Transport,' *Lloyd's Maritime and Commercial Law Quarterly*, 2002, Part 3, pp. 339–404.

Aminoff, J., 'Article 71 of the Brussels I Regulation and the Application of Transport Law Conventions in the Light of Some Judgments of the European Court of Justice,' *Tidskrift utgiven av Juridiska Föreningen i Finland (JFT)*, 2014, Volume 6, pp. 420–441.

Angus, W., 'Legal Implications of "The Container Revolution" in International Carriage of Goods', *McGill Law Journal*, 1968, Volume 14, pp. 395–429.

Atamer, K., 'Construction Problems in the Rotterdam Rules regarding the Performing and Maritime Performing Parties', *Journal of Maritime Law & Commerce*, 2010, Volume 41, Issue 4, pp. 469–497.

Bask, A. and Eftestøl-Wilhelmsson, E., 'Is a Harmonised Liability System a Necessary Prerequisite for European Multimodal Transport? The Finnish Logistic Service Providers' Point of View', in Mäenpää, O. et al., *Oikeuden Historiaasta Tulevaisuuden Eurooppaan*, Suomalainen Lakimiesyhdistys ja kirjoittajat, 2014, pp. 41–50.

Beare, S., 'Liability Regimes, Where We Are, How We Got There and Where We Are Going', *Lloyd's Maritime and Commercial Law Quarterly*, 2002, Volume 3, pp. 306–315.

Berlingieri, F., 'Uniformity in Maritime Law and Implementation of International Conventions', *Journal of Maritime Law and Commerce*, 1987, Volume 18, Issue 3, pp. 317–350.

Berlingieri, F., 'Multimodal Aspects of the Rotterdam Rules', paper presented at the Colloquium of the Rotterdam Rules 2009, 21 September 2009, De Doelen. Available online at http://www.rotterdamrules2009.com/cms/uploads/Def.%20tekst%20F.%20Berlingieri%2013%20OKT29.pdf (accessed 15 May 2015).

Berlingieri, F., 'Revisiting the Rotterdam Rules', *Lloyd's Maritime and Commercial Law Quarterly*, 2010, Volume 6, pp. 583–639.

Bonell, M., 'International Uniform Law in Practice – Or Where the Real Trouble Begins', *The American Journal of Comparative Law*, 1990, Volume 38, pp. 865–888.

Brunnee, J., 'Of Sense and Sensibility: Reflections on International Liability Regimes as Tools for Environmental Protection', *International and Comparative Law Quarterly*, 2004, Volume 53, pp. 351–368.

Cariou, P., 'Is Slow Steaming a Sustainable Mean for Reducing Liner Shipping CO_2 Emissions? paper presented at EUROMED MANAGEMENT MARE FORUM,

14 September 2010, Marseilles. Available online at http://www.mareforum.com/EUROMED_PRESENTATIONS_2010/CARIOU_paper.pdf (accessed).

Clarke, M., 'A Conflict of Conventions: The UNCITRAL/CMI Draft Transport Instrument on Your Doorstep', *The Journal of International Maritime Law*, 2003, Volume 9, pp. 28–39.

Corbett, J., 'The Role of International Policy in Mitigating Global Shipping Emission', *Brown Journal of World Affairs*, 2010, Volume XVI, Issue II, pp. 143–154.

Crowley, J., 'Inland Transport in the European Community following 1992', *The Antitrust Bulletin*, 1992, pp. 453–480.

Crowley, M., 'The Limited Scope of the Cargo Liability Regime Covering Carriage of Goods by Sea: The Multimodal Problem', *Tulane Law Review*, 2005, Volume 79, pp. 1461–1504.

Damar, D., 'Breaking the Liability Limits in Multimodal Transport', *Tulane Maritime Law Journal*, 2012, Volume 36, pp. 659–683.

Dempsey, P., 'The Law of Intermodal Transportation: What It Was, What It Is, What It Should Be', *Transportation Law Journal*, 2000, Volume 27, pp. 367–417.

Devia, N.M., *The Multimodal Transport System in the Andean Community – An Analysis from a Legal Perspective*, Erasmus University 2008.

Diamond, A., 'The Next Sea Carriage Convention?' *Lloyd's Maritime and Commercial Law Quarterly*, 2008, Part 1, pp. 135–187.

Diamond, A, 'The Rotterdam Rules', *Lloyd's Maritime and Commercial Law Quarterly*, 2009, Part 4, pp. 445–536.

Driscoll, W. and Larsen B., 'The Convention on International Multimodal Transport of Goods', *Tulane Law Review*, 1982, Volume 5, pp. 193–280.

Eftestøl-Wilhelmsson, E., 'European Sustainable Freight: The Role of Contract Law', in Wetterstein, P. and Rak, H. (eds), *Environmental Liabilities in Ports and Coastal Areas – Focus on Public Authorities and Other Actors*, Institute of Maritime and Commercial Law Åbo Akademi University, 2011, pp. 229–245.

Eftestøl-Wilhelmsson, E., 'The Rotterdam Rules in a European Multimodal Context', *Journal of International Maritime Law*, Gyldendal Akademisk 2010, Volume 16, pp. 274–288.

Eftestøl-Wilhelmsson, E., *Fra etterprovision til avgangsvederlag*, Norwegian Bokmal, 2005.

Eftestøl-Wilhelmsson, E., Bask, A. and Rajahonka, M., 'Intermodal Transport Research A Law and Logistics Literature Review with EU Focus', *European Transport Law*, 2014, Volume XLIX, Issue 6, pp. 609–674.

Faghfouri, M., 'International Regulation of Liability for Multimodal Transport – in Search of Uniformity', *WMU Journal of Maritime Affairs,* 2006, Volume 5, Issue 1, pp. 95–114.

Falkanger, T., Bull, H.B. and Brautaset, L., *Scandinavian Maritime Law. The Norwegian Perspective*, 3rd edn, Universitetsforlaget, 2011.

Faria, J., 'Uniform Law and Functional Equivalence: Diverting Paths or Stops Along the Same Road? Thoughts on a New International Regime for Transport Documents', *Elon Law Review*, 2011, Volume 2, Issue 1, pp. 1–37.

Force, R., 'The Aftermath of *Norfolk Southern Railway v. James N. Kirby, Pty Ltd.*: Jurisdiction and Choice of Law Issues', *Tulane Law Review*, 2008–2009, Volume 83, pp. 1393–1433.

Force, R., 'The Regal-Beloit Decision: What, If Anything, Would Happen to the Legal Regime for Multimodal Transport in the United States If It Adopted the Rotterdam Rules', *Tulane Maritime Law Journal*, Volume 36, 2011–2012, pp. 685–706.

Fujiati, T., 'The Comprehensive Coverage of the new Convention: Performing Parties and the Multimodal Implications', *Texas International Law Journal*, 2009, Volume 44, pp. 349–373.

Glass, D. and Nair, M., 'Towards Flexible Carriage Documents? Reducing the Need for Modally Distinct Documents in International Goods Transport', *The Journal of International Maritime Law*, 2009, Volume 15, pp. 1–28.

Greaves, R., *EC Transport Law*, Longman, 2000.

Grönfors, K., *Successiva transporter*, P.A Norsted & Söners Förlag, 2008.

Haak, K.F., 'The Harmonization of Intermodal Liability Arrangements', *European Transport Law*, 2005, pp. 13–51.

Haak, K.F., 'Carriage Preceding or Subsequent to Sea Carriage under the Rotterdam Rules', *European Journal of Commercial Contract Law*, 2010, Volume 2, Issue 1/2, pp. 63–71.

Hancock, C., 'Multimodal Transport and the New UN Convention on the Carriage of Goods', *Journal of International Maritime Law*, 2008, Volume14, pp. 484–495.

Harllee, J, Nemirow, S. and Jerome, B., 'Current Regulation and Modern Transportation Schemes', *The Transportation Law Journal*, 1969, Volume 1, pp. 39–50.

Herber, R., 'The European Legal Experience with Multimodalism', *Tulane Law Review*, 1989–1990, Volume 64, Issues 2 & 3, pp. 611–629.

Herber, R., 'The New German Transport Legislation', *European Transport Law*, 1998, Volume XXXIII, Issue 5, pp. 591–606.

Hoeks, M., 'Multimodal Carriage with a Pinch of Sea Salt: Door to Door under the UNCITRAL Draft Instrument', *European Transport Law*, 2008, Volume 43, pp. 257–280.

Hoeks, M., *Multimodal Transport Law – The Law Applicable to the Multimodal Contract for the Carriage of Goods*, Kluwer Law International, 2010.

Hoeks, M., 'Liability, Jurisdiction and Enforcement Issues in International Road Carriage: CMR-Carrier Liability in the Netherlands and Germany and the Influence of the EU', in Soyer, B. and Tettenborn, A. (eds), *Carriage of Goods by Sea, Land and Air. Unimodal and Multimodal Transportation in the 21st Century*, Informa Law from Routledge, 2013, pp. 45–64.

Hooper, C., 'Ratification of the Rotterdam Rules and their Implications for International Shipping'. Available online at http://www.skuld.com/documents/library/beacon/beacon_2_2012_rotterdam_rules.pdf (accessed 15 May 2015).

Johansson, S.O., *An Outline of Transport Law*, 2nd edn, Stockholm, 2014.

Lamont-Black, S., 'Claiming Damages in Multimodal Transport: A Need for Harmonisation', *Tulane Maritime Law Journal*, 2012, Volume 36, pp. 707–724.

Kiantou-Pampouki, A., 'Multimodal Transport Carrier Liability and Issues Related to Bills of Lading', in Kiantou-Pampouki, A. (ed.), *Multimodal Transport. Carrier Liability and Issues Related to Bills of Lading*, XVth International Congress of Comparative Law, 26 July–1 August 1998, Bristol, Brussels, 2000, pp. 3–66.

Krämer, L., 'Give a Voice to the Environment by Challenging the Practice of Integrating Environmental Requirements into other EU Policies'. Available online at http://www.clientearth.org/aarhus-centre-documents/lk-integrating-requirements.pdf (accessed 15 May 2015).

Legros, C., 'Relations Between the Rotterdam Rules and the Convention on the Carriage of Goods by Road', *Tulane Maritime Law Journal*, 2012, Volume 36, pp. 725–740.

Leloudas, G., 'Multimodal Transport under the Warsaw and Montreal Convention Regimes: A Velvet Revolution?' in Soyer, B. and Tettenbom, A. (eds), *Carriage of Goods By Sea, Land and Air – Unimodal and Multimodal Transport in the 21st Century*, Informa Law from Routledge, 2013, pp. 77–110.

Lorenzon, P. 'The European Contract Law Project and Maritime Law in The Emerging European Maritime Law', Proceedings from the Third European Colloquium on Maritime Law Research', 17–18 September 2004, Ravenna, *MarIus* 2005, No. 333, pp. 137–158.

Mankowski, P., 'The Rotterdam Rules – Scope of Application and Freedom of Contract', *European Journal of Commercial Contract Law*, 2010, Volume 2, Issue 1/2, pp. 9–21.

Marten, B., 'A Multimodal Transport Reform and the European Union: A Minimalist Approach', *European Transport Law*, 2012, Volume XLVII, Issue 2, pp. 129–152.

Masud, R., 'The Emerging Legal Regime for Multimodal Transport', *Int'l Business Law Journal*, 1992, Volume 7, pp. 825–834.

Moens, G. and Trone, J., *Commercial Law of the European Union*, Springer, 2010.

Munari, F. and La Mattina, A., 'The Rotterdam Rules and their Implications for Environmental Protection, *Journal of International Maritime Law*, 2010, Volume 16, pp. 370–379.

Myrburgh, P., 'Uniformity or Unilateralism in the Law of Carriage of Goods by Sea?' *Victoria University of Wellington Law Review*, 2000, Volume 31, pp. 355–382.

Nikaki, T., 'The Fundamental Duties of the Carrier under the Rotterdam Rules', *The Journal of International Maritime Law*, 2008, Volume 14, pp. 512–523.

Nikaki, T., 'The Carrier's Duties Under the Rotterdam Rules: Better the Devil You Know?', *Tulane Maritime Law Journal*, 2010, Volume 35, Issue 1, pp. 1–44.

Nikaki, T. and Soyer, B., 'New International Regime for Carriage of Goods by Sea: Contemporary, Certain, Inclusive AND Efficient, or Just Another One for the Shelves?', *Berkeley J. Int'l L.*, 2012, Volume 30, pp. 303–348.

Queinnec, Y., 'Sustainable Contracts Concept's Outlines and Exploration Tracks', January 2010. Available online at http://www.reports-and-materials.org/sites/default/files/reports-and-materials/Sherpa-on-sustainable-contracts-Jan-2010.pdf (accessed 15 May 2015).

Ramberg, J., 'The Law of Carriage of Goods – Attempts of Harmonization', *Scandinavian Studies in Law* 1973, Volume 17, pp. 211–252.

Ramberg, J. , 'The Future of International Unification of Transport Law', *Scandinavian Studies in Law*, 2001, Volume 41, pp. 453–458.

Ramberg, J., 'The Future Law of Transport Operators and Service Providers', *Scandinavian Studies in Law*, 2004, Volume 46, pp. 135–151.

Ramberg, J., *The Law of Transport Operators in International Trade*, 2005.

Rasmussen, U., 'Additional Provisions Relating to Particular Stages of Carriage', in von Ziegler, A., Schelin, J. and Zunarelli, S. (eds), *The Rotterdam Rules 2008*, Kluwer, 2010, pp. 93–132.

Schmidt, M. and Giorgi, L., 'Successes, Failures and Prospects for the Common Transport Policy', *Innovation*, 2001, Volume 14, Issue 4, pp. 293–313.

Reich, N., *General Principles of EU Civil Law*, Intersentia, 2014.

Roost, L.A., *Multimodale Transporter*, Jurist of Økonomtorbundet, 2012.

Rosas, A., 'EU Law and International Agreements Concluded by EU Member States, with Particular Emphasis on Maritime Law', in Rak, H. and Wetterstein, P. (eds), *Environmental Liabilities in Ports and Coastal Areas – Focus on Public Authorities and Other Actors*, ÅBO Akademi University Turku, 2011, pp. 9–47.

Røsæg, E., 'The Rotterdam Rules as a Model for Multimodal Transport Law', *European Journal of Commercial Contract Law*, 2010, Volume 1/2, pp. 94–97.

Schmidt, M. and Giorgi, L., 'Successes, Failures and Prospects for the Common Transport Policy', *The European Journal of Social Science*, 2001, Volume 1, Issue 4, pp. 293–313.

Schoenbaum, T., 'Important New U.S. Supreme Court Case on the Multimodal Carriage of Goods', *The Journal of International Maritime Law*, 2010, Volume 16, pp. 184–185.

Schoenbaum, T., 'An Evaluation of the Rotterdam Rules', *The Hamburg Lectures on Maritime Affairs*, 2011–2013, Volume 28, pp. 21–43.

Sjåfjell, B., *Towards a Sustainable European Company Law. A Normative Analysis of the Objectives of EU Law, with the Takeover Directive as a Test Case*, Kluwer Law International, 2009, Part III.

Sjåfjell, B., 'The Legal Significance of Article 11 TFEU for EU Institutions and Member States', in Sjåfjell, B. and Wiesbrock, A. (eds), *The Greening of European Business under EU Law. Taking Article 11 TFEU Seriously*, Routledge, 2015, pp. 51–71.

Smith, D., 'The European Union's Commitment to Sustainable Development: Is the Commitment Symbolic or Substantive in the Context of Transport Policy?', *Colo. J. Int'l Envtl. & Pol'y*, 2002, Volume 13, pp. 242–331.

Sturley, M., 'Jurisdiction Under the Rotterdam Rules', *Uniform Law Review*, 2009, Volume 14, Issue 1/2, pp. 1–36.

Sturley, M., 'Maritime Cases About Train Wrecks: Applying Maritime Law to the Inland Damage of Ocean Cargo', *Journal of Maritime Law & Commerce*, 2009, Volume 40, Issue 1, pp. 1–43.

Tetley, W., 'Uniformity of International Private Maritime Law – The Pros, Cons, and Alternatives to International Conventions – How to Adopt an International Convention', *International Maritime Law*, 2000, Volume 24, pp. 775–856.

Tetley, W., 'A Summary of General Criticisms of the UNCITRAL Convention (The Rotterdam Rules)' (20 December 2008). Available online at http://www.mcgill.ca/files/maritimelaw/Summary_of_Criticism_of_UNCITRAL__No_1.pdf (accessed 15 May 2015).

Teubner, G., 'Legal Irritants: Good Faith in British Law or How Unifying Law Ends Up in New Differences', *Modern Law Review*, 1998, Volume 61, pp. 11–32.

Trappe, J., 'The Reform of German Transport Law', *Lloyd's Maritime and Commercial Law Quarterly*, 2001, Part 3 pp. 392–405.

Ulfbeck, V., 'Multimodal Transport in the United States and Europe – Global or Regional Liability Rules?' *Tulane Maritime Law Journal*, 2009, Volume 34, pp. 37–90.

Ulfbeck, V., 'Options in Contracts of Carriage. The Air/Road Combination in Recent European Case Law', *Transportrecht*, 2010, Volume 10, pp. 370–376.

Weatherill, S., 'European Private Law and the Constitutional Dimension', in F. Cafaggi (ed.), *The Institutional Framework of European Private Law*, Oxford University Press, 2006, pp. 79–106.

Wouters, J., Coppens, D. and De Meester, B., 'The European Union's External Relations after the Lisbon Treaty', in Griller, S. and Ziller, J. (eds), *The Lisbon Treaty. EU Constitutionalism without a Constitutional Treaty? Springer*, 2008, pp. 144–203.

De Witt, R., *Multimodal Transport*, Lloyd's Shipping Law Library, 1995.

Yuzhou, S. and Hai Li, H., 'The New Structure of the Basis of Liability for the Carrier', paper presented at the Colloquium of the Rotterdam Rules 2009, 21 September

2009, De Doelen. Available online at www.rotterdamrules2009.com/cms/index.php?page=text-speakers-rotterdam-rules-2009 (accessed 15 May 2015).

Von Bar, C., Clive, E. and Schulte Nölke, H. (eds), *Principles, Definitions and Model Rules of European Private Law. Draft Common Frame of Reference (DCFR)*, Sellier, 2009.

von Ziegler, A., 'Liability of the Carrier for Loss, Damage or Delay', in von Ziegler, A., Schelin, J. and Zunarelli, S. (eds), *The Rotterdam Rules 2008*, Wolters Kluwer, 2010, pp. 93–132.

Ziel van der, G.J., 'Multimodal Aspects of the Rotterdam Rules', *CMI Yearbook*, 2009, Part II.

Zunarelli, S., 'The Carrier and the Maritime Performing Party in the Rotterdam Rules', *Uniform Law Review*, 2009, Volume 14, pp. 1011–1023.

Official documents

EU documents

Green papers

Green Paper on The Impact of Transport on the Environment – A Community strategy for 'sustainable mobility' COM (92) 46 final.

Green Paper from the Commission on policy options for progress towards a European Contract Law for consumers and businesses COM (2010) 348 final (not published in the OJ).

White papers

Completing the Internal Market: White Paper from the Commission to the European Council, COM (85) 310 final.

White Paper, European Transport Policy for 2010: Time To Decide, COM (2001) 370 final.

White Paper, Roadmap to a Single European Transport Area – Towards a competitive and resource efficient transport system, COM (2011) 144 final.

Communications

Communication from the Commission – the future development of the common transport policy – A global approach to the construction of a Community framework for sustainable mobility, COM (92) 494 final.

Communication from the Commission to the Council, the European Parliament, the Economic and Social Committee and the Committee of the Regions – Intermodality and intermodal freight transport in the European Union – A systems approach to freight transport – Strategies and actions to enhance efficiency, services and sustainability, COM (97) 243 final.

Communication from the Commission to the Council and the European Parliament on European Contract Law, COM (2001) 398 final, OJ C 255/2001 s. 1-44.

Communication from the Commission to the European Parliament and the Council – A more coherent European contract law – An action plan, COM (2003) 68 final, OJ C 63/2003 s. 1-44.

Communication from the Commission – Freight Transport Logistics Action Plan, COM (2007) 607 final (not published in the OJ).

Working Documents

Commission Staff Working Document, Accompanying Document to the Communication from the Commission – Freight Transport Logistics Action Plan – Impact Assessment, SEC (2007) 1320 final.

Commission Staff Working Document, Accompanying the White Paper – Roadmap to a Single European Transport Area – Towards a competitive and resource efficient transport system, SEC (2011) 391 final.

Communication from the Commission to the European Parliament and the Council. Keep Europe moving – Sustainable mobility for our continent. Mid-term review of the European Commission's 2001 Transport White Paper COM (2006) 314 final.

EU initiated studies

Intermodal Transportation and Carrier Liability, Asariotis, R., Bull, H.J., Clarke, M.A., Herbert, R., Kiantou-Pampouki, A., Morán-Bovio, D., Ramberg, J., deWitt, R. and Zunarelli, S., European Communities, Office for Official Publications of the European Communities, 1999.

The Economic Impact of Carrier Liability in Intermodal Freight Transport, IM Technologies (England) and Studiengesellschaft für den kombinierten Verkehr e.V (Germany), London 2001.

Study on Freight Integrators: Final Report, Commission of the European Communities, Berlin 2003.

Integrated Services in the Multimodal Chain (ISIC) Final Report Task B: Multimodal liability and documentation. Research report commissioned by the European Commission – DG TREN provided by an independent panel of legal experts, published by ECORYS Nederland BV, Rotterdam 2005.

Commission decisions

Commission Decision (93/45/EEC) of 22 December 1992 concerning the granting of financial support for pilot schemes to promote combined transport [1992] OJ L 16/55

UNCTAD documents

United Nations Conference on Trade and Development, Implementation of Multimodal Transport Rules, Report prepared by the UNCTAD secretariat, UNCTAD/SDTE/TLB/2, 27 June 2001.

United Nations Conference on Trade and Development (UNCTAD), Multimodal Transport: The Feasibility of an International Legal Instrument, Report by the UNCTAD secretariat, UNCTAD/SDTE/TLB/2003/1, 13 January 2003.

Others

Gjennomføringen av Rotterdamreglene i sjøloven. Norges offentlige utredninger, NOU 2012:10 [The implementation of the Rotterdam Rules in the Norwegian Maritime Code. Norwegian public report 2012:10].

World Commission on Environment and Development, *Our Common Future*, Oxford University Press, 1987.

Table of treaties

Table of cases

National cases

Denmark

England and Wales

Germany

The Netherlands

The USA

Court of Justice of the European Union

Table of legislation

EU legislation

National legislation

Denmark

Germany

Holland

Norway

United States

Index

For Product Safety Concerns and Information please contact our EU
representative GPSR@taylorandfrancis.com
Taylor & Francis Verlag GmbH, Kaufingerstraße 24, 80331 München, Germany

www.ingramcontent.com/pod-product-compliance
Ingram Content Group UK Ltd.
Pitfield, Milton Keynes, MK11 3LW, UK
UKHW011015180926
475701UK00004B/758
* 9 7 8 1 1 3 8 6 1 4 4 2 0 *